How to Remove a PC's Case

1. Turn off the computer, monitor, and peripherals (modem, CD-ROM, and so on). Make sure that everything attached to your computer is turned off and unplugged.

2. Unplug your computer. Unplug your computer's power cord from the wall.

3. Remove four or five screws from the outside edges. The older your PC, the more screws you'll find on the back of it. See the four screws closest to each corner, like in the figure? Those outside-edge screws hold the cover onto the case; ignore the others. Turn each screw counterclockwise to loosen it. If there's a screw along the top edge, midway between the corners, remove that one, too.

    Place the screws in a safe place, where you'll be able to find them later (and where they won't fall and lodge themselves in your PC's guts).

4. Slide off the cover. On some computers, the cover slides toward the front. You may need to pull pretty hard. Try lifting up a little on the cover from the back.

    On other computers, the cover lifts up and off.

5. Clean inside the computer. Use a can of compressed air to blow out all the dust while you're in there. Clean any dust remnants from where they cling to the power supply's fan in the back.

To replace the cover, reverse these steps. (Don't put the dust back in, though.)

I Can Access My PC's CMOS or Setup Program by Doing This

(circle one)

Pressing the Delete key when the computer boots up

Pressing Ctrl-Alt-Enter simultaneously

Pressing Ctrl-Alt-Esc simultaneously

(write your own method here)

_____

_____

_____

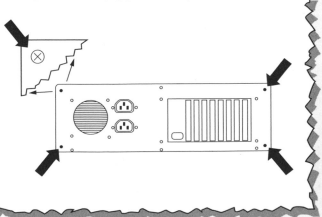

...For Dummies: #1 Computer Book Series for Beginners

COMPUTER
BOOK SERIES
FROM IDG

Upgrading & Fixing PCs For Dummies, 3rd Edition

Cheat Sheet

Steps for Working on Your PC

1. Back up any important information on your hard drive to a floppy disk for safekeeping. (To be really safe, back up the whole hard drive.)

2. Read any instructions that came with your new part.

3. Exit any running programs, turn off your PC, and unplug it from the wall.

4. Clean off the desk space next to your computer.

5. Put your tools next to the computer.

6. Remove your PC's cover.

7. Touch an unpainted part of the computer's case to discharge any static electricity that may have built up. This keeps static electricity from damaging your computer's sensitive internal parts.

8. Remove the old item and insert the new one.

9. Plug in the PC, turn it on, and carefully test the new part to see whether it works.

10. Turn off the PC, unplug it, and put the case back together.

11. Plug in the PC and put away your tools.

Always Remember These Things

Turn off and unplug your computer before taking off its cover.

Please. This one's the most important step of all. You can damage both yourself *and* your computer if you forget to turn off and unplug the computer.

The red (or colored) wire is positive.

Look for a little + sign on the socket that the wires plug into. The red or colored wire plugs into the pin marked by the + sign.

The positive/red wire connects to Pin 1.

Look for little numbers printed along the edge of a socket.

The positive wire — always the red or colored wire — always fits onto the pin marked as number 1.

Can't see the number 1? Then push the plug into the socket with the red wire facing toward the *low* numbers on the socket.

The two black wires almost always go next to each other on a motherboard's power connector.

When pushing power-supply cables into the motherboard's sockets, arrange the two cables so the two black wires are next to each other.

The Back of a PC

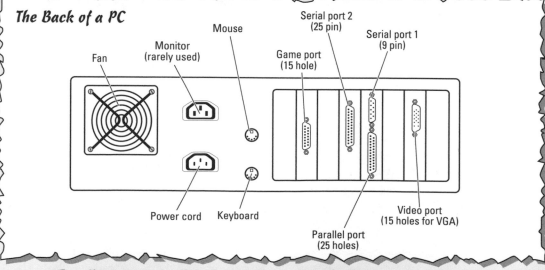

Fan

Monitor (rarely used)

Mouse

Game port (15 hole)

Serial port 2 (25 pin)

Serial port 1 (9 pin)

Power cord   Keyboard

Parallel port (25 holes)

Video port (15 holes for VGA)

...For Dummies: #1 Computer Book Series for Beginners

UPGRADING & FIXING PCs FOR DUMMIES®

3RD EDITION

by Andy Rathbone

IDG Books Worldwide, Inc.
An International Data Group Company

Foster City, CA ♦ Chicago, IL ♦ Indianapolis, IN ♦ Southlake, TX

Upgrading & Fixing PCs For Dummies® 3rd Edition

Published by
IDG Books Worldwide, Inc.
An International Data Group Company
919 E. Hillsdale Blvd.
Suite 400
Foster City, CA 94404
www.idgbooks.com (IDG Books Worldwide Web site)
www.dummies.com (Dummies Press Web site)

Library of Congress Catalog Card No.: 97-72405

ISBN: 0-7645-0129-1

Printed in the United States of America

10 9 8 7 6 5 4 3 2

3B/SS/RQ/ZX/IN

Distributed in the United States by IDG Books Worldwide, Inc.

Distributed by Macmillan Canada for Canada; by Transworld Publishers Limited in the United Kingdom; by IDG Norge Books for Norway; by IDG Sweden Books for Sweden; by Woodslane Pty. Ltd. for Australia; by Woodslane Enterprises Ltd. for New Zealand; by Longman Singapore Publishers Ltd. for Singapore, Malaysia, Thailand, and Indonesia; by Simron Pty. Ltd. for South Africa; by Toppan Company Ltd. for Japan; by Distribuidora Cuspide for Argentina; by Livraria Cultura for Brazil; by Ediciencia S.A. for Ecuador; by Addison-Wesley Publishing Company for Korea; by Ediciones ZETA S.C.R. Ltda. for Peru; by WS Computer Publishing Corporation, Inc., for the Philippines; by Unalis Corporation for Taiwan; by Contemporanea de Ediciones for Venezuela; by Computer Book & Magazine Store for Puerto Rico; by Express Computer Distributors for the Caribbean and West Indies. Authorized Sales Agent: Anthony Rudkin Associates for the Middle East and North Africa.

For general information on IDG Books Worldwide's books in the U.S., please call our Consumer Customer Service department at 800-762-2974. For reseller information, including discounts and premium sales, please call our Reseller Customer Service department at 800-434-3422.

For information on where to purchase IDG Books Worldwide's books outside the U.S., please contact our International Sales department at 415-655-3200 or fax 415-655-3295.

For information on foreign language translations, please contact our Foreign & Subsidiary Rights department at 415-655-3021 or fax 415-655-3281.

For sales inquiries and special prices for bulk quantities, please contact our Sales department at 415-655-3200 or write to the address above.

For information on using IDG Books Worldwide's books in the classroom or for ordering examination copies, please contact our Educational Sales department at 800-434-2086 or fax 817-251-8174.

For press review copies, author interviews, or other publicity information, please contact our Public Relations department at 415-655-3000 or fax 415-655-3299.

For authorization to photocopy items for corporate, personal, or educational use, please contact Copyright Clearance Center, 222 Rosewood Drive, Danvers, MA 01923, or fax 508-750-4470.

About the Author

Andy Rathbone started geeking around with computers in 1985 when he bought a boxy CP/ M Kaypro 2X with lime-green letters. Like other budding nerds, he soon began playing with null-modem adaptors, dialing up computer bulletin boards, and working part-time at Radio Shack.

In between playing computer games, he served as editor of the *Daily Aztec* newspaper at San Diego State University. After graduating with a comparative literature degree, he went to work for a bizarre underground coffee-table magazine that sort of disappeared.

Andy began combining his two interests, words and computers, by selling articles to a local computer magazine. During the next few years, Andy started ghostwriting computer books for more famous computer authors, as well as writing several hundred articles about computers for technoid publications like *Supercomputing Review, CompuServe Magazine, ID Systems, DataPro,* and *Shareware.*

In 1992, Andy and *DOS For Dummies* author/legend Dan Gookin teamed up to write *PCs For Dummies,* which was runner-up in the Computer Press Association's 1993 awards. Andy subsequently wrote the first edition of *Windows For Dummies* plus *OS/2 For Dummies, Upgrading & Fixing PCs For Dummies, Multimedia & CD-ROMs For Dummies, MORE Windows For Dummies,* and *Windows 95 For Dummies.* He also cowrote *Windows NT 4 For Dummies* with Sharon Crawford.

Andy lives with his most-excellent wife, Tina, and their cat in San Diego, California. When not writing, he fiddles with his MIDI synthesizer and tries to keep the cat off both keyboards.

ABOUT IDG BOOKS WORLDWIDE

Welcome to the world of IDG Books Worldwide.

IDG Books Worldwide, Inc., is a subsidiary of International Data Group, the world's largest publisher of computer-related information and the leading global provider of information services on information technology. IDG was founded more than 25 years ago and now employs more than 8,500 people worldwide. IDG publishes more than 275 computer publications in over 75 countries (see listing below). More than 60 million people read one or more IDG publications each month.

Launched in 1990, IDG Books Worldwide is today the #1 publisher of best-selling computer books in the United States. We are proud to have received eight awards from the Computer Press Association in recognition of editorial excellence and three from *Computer Currents*' First Annual Readers' Choice Awards. Our best-selling *...For Dummies*® series has more than 30 million copies in print with translations in 30 languages. IDG Books Worldwide, through a joint venture with IDG's Hi-Tech Beijing, became the first U.S. publisher to publish a computer book in the People's Republic of China. In record time, IDG Books Worldwide has become the first choice for millions of readers around the world who want to learn how to better manage their businesses.

Our mission is simple: Every one of our books is designed to bring extra value and skill-building instructions to the reader. Our books are written by experts who understand and care about our readers. The knowledge base of our editorial staff comes from years of experience in publishing, education, and journalism — experience we use to produce books for the '90s. In short, we care about books, so we attract the best people. We devote special attention to details such as audience, interior design, use of icons, and illustrations. And because we use an efficient process of authoring, editing, and desktop publishing our books electronically, we can spend more time ensuring superior content and spend less time on the technicalities of making books.

You can count on our commitment to deliver high-quality books at competitive prices on topics you want to read about. At IDG Books Worldwide, we continue in the IDG tradition of delivering quality for more than 25 years. You'll find no better book on a subject than one from IDG Books Worldwide.

John Kilcullen
CEO
IDG Books Worldwide, Inc.

Steven Berkowitz
President and Publisher
IDG Books Worldwide, Inc.

Eighth Annual
Computer Press
Awards ≥1992

Ninth Annual
Computer Press
Awards ≥1993

Tenth Annual
Computer Press
Awards ≥1994

Eleventh Annual
Computer Press
Awards ≥1995

IDG Books Worldwide, Inc., is a subsidiary of International Data Group, the world's largest publisher of computer-related information and the leading global provider of information services on information technology. International Data Group publishes over 275 computer publications in over 75 countries. Sixty million people read one or more International Data Group publications each month. International Data Group's publications include: **ARGENTINA:** Buyer's Guide, Computerworld Argentina, PC World Argentina; **AUSTRALIA:** Australian Macworld, Australian PC World, Australian Reseller News, Computerworld, IT Casebook, Network World, Publish, Webmaster; **AUSTRIA:** Computerwelt Österreich, Networks Austria, PC Tip Austria; **BANGLADESH:** PC World Bangladesh; **BELARUS:** PC World Belarus; **BELGIUM:** Data News; **BRAZIL:** Annuário de Informática, Computerworld, Connections, Macworld, PC Player, PC World, Publish, Reseller News, Supergamepower; **BULGARIA:** Computerworld Bulgaria, Network World Bulgaria, PC & MacWorld Bulgaria; **CANADA:** CIO Canada, Client/Server World, ComputerWorld Canada, InfoWorld Canada, NetworkWorld Canada, WebWorld; **CHILE:** Computerworld Chile, PC World Chile; **COLOMBIA:** Computerworld Colombia, PC World Colombia; **COSTA RICA:** PC World Centro America; **THE CZECH AND SLOVAK REPUBLICS:** Computerworld Czechoslovakia, Macworld Czech Republic, PC World Czechoslovakia; **DENMARK:** Communications World Danmark, Computerworld Danmark, Macworld Danmark, PC World Danmark, Techworld Denmark; **DOMINICAN REPUBLIC:** PC World Republica Dominicana; **ECUADOR:** PC World Ecuador; **EGYPT:** Computerworld Middle East, PC World Middle East; **EL SALVADOR:** PC World Centro America; **FINLAND:** MikroPC, Tietoverkko, Tietoviikko; **FRANCE:** Distributique, Hebdo, Info PC, Le Monde Informatique, Macworld, Reseaux & Telecoms, WebMaster France; **GERMANY:** Computer Partner, Computerwoche, Computerwoche Extra, Computerwoche FOCUS, Global Online, Macwelt, PC Welt; **GREECE:** Amiga Computing, GamePro Greece, Multimedia World; **GUATEMALA:** PC World Centro America; **HONDURAS:** PC World Centro America; **HONG KONG:** Computerworld Hong Kong, PC World Hong Kong, Publish in Asia; **HUNGARY:** ABCD CD-ROM, Computerworld Szamitastechnika, Internetto online Magazine, PC World Hungary, PC-X Magazin Hungary; **ICELAND:** Tolvuheimur PC World Island; **INDIA:** Information Communications World, Information Systems Computerworld, PC World India, Publish in Asia; **INDONESIA:** InfoKomputer PC World, Komputek Computerworld, Publish in Asia; **IRELAND:** ComputerScope, PC Live!; **ISRAEL:** Macworld Israel, People & Computers/Computerworld; **ITALY:** Computerworld Italia, Macworld Italia, Networking Italia, PC World Italia; **JAPAN:** DTP World, Macworld Japan, Nikkei Personal Computing, OS/2 World Japan, SunWorld Japan, Windows NT World, Windows World Japan; **KENYA:** PC World East African; **KOREA:** Hi-Tech Information, Macworld Korea, PC World Korea; **MACEDONIA:** PC World Macedonia; **MALAYSIA:** Computerworld Malaysia, PC World Malaysia, Publish in Asia; **MALTA:** PC World Malta; **MEXICO:** Computerworld Mexico, PC World Mexico; **MYANMAR:** PC World Myanmar; **NETHERLANDS:** Computer! Totaal, LAN Internetworking Magazine, LAN World Buyers Guide, Macworld Netherlands, Net, WebWereld; **NEW ZEALAND:** Absolute Beginners Guide and Plain & Simple Series, Computer Buyer, Computer Industry Directory, Computerworld New Zealand, MTB, Network World, PC World New Zealand; **NICARAGUA:** PC World Centro America; **NORWAY:** Computerworld Norge, CW Rapport, Datamagasinet, Financial Rapport, Kursguide Norge, Macworld Norge, Multimediaworld Norge, PC World Ekspress Norge, PC World Nettverk, PC World Norge, PC World ProduktGuide Norge; **PAKISTAN:** Computerworld Pakistan; **PANAMA:** PC World Panama; **PEOPLE'S REPUBLIC OF CHINA:** China Computer Users, China Computerworld, China InfoWorld, China Telecom World Weekly, Computer & Communication, Electronic Design China, Electronics Today, Electronics Weekly, Game Software, PC World China, Popular Computer Week, Software Weekly, Software World, Telecom World; **PERU:** Computerworld Peru, PC World Profesional Peru, PC World SoHo Peru; **PHILIPPINES:** Click!, Computerworld Philippines, PC World Philippines, Publish in Asia; **POLAND:** Computerworld Poland, Computerworld Special Report Poland, Cyber, Macworld Poland, Networld Poland, PC World Komputer; **PORTUGAL:** Cerebro/PC World, Computerworld/Correio Informático, Dealer World Portugal, Mac*In/PC*In Portugal, Multimedia World; **PUERTO RICO:** PC World Puerto Rico; **ROMANIA:** Computerworld Romania, PC World Romania, Telecom Romania; **RUSSIA:** Computerworld Russia, Mir PK, Publish, Seti; **SINGAPORE:** Computerworld Singapore, PC World Singapore, Publish in Asia; **SLOVENIA:** Monitor; **SOUTH AFRICA:** Computing SA, Network World SA, Software World SA; **SPAIN:** Communicaciones World España, Computerworld España, Dealer World España, Macworld España, PC World España; **SRI LANKA:** Infolink PC World; **SWEDEN:** CAP&Design, Computer Sweden, Corporate Computing Sweden, Internetworld Sweden, it.branschen, Macworld Sweden, MaxiData Sweden, MikroDatorn, Nätverk & Kommunikation, PC World Sweden, PCaktiv, Windows World Sweden; **SWITZERLAND:** Computerworld Schweiz, Macworld Schweiz, PCtip; **TAIWAN:** Computerworld Taiwan, Macworld Taiwan, NEW ViSiON/Publish, PC World Taiwan, Windows World Taiwan; **THAILAND:** Publish in Asia, Thai Computerworld; **TURKEY:** Computerworld Turkiye, Macworld Turkiye, Network World Turkiye, PC World Turkiye; **UKRAINE:** Computerworld Kiev, Multimedia World Ukraine, PC World Ukraine; **UNITED KINGDOM:** Acorn User UK, Amiga Action UK, Amiga Computing UK, Apple Talk UK, Computing, Macworld, Parents and Computers UK, PC Advisor, PC Home, PSX Pro, The WEB; **UNITED STATES:** Cable in the Classroom, CIO Magazine, Computerworld, DOS World, Federal Computer Week, GamePro Magazine, InfoWorld, I-Way, Macworld, Network World, PC Games, PC World, Publish, Video Event, THE WEB Magazine, and WebMaster; online webzines: JavaWorld, NetscapeWorld, and SunWorld Online; **URUGUAY:** InfoWorld Uruguay; **VENEZUELA:** Computerworld Venezuela, PC World Venezuela; and **VIETNAM:** PC World Vietnam.   3/24/97

Dedication

To that sense of satisfaction felt when fixing it yourself.

Acknowledgments

Special thanks to the cat, for staying off the keyboard this time.

Publisher's Acknowledgments

We're proud of this book; please register your comments through our IDG Books Worldwide Online Registration Form located at `http://my2cents.dummies.com`.

Some of the people who helped bring this book to market include the following:

Acquisitions, Development, and Editorial

Project Editor: Tere Drenth

Acquisitions Editor: Michael Kelly

Copy Editor: Jennifer Davies

Technical Editor: Jamey Marcum

Editorial Manager: Seta K. Frantz

Editorial Assistants: Donna Love, Darren Meiss

Production

Project Coordinator: Regina D. Snyder

Layout and Graphics: Linda M. Boyer, Dominique DeFelice, Angela F. Hunckler, Todd Klemme, Brent Savage

Proofreaders: Ethel M. Winslow, Melissa D. Buddendeck, Renee Kelty, Betty Kish, Christine D. Berman, Joel K. Draper, Rachel Garvey, Robert Springer, Karen York

Indexer: Nancy Anderman Guenther

Special Help

Colleen Rainsberger, Senior Project Editor

General and Administrative

IDG Books Worldwide, Inc.: John Kilcullen, CEO; Steven Berkowitz, President and Publisher

IDG Books Technology Publishing: Brenda McLaughlin, Senior Vice President and Group Publisher

Dummies Technology Press and Dummies Editorial: Diane Graves Steele, Vice President and Associate Publisher; Mary Bednarek, Acquisitions and Product Development Director; Kristin A. Cocks, Editorial Director

Dummies Trade Press: Kathleen A. Welton, Vice President and Publisher; Kevin Thornton, Acquisitions Manager

IDG Books Production for Dummies Press: Beth Jenkins, Production Director; Cindy L. Phipps, Manager of Project Coordination, Production Proofreading, and Indexing; Kathie S. Schutte, Supervisor of Page Layout; Shelley Lea, Supervisor of Graphics and Design; Debbie J. Gates, Production Systems Specialist; Robert Springer, Supervisor of Proofreading; Debbie Stailey, Special Projects Coordinator; Tony Augsburger, Supervisor of Reprints and Bluelines; Leslie Popplewell, Media Archive Coordinator

Dummies Packaging and Book Design: Patti Crane, Packaging Specialist; Lance Kayser, Packaging Assistant; Kavish + Kavish, Cover Design

♦

The publisher would like to give special thanks to Patrick J. McGovern, without whom this book would not have been possible.

♦

Contents at a Glance

Cartoons at a Glance

By Rich Tennant

The 5th Wave — By Rich Tennant

In the wee hours of the morning, confused with fatigue, Gary, the chocolate junky, discovers, the hard way, how similar in appearance are his new expanded memory circuit boards, and an unwrapped Nestle Crunch bar.

page 151

The 5th Wave — By Rich Tennant

"I'M WAITING FOR MY AUTOEXEC FILE TO RUN, SO I'M GONNA GRAB A CUP OF COFFEE, MAYBE MAKE A SANDWICH, CHECK THE SPORTS PAGE, REGRIND THE BRAKEDRUMS ON MY TRUCK, BALANCE MY CHECKBOOK FOR THE PAST 12 YEARS, LEARN SWAHILI, ..."

page 253

The 5th Wave — By Rich Tennant

"HOLD ON, THAT'S NOT A PROGRAM ERROR, IT'S JUST A BOOGER ON THE SCREEN."

page 309

The 5th Wave — By Rich Tennant

"YEAH, I USED TO WORK ON REFRIGERATORS, WASHING MACHINES, STUFF LIKE THAT—HOW'D YOU GUESS?"

page 7

The 5th Wave — By Rich Tennant

"Now, when someone rings my doorbell, the current goes to a scanner that digitizes the audio impulses and sends the image to the PC where it's converted to a Pict file. The image is then animated, compressed, and sent via high-speed modem to an automated phone service that sends an e-mail message back to tell me someone was at my door 40 minutes ago."

page 89

Fax: 508-546-7747 • **E-mail:** the5wave@tiac.net

Table of Contents

Part II: The PC Parts You Can See (Peripherals) 89

Introduction

∙ ∙

*Y*ou're no dummy; we both know that. But something about computers makes you feel like a dummy. And that's perfectly understandable. Unlike today's MTV-drenched kids, you didn't start learning about computers while at the day-care center. And you haven't spent much time trying to catch up, either.

You haven't missed much, though. Computers are still as cryptic as they were the day you first saw one. They haven't gotten any friendlier, either. At least a bank's ATM rewards its users with a $20 bill after they've figured out which keys to press. Computers just *take* your money.

In fact, your computer's probably asking for some more of your cash right now, and that's why you're flipping through this book's Introduction.

Most of today's computer owners face at least one of the following problems:

- Your new software comes on those small shirt-pocket-sized disks, and your old computer only takes the big black ones.
- Somebody says that you "need more RAM."
- Even if your software *did* come on the right-sized disks, your hard drive isn't big enough to hold the software.
- Your computer made three long beeps, and now it won't work anymore.
- You want to see and hear some of those fun multimedia programs that everybody's talking about.
- Sighing deeply, you decide it's your turn to join the Internet and send e-mail to long-lost relatives.
- You're wondering why you should pay the repair shop $75 an hour to install a part that only costs half that much.

About This Book

That's where this book comes in handy. With this book in one hand and a screwdriver in the other, you can repair your own computer or add new parts to it. Best yet, this book doesn't force you to learn anything during the process.

Instead, this book is a reference filled with nuggets of information — sort of a mini-encyclopedia. For example, if your floppy drive starts acting weird, just flip through to the section dealing with weird-acting floppy drives. There, you find simple instructions for jump-starting your floppy drive back into action.

Floppy drive still won't work? Then follow the clearly numbered steps to pull out your old floppy drive and stick in a new one. You won't find any techno-babble blocking the way, either. Instead, you can just jump to the details you need to know now: Which screws do you need to remove? Which cable plugs into which hole? How do you put the computer back together? And what happens if you lose an important screw in the shag carpet somewhere beneath the desk?

Unlike other computer repair books, this book steers clear from headings like "Integrated I/O Circuitry on the Mainboard" or "Procedures for Measuring Capacitor Flow." Who cares?

How to Use This Book

Suppose your keyboard's on the fritz. Don't know how a healthy keyboard's supposed to act? Then head to Chapter 3 for a quick rundown. (That's the chapter that explains all the computer stuff everybody thinks you already know.)

Then when you're ready, flip to Chapter 5, the keyboard chapter, to hear about common keyboard foul-ups, as well as tips on how to make your keyboard work again. In that chapter, you find fixes for problems like these:

- ✔ When I turn on my computer, the screen says `Keyboard not found —` `Press <F1> to continue` or something equally depressing!

- ✔ Some of the keys stick after I spilled a Hansen's Natural Raspberry Soda over them!

- ✔ My arrow keys don't move the cursor — they make numbers!

- ✔ My keyboard doesn't have F11 and F12 keys, and Microsoft Word for Windows uses those!

If your keyboard's truly beyond repair, head for Chapter 5's "How Do I Install a New Keyboard?" section. There, you discover which tools you need (if any) and how much money this setback will cost you. Finally, you see a list of clearly numbered steps explaining everything you need to do to get that new keyboard installed and ready for hunting and pecking.

Type This Stuff Here

If you need to type anything into your computer, you see the text you need to type displayed like this:

```
C:\> TYPE THIS IN
```

Here, you type the words **TYPE THIS IN** after the C:\> thing and then press the Enter key. If the material you're supposed to type is particularly awkward, a description of what you're supposed to type follows so that there's no confusion (well, as little confusion as possible, anyway).

Words or commands that appear on the screen appear in the book like this: `These words appear on the screen.`

Read These Parts

If you're lucky (and your computer's healthy), you won't have to read very much of this book. But, when something weird happens, this book can help you figure out what went wrong, whether it can be repaired, or whether you have to replace it.

Along the way, you may find helpful comments or warnings explaining the process in more detail.

You find tips like this scattered throughout the book. Take a look at them first. In fact, one tip may spare you from having to read more than a paragraph of a computer book — a worthy feat indeed!

Don't Read These Parts

Okay, I lied a little bit. I did stick some technobabble in this book. After all, I'm a computer geek. (Whenever I sit down in a restaurant, my palmtop computer shoots out the top of my back pocket and clatters on the floor.) Luckily for you, however, I have neatly cordoned off all the technical drivel.

Any particularly odious technical details are isolated and posted with this icon so you can avoid them easily. If a computer nerd drops by to help with your particular problem, just hand the computer nerd this book. With these icons, he or she will know exactly which sections to look for.

How This Book Is Organized

This book has five major parts. Each part is divided into several chapters. And each chapter covers a major topic, which is divided into specific sections.

The point? Well, this book's indexer sorted all the information with an extra-fine-tooth flea comb, making it easy for you to find the exact section you want, when you want it. Plus, everything's cross-referenced. If you need more information about a subject, you can figure out exactly which chapter to head for.

Here are the parts and what they contain:

Part I: Biting Your Fingernails

You find the basics in here. One chapter explains your computer's basic anatomy so that you'll know which parts are *supposed* to make noise. Another chapter helps you figure out which part of your computer isn't working right. Plus, the very first chapter offers a few ego-boosting tips. Yes, you *can* upgrade and fix your computer by yourself.

Part II: The PC Parts You Can See (Peripherals)

Here you find "fix-it" information on the parts of your PC that are in plain sight: your monitor, for example, as well as your printer, keyboard, and other stuff you have to wipe the dust off of every once in a while. Each chapter starts off with repair tips and — if the thing still won't work right — detailed instructions on how to yank parts out and stick in new ones.

Part III: The Stuff Hiding Inside Your PC

Your PC's more mysterious parts lurk inside its big case, hidden from sight. Tilt down the brim of your safari hat as you rummage through the inside of your PC to replace floppy drives, add memory chips, or add fun computer toys like compact disc players.

Part IV: Telling Your Computer What You've Done

If anybody's a dummy here, it's your computer. Even after you've stuck a new part in its craw, your computer probably won't know that the part is there. This part of the book explains how to tell your computer that it has just received a new part and that it should start groping around for it.

Part V: The Part of Tens

Some information just drifts away when it's buried deep within a paragraph. That's why these tidbits are stacked up in lists of ten (give or take a few). Here, you find lists like "Ten Cheap Fixes to Try First," "Ten Ways to Make Your PC Run Better," "The Ten Easiest Things to Upgrade," and other fun factoids.

Icons Used in This Book

This book's most exceptional parts are marked by icons — little eye-catching pictures in the margins:

This icon warns of some ugly technical information lying by the side of the road. Feel free to drive right by. The information is probably just a more complex discussion of something already explained in the chapter.

Pounce on this icon whenever you see it. Chances are that it marks a helpful paragraph worthy of a sticky note.

If you've forgotten what you were supposed to remember, keep an eye toward the margins for this icon.

Better be careful when doing stuff marked by this icon. In fact, this icon usually warns you about stuff you *shouldn't* be doing, like squirting WD-40 into your floppy drive.

Sometimes computer parts don't live well together. Computer upgrades that sometimes lead to even *more* repairs or purchases are pegged with this icon.

Still pounding the keys on an ancient hand-me-down? Picked up a lumbering oldster at a garage sale? This icon flags specific fixes and tips for people stuck with those old monsters. (Windows-snubbing DOS users can also find helpful tips here.)

Auto mechanics can find the most helpful sections in their manuals by just looking for the greasiest pages. So, by all means, draw your own icons next to the stuff that you find particularly helpful. Scrawl in some of your own observations, as well.

Where to Go from Here

I'm not going to kid you. You won't be able to replace and/or fix *every* part in your PC. For example, most repair shops don't fix monitors or power supplies. Those items are just too complicated (and dangerous) to mess with. You have to buy new ones.

In fact, this book tells you which parts of your PC you can fix *yourself* (most of them) and which parts are probably over your head. That way, you know which repairs you should parcel out to the technoweenies in the shop. You won't have to worry about attempting any repairs that are simply beyond your mortal abilities.

Also, your path will be easier if you're briefly familiar with your PC. For example, you need to know how to see a directory of the files on a floppy disk. Don't know? You type this at the A:\> prompt:

```
A:\> DIR
```

That's the word **DIR** followed by a press of the Enter key. Your computer displays the names of that disk's files. If these concepts seem foreign to you, pick up a copy of this book's great-grandfather, *DOS For Dummies,* 2nd Edition, by Dan Gookin (IDG Books Worldwide, Inc.). It's chock-full of introductory PC dance steps.

Ready to go? Then grab this book and a screwdriver. Your computer's ready whenever you are. Good luck.

Part I
Biting Your Fingernails

The 5th Wave   By Rich Tennant

"YEAH, I USED TO WORK ON REFRIGERATORS, WASHING MACHINES, STUFF LIKE THAT–HOW'D YOU GUESS?"

In this part . . .

xcited about electrolytic capacitors?

All agog over Schottky Integrated Circuits?

Then back up and keep reading those two sentences. You won't find any words like that in the *rest* of this book.

Chapter 1

Are You Nerdy Enough to Do It Yourself?

. . . .

In This Chapter

▶ Computers are difficult to destroy

▶ PCs are easier to fix than cars

▶ Can you save money by upgrading your PC yourself?

▶ PCs aren't as scary after you've fixed one

▶ When should you upgrade?

▶ When shouldn't you upgrade?

▶ What happens if parts don't work together?

. . . .

*H*ere's the secret: If you can open a bag of Cheetos, then you can upgrade and repair your PC. You don't need to be a technoweenie with a vacant stare.

In fact, upgrading a PC is almost always easier than trying to use one. I know a guy who can turn a box of spare parts into a whole PC in less time than it takes to print a three-column page in WordPerfect.

Still not convinced? Then let this chapter serve as a little confidence booster. Remember, you don't *have* to be a computer wizard to upgrade or repair your PC.

You Probably Won't Kill Your PC by Accident

Are you afraid that you'll mess something up if you take off your computer's case? Actually, there's very little that can go wrong. As long as you don't leave a dropped screw rolling around in your computer's innards, you don't have much to worry about. (And I tell you how to retrieve the dropped screw in Chapter 2.)

Do safety concerns keep you from prodding around inside your PC? Not only is the computer safe from your fingers, but your fingers are safe from your computer. After you unplug the beasts, computers are safer than an un-plugged blender. You're not going to get a frizzy new hairstyle by acciden-tally touching the wrong part. Besides, you can fix a lot of your computer's problems without even taking off the case.

Are you afraid that you may accidentally put the wrong wire in the wrong place? Don't worry about it. Most of the wires in your PC are color coded. You can easily tell which wire goes where. The computer designers even catered to groggy engineers: Most of the cables only fit into their plugs one way — the right way.

If you can change a coffee filter (even one of those expensive, gold-plated coffee filters), then you can change the parts of your PC.

- ✔ The PC was designed to be *modular* — all the parts slip in and out of their own special areas. You can't accidentally install your hard drive where the power supply is supposed to go. Your hard drive simply won't fit. (Just to be sure, I tried it just now and it didn't work.)

- ✔ Although computers suck 110 volts from a wall outlet — the same as any household appliance — they don't actually use that much electric-ity. A computer's power supply turns 120 volts into 5 or 12 volts, which is less than the amount that some freebie Radio Shack flashlights use. This way, computers are a little less dangerous.

- ✔ Your PC won't explode if you install a part incorrectly; it just won't work. Although a computer that doesn't work can lead to serious head scratching, it won't lead to any head bandaging. Simply remove the misinstalled part and try installing it again from scratch. Then be careful to follow this book's step-by-step instructions. (And keep an eye out for the troubleshooting tips found in nearby paragraphs.)

- ✔ When IBM built its first PC microcomputer about 15 years ago, the engineers designed it to be thrown together quickly with common parts. It's still like that today. You can install most computer upgrades with just a screwdriver, and other parts just snap in place just like expensive Lego blocks.

Just as wicked witches don't like water, computer chips are deathly afraid of static electricity. A little static zap may scare you into dropping your pencil, but that zap can be instant death for a computer chip. Be sure to touch something metal — the edge of a metal desk, a file cabinet, or even your PC's chassis — before touching anything inside your computer. Live in a particularly static-prone environment? Some stores sell static-grounding straps: little wrist bracelets that screw onto your PC's chassis to keep you grounded at all times.

Upgrading a PC Beats Working on a Car

Forget about the mechanic's overalls; computers are *much* easier to work on than cars for several reasons. Ninety percent of the time, you can upgrade a PC by using a screwdriver from your kitchen's junk drawer. No need for expensive tools, protective gloves, or noisy wrenches. You don't even have to grunt, spit, or wipe your hands on your pants, unless you already do that stuff anyway.

Also, computer parts are easier to find than car parts. Every year, cars use a different kind of bumper or a new air filter. But, with a PC, all the parts are pretty much the same. You can take a mouse off a friend's computer and plug it into your computer without any problem (unless your friend sees you doing it).

With PC repair, you never encounter any heavy lifting. And you never have to roll under your computer either, unless you're laptopping at the beach.

✔ If you have an old car, you're probably stuck buying parts from a hard-to-find garage in New Jersey. But, if you have an old computer, just grab the floppy drive sitting on the computer store shelf. With a few rare exceptions, you won't have to search old IBM heaps for an '87 floppy drive for a TurboChunk 286.

✔ There aren't any pipes to drop bolts into, like I did when I foolishly tried to replace the carburetor on my '65 VW van. After watching the tow truck haul my car away, I decided to stick with PCs: Computers don't have any open pipes, they don't use bolts, and they smell a lot better than carburetor cleaner. Plus, PCs don't have as many moving parts to catch your sleeve and drag you perilously close to whirling gears.

✔ Here's one more difference: Car mechanics *repair* stuff. If something inside the engine breaks, the mechanic laboriously takes apart the engine, replaces the bad part with a good one, and laboriously puts the engine back together. But, with PCs, you *replace* stuff. If your PC's video card dies, throw it away and screw in a new one. Much less fuss. And it's cheaper, too.

✔ Finally, you can sometimes fix your PC without even opening the case. Some software can automatically probe inside your computer, find any culprits, and fix them.

Can You Really Save Bundles of Money?

Many people think that they can build their own PCs from scratch and save a bundle. But it just doesn't work that way. Nobody can save money on a Corvette by picking up all the parts at the Chevy dealer's parts window and bolting them together. The same holds true for a PC.

Today's computer dealers buy zillions of parts at a bulk rate discount, slap 'em all together in the back room, and stick the finished product in the store window 20 minutes later. Without all those bulk discounts on the parts though, a self-made computer costs about as much as a brand-new one — maybe even a little more.

✔ If your computer is so old that you want to replace *everything,* go for it. But replace everything by buying a *brand new computer.* You not only save money and time, but you probably get some free software — and a new warranty — tossed in as well.

✔ It's almost always cheaper to *replace* a part than to *repair* it. Most repair shops charge upwards of $75 an hour; a long repair job can cost more than a new part. And many shops don't even bother trying to repair the really scary stuff, like monitors or power supplies. It's cheaper (and easier) for the shops to just sell you new ones.

✔ So why bother upgrading your computer yourself? Because you can save cash on repair bills. Plus your computer will be up and running more quickly: It won't be stuck in a backlogged repair shop while you're stuck with no computer. Horrors!

PCs Aren't as Scary After You've Fixed One

When I was a kid, my mom took the car into the shop because it made a strange rattling sound while she turned corners. My mom didn't have any idea what could be causing the problem. The car's rattles and pops *all* sounded scary and mysterious to her.

The mechanic couldn't find anything wrong, though, so my mom took him on a test drive. Sure enough, when the car rounded a sharp corner, the rattling noise appeared. The mechanic cocked his ear for a few seconds and then opened the metal ashtray on the dashboard. He removed a round pebble and the sound at the same time.

My mom was embarrassed, of course. And, luckily, the auto shop didn't charge for the fix. But this anecdote proves a point: If my mom had known a little bit more about her car, the rattling sound wouldn't have been scary, and she could have saved herself a trip to the shop.

"So what's your point?" you ask. Well . . .

✔ After you open your PC's case and see what's inside, your PC isn't as mysterious or scary to you. You see that it's just a collection of parts, like anything else.

✔ After you fiddle with a PC, you feel more confident about working with your computer and its software. Fiddling with PCs doesn't have to become a hobby, heaven forbid. But you won't be afraid that if you press the wrong key, the monitor will explode like it did on *Star Trek* last week. (And come to think of it, the week before that, too.)

✔ If you're going to bring small rocks back from the desert, put them in the glove compartment. They don't rattle as loudly in there.

When Should You Upgrade?

Your computer will tell you when you need to upgrade. You may have already seen some of the following warning signs:

When Windows demands it

Everybody's using Windows, or at least that's what the folks who sell Windows say. And finicky Windows works best on one of those big, new, sporty computers with a fast Central Processing Unit (CPU), a big hard drive, and large smokestacks. If you want to upgrade to Windows 95 or Windows NT, then upgrade your computer as well.

When you keep waiting for your PC to catch up

You press a button and wait. And wait. Or, if you're using Windows, you click on a button and watch the little hourglass sit on the screen. When you're working faster than your PC, it's time to give the little fellow a boost with some extra memory, a larger hard drive, or a faster CPU.

When you can't afford a new computer

When you're strapped for cash and can't afford a new computer, buy the parts one at a time. For example, add that new hard drive now and add other parts a few months later when your credit card's not as anemic.

When your old equipment becomes tired

Is your mouse hopping across the screen? Are the keys on your keyboard stickingggg? Do your disk drives burp on your floppy disks? Is your old hard drive sending you weird messages? If so, chances are that the parts are saying, "Replace me quick, before I pack my bags and take all your reports, spreadsheets, and high-game scores with me."

When you want a new part in a hurry

Computer repair shops aren't nearly as slow as stereo repair shops. Still, do you really want to wait four days for them to install that hot new video card? Especially when you have a nagging suspicion that you could do it yourself in less than 15 minutes?

Also, if you're buying your parts through the mail to save some bucks, count on sticking them inside the computer yourself.

When there's no room for new software

When five people head to the restaurant in a single car, three friends cram into the back seat and ride with their knees in the air.

Computer software won't be nearly as neighborly. Each program stakes out its own portion of your computer's hard drive, and it doesn't share.

When you run out of hard disk space for new programs, you have two options: Delete software you no longer use or buy a hard disk big enough to hold all your programs comfortably.

When Shouldn't You Upgrade?

Sometimes, you shouldn't work on your computer yourself. Take caution under the following circumstances:

When a computer part breaks while your computer is under warranty

If your computer is under warranty, let *them* fix the part. In fact, fixing a part yourself may void the warranty on the rest of your computer.

When the dealer says, "I'll install the part for free, within 15 minutes!"

Fifteen minutes? By all means, take the dealer up on the offer before he or she wises up and starts charging, like all the other dealers. (Make sure you compare prices with other dealers, however; a higher-priced part may make up for the free installation.)

On a Friday

Never try to install a new computer part on a Friday afternoon. When you discover that the widget needs a *left* bracket too, most repair shops will be closed, leaving you with a desktop full of detached parts until Monday morning.

When your computer is ancient

Not all computers can be upgraded. If you're using an old XT or AT computer (which I describe in Chapter 3), it's probably cheaper to buy a new computer than to replace all the old parts individually. In fact, if you're thinking about upgrading a computer that's more than two years old, try this: Total the amount of new equipment you need (bigger hard drive, better video card and monitor, faster modem, and other goodies) and compare it to the cost of a new computer. Chances are, the two figures won't be far off.

When you need your computer up and running within 90 minutes

Just like kitchen remodeling, computer upgrading and repairing takes at least twice as long as you originally thought. Don't try to work on your computer under deadline pressure, or you'll wind up steam-cleaning your ears when your head explodes.

When you haven't optimized your computer's software

Hey, your computer may not need expensive new hardware in order to run better. You may be able to run some "test and fix" software that ferrets out any software problems and fixes them for you. (Chapter 19 describes some of these.)

Beware of the Chain Reaction

One upgrade often leads to another. Like quarreling office workers, some computer parts refuse to work together — even though they're designed for *IBM compatible* computers.

For example, you buy a new hard drive, install it, and wonder why it doesn't work. Then you discover that your computer has a *controller card,* and it's not compatible with the hard drive you've just installed.

Luckily, controller cards are relatively cheap. However, compatibility is still something to be aware of. When you see the Chain Reaction icon in this book, be aware that you may have to buy yet another part before the upgrade will work.

- ✔ Chain reactions can pop up with just about any part, unfortunately. For example, sometimes you have to replace *all* of your memory chips instead of just plugging in a few new ones, as you had hoped. Or sometimes buying a new video card means that you have to buy a new monitor, too: Your old monitor may still work, but it probably won't take advantage of all your new card's whiz-bang features.

- ✔ None of this stuff is *your* fault, though. The same chain reaction can happen even if you let the folks at the repair shop upgrade your computer. The only difference is that you hear the sorry news over the phone, just like when the mechanic calls the office saying that you need a new radiator when you only took the car in for a new set of shocks. Yep, those are some shocks all right.

- ✔ If a part doesn't work in your computer, there's still hope. You can almost always return computer parts for a refund just as if the parts were sweaters that didn't fit. If you don't feel like replacing all the incompatible parts, just take back your new part for a refund. As long as you return it within a reasonable amount of time and in good working order, you shouldn't have a problem. (As a precaution, however, always check the return policy before buying a part.)

Chapter 2
The *Right* Way to Fix Your PC

. . . .

In This Chapter

▶ Ten steps for upgrading your PC

▶ Where you should work on your PC

▶ The tools you need

▶ How to make a System disk

▶ Things to do when working on your PC

▶ Things *not* to do when working on your PC

▶ How to fish out dropped screws

. . . .

*W*hen I was a little kid, my sister and I met a guy who lived by the beach and liked to fiddle around with gadgets. One day, he cut the power cord off an old lamp and tied a big nail to the ends of each wire.

Then he stuck one nail in each end of a hot dog and plugged the cord back into the wall. Sure enough, the hot dog cooked. Sizzled, even, and made some sputtering sounds. But we didn't eat the hot dog. In fact, we kind of gave the guy a wide berth after that.

My sister and I knew there was a *right* way to do things and a *wrong* way. This chapter points out the difference between the two when you're working on your computer.

The Ten Steps for Upgrading Your PC

Those technodrones in the back room can charge you $75 an hour for replacing a part, but they're merely following simple steps they learned at Computer School. Consider these steps from the Cliffs Notes of Upgrading (in fact, you can find them repeated in the handy Cheat Sheet at the front of this book):

1. Back up your hard drive so you won't lose any data.

Whenever you drop a new part into your PC, you run the risk of upsetting its stomach. Your PC probably won't wipe out any information on your hard drive for revenge, but wouldn't you feel like a dweeb if something *did* happen? Make sure that you have a backup copy of everything on your hard drive. Of course, you've been backing up your data every day, so this shouldn't be too much of a chore. (You *have* been backing up your data, haven't you?)

If you're tired of copying everything onto floppy disks, consider buying one of several types of *backup units.* They're special little gizmos that quickly and automatically record all your information onto special computerized cassette tapes or disks. They can even back up your hard drive automatically at the end of each day, so you don't have to remember anything. (Ready to install one? Then head to Chapter 13.)

2. Read the instructions that come with the part.

After you tear open the box, look at the installation instructions. Chances are that the instructions booklet has a page in the front labeled "At Least Read This Part." This page is for people who are too excited about their new computer part to wade through the boring manual.

Next, look for any enclosed computer disks. Find one? Then stick it into your floppy drive and look for a file called README.TXT, README.COM, or something similar. Manufacturers often update their equipment more often than they update their manuals, so they stick the most up-to-date information on the floppy disk. (Double-click on the file's name from within the Windows 95 My Computer or Windows Explorer programs to bring the file to the screen.)

If you find a file that says README.COM and you aren't using Windows, type the following at the prompt and then press Enter:

```
A:\> README
```

The program brings some last-minute information to your screen.

If you find a file called README.TXT and you aren't using Windows, then type this at the prompt:

```
A:\> TYPE README.TXT | MORE
```

(That weird | thing between README.TXT and MORE is on the slash key near the Enter key.) When you press Enter after typing the word MORE, your computer brings the information to your screen and pauses thoughtfully at each page. Press the spacebar to advance to the next page.

See any information that might come in handy down the road? Then write it down or print it out. Otherwise, head for the next step.

3. **Exit any programs, turn off your PC, and unplug it from the wall.**

Don't ever turn off your PC while it has a program on the screen. That's like plucking a kid off the merry-go-round before it stops turning — potentially dangerous and certainly hard on the ears.

Make sure that you exit any currently running programs — especially Windows. When Windows 95 says it's okay to turn off your computer (or when a DOS computer simply shows the C:\> prompt on the screen), you can safely head for the off switch. Just to make sure that nobody trips over the cord, unplug it from the wall, too.

Don't know how to turn off your computer in Windows 95? Click the Start button and choose the Sh<u>u</u>t down button from the list that pops up. Make sure the <u>S</u>hut down the computer button is checked and click <u>Y</u>es to make Windows 95 go to sleep.

4. **Clean off the counter space next to your computer.**

Dump the junk mail and shelve any stray floppy disks. You need an empty place to set things so you don't have to stack stuff on top of each other.

Don't keep any liquids near your repair area where you can spill them into your case. A spilled beverage will almost certainly destroy your computer.

5. **Find your tools and put them next to the computer.**

After you start to install that new part, the adrenaline begins to flow. You don't want to lose momentum while hunting for a screwdriver, so make sure that all your tools are within reach. What tools? Check out the "What Tools Do You Need?" section later in this chapter.

6. **Remove the cover of your PC.**

On some of the older models, you remove the four screws around the bottom sides of the case (two along each side). Sometimes, you can find a screw or two in the back as well. Other computer cases — the ones that stand up like a brick — have a single screw in the top of their back panel and a few plastic tabs. If you're lucky with the screws, the case slides off like butter on a hot pancake. Other times, the case sticks like gum under the table. Check this book's Cheat Sheet for full details.

Touch an unpainted part of the computer's case to discharge any static electricity that may have built up. This keeps static electricity from damaging your computer's sensitive internal parts.

7. **Pull out the old item and insert the new.**

   You may want to take notes on a scratch pad so you can remember which wires go where. Cables and plugs usually only fit one way, but you may feel more confident if you draw your own picture.

8. **Plug in your computer and fire up the gizmo to see whether it works.**

   What? Plug in the computer and turn it on when the case is *off?* Yes. Just don't touch anything inside the case and you'll be safe. For example, if you replace a video card, you can check to make sure that you see stuff on your monitor when you turn on your computer.

   If the new part works, head for Step 9. If it doesn't, turn the computer off, unplug it, and start troubleshooting. Perhaps you forgot to connect a cable. Or you may need to flip a switch somewhere, which I describe in Chapter 18.

9. **Unplug the computer and put the PC back together.**

   Done? Then check to make sure that you don't have any leftover screws or, even worse, any leftover holes *without* screws. If a forgotten screw is wedged in the wrong place inside the case, your computer may fry like an electrocuted hot dog.

   You can find tips on fishing out stubborn screws later in this chapter.

10. **Plug the PC back into the wall and give it a final test.**

    The part's installed, the case is back on, and all the cables are plugged back in. Does the computer still work? *Whew.* If not, check the cables to make sure that you pushed them in all the way.

By carefully following these ten steps, you can avoid problems. The key is to proceed methodically, step-by-step. Not watching television at the same time can help, too.

Making a Garage for Your PC

PCs don't need much of a garage. For the most part, your desktop works fine. Just make sure that it has plenty of elbow room.

If your desktop is too small, consider moving the computer to the dining room table. Actually, the tablecloth can help out: Screws won't roll as far when they're dropped. Plus, the extra padding, no matter how slight, helps protect your PC's more sensitive parts when you set them down.

What Tools Do You Need?

All the tools required to fix a PC can fit into a single pocket protector: A small Phillips screwdriver handles 90 percent of the operating room chores, although a few other tools occasionally come in handy (like the plain old screwdriver in your fix-it drawer).

Feeling particularly sporty? Drop by a computer shop and pick up a computer tool kit. You can get most of the tools mentioned below and a snazzy, zip-up black case to keep them in, and most kits cost less than $20.

Small Phillips screwdriver

The Phillips screwdriver needs to be able to handle a screw that's the size of the one shown in Figure 2-1. (Phillips screwdrivers are the kind with the little square cross on their tip, not a flat blade.)

Itty-bitty flathead screwdriver

Printer cables, monitor cables, and mouse tails all plug into the back of your PC. Most cables have tiny screws on the end to keep them from falling off their plugs. You need a screwdriver to handle screws the size of the one shown in Figure 2-2.

Medium Phillips screwdriver

Sometimes an overeager computer nerd will really bear down on the screws that hold on your computer's case. In that case, a slightly larger Phillips screwdriver can give you better leverage. Check out the size of the screws on your PC's case and shop accordingly.

Paper clip

Believe it or not, tiny elves design and build many computer parts. That's the reason the special switches, called DIP switches, are so small. A bent paper clip helps to move these switches back and forth. You often need to *flip a DIP* when adding a new part to your computer. The switches are really as small as they look in Figure 2-3.

The manual bundled with Toshiba's 3401 CD-ROM drive shows a paper clip being used for the Emergency Eject Procedure that extracts stubborn compact discs.

Figure 2-1:
Most of the screws holding your PC together are this size.

⊕

Figure 2-2:
The screws holding your cables to the back of your computer are really this tiny.

⊖

Figure 2-3:
A bent paper clip comes in handy for flipping tiny switches like these.

Other handy tools

The following items aren't crucial, but feel free to pick them up if you spot them at a garage sale or a Pic 'n Save.

Small flashlight

Some of the stuff in your computer is jammed in pretty close together. A flashlight can help you read important labels or spot fallen screws.

Magnetized screwdriver

A magnetized screwdriver makes it easier to grab a fallen screw you've just spotted with the flashlight. Just touch the screw with the end of the screwdriver and gently lift it out when it sticks to the end of the screwdriver.

Anything with a magnet can wipe out any information on your floppy disk. To avoid problems, don't keep your magnetized screwdriver near your work area. Just grab it when you need to fetch a dropped screw and then put it back on the other side of the room.

Empty egg carton

Most people use a coffee cup to hold screws. But an empty egg carton is more fun because you can put screws from different parts into different depressions.

Compressed air canister

Your computer's fan constantly sucks in fresh air through your PC's vents. That means it's also sucking in dust, lint, and occasionally, dried fern leaves. PC repair geeks can instantly tell which PC owners have cats by simply looking at the layers of hair inside a PC's case. A cigarette smoker's computer looks even worse.

PC repair shops and art supply shops sell compressed air in canisters so you can blow all the dust out of the inside of your PC. Adventurous souls can also squirt coworkers in the back of the head when they're not looking.

Don't blow on your PC's innards to remove dust. Although you're blowing air, you're also blowing moisture, which can be even worse for your PC than dust.

Every few months, pull off the dust balls that clog the air vent on the back of your PC. The cooler you can keep your PC, the longer it will last.

Pencil and paper

Sometimes a pad of paper and a pencil can be handy for writing down part numbers — or writing angst-ridden poetry when things aren't going according to plan.

Spare computer parts

A spare parts collection is something you can only build up through time. Repair shops are filled with extra computers and have stacks of parts lying around in boxes. If a part doesn't work in one computer, the repair person pulls out the part and tries it in another. Through the process of elimination, repair shops figure out which parts are bad.

You don't have that many boxes of parts. Yet . . .

Making a "Startup" or "System" Disk

Anytime you're working on a hard drive, you need a "Startup" disk, also called a *System disk,* or *Boot disk.* Whenever you turn on your computer, it looks for hidden "who, what, and where am I?" information stored on your hard drive.

If a floppy disk is sitting in the disk drive when you turn on your computer, it cannot find that hidden information and sends a message like this:

```
Non-System disk or disk error
Replace and press any key when ready
```

Your computer is saying that it couldn't find its hidden information on the floppy disk, so it gave up and stopped working. (The information was on the hard drive, but the computer was too lazy to look there.)

However, you can copy that important *system* information to a regular floppy disk. Then you can use that floppy disk to start up your computer, even if your hard drive is on the fritz.

Windows 95 can create a special type of Startup disk for fixing problems. To create one, follow these steps:

1. **Insert a blank disk (or a disk with information you're trying to get rid of) into drive A and close its latch.**

   The latches usually close automatically on the 3¹/₂-inch disk drives. Make sure that the disk matches your floppy drive's capacity — either high or low. Finally, only use drive A. Your computer never bothers to look for its hidden information in drive B, no matter how hard you try to make it do so.

2. **Click Windows 95's Start menu and choose <u>C</u>ontrol Panel from the <u>S</u>ettings menu.**

3. **Double-click the Add/Remove Programs icon and click the Startup Disk tab from the window's top.**

4. **Click the <u>C</u>reate Disk button and follow the instructions.**

   Now, twiddle your thumbs. Eventually, the computer wipes its hands on its pants and simply finishes — without telling you that it's finished.

5. **Remove the disk and use a felt-tip pen to write *System disk* on the label.**

   Now, if your computer refuses to start some cold morning, you have a weapon: Stick your System disk into drive A and press the Reset button. Hopefully, that will get the computer back on the racetrack.

Still using DOS instead of Windows 95? Then here's how to make a DOS system disk:

1. **Insert a blank disk (or a disk with information you're trying to get rid of) into drive A and close its latch.**

   The latches usually close automatically on the 3¹/₂-inch disk drives. Make sure that the disk matches your floppy drive's capacity — either high or low.

   Only use drive A. Your computer never bothers to look for its hidden information in drive B, no matter how hard you try to make it do so.

2. **At the DOS prompt, type the following and then press Enter:**

   ```
   C:\> FORMAT A: /S
   ```

   That is, type the word FORMAT, a space, an A, a colon, a space, a forward slash (found near the right Shift key), and then an S. Got it? Then press Enter.

   Now, twiddle your thumbs. Eventually, the computer says, System transferred, which means it's through. Almost . . .

   Then your computer asks you to enter something called a volume label.

3. **Type the following at the prompt:**

```
Volume label (11 characters, ENTER for none)? SYSTEM
        DISK
```

That is, after the question mark, type SYSTEM, a space, and DISK.

4. **Press Enter when you're through and ignore the next few lines of gibberish that the computer hurls your way.**

5. **When asked to** `Format another (Y/N)?`, **press the N key.**

One System disk is enough for today. The computer leaves you at the DOS prompt.

6. **Now type these commands, one after another, and press Enter after each command:**

```
c:\> COPY \DOS\FORMAT.COM A:
c:\> COPY \DOS\FDISK.EXE A:
```

Two important DOS commands are copied to your System disk for safekeeping. You need those two commands if you ever replace your hard drive or add another one, a task I tackle in Chapter 13.

7. **Remove the disk and use a felt-tip pen to write *System disk* on the label.**

Now, if your computer refuses to start some cold morning, slide your System disk into drive A and aim your finger toward the Reset button. Hopefully, that combination will get the computer back on its feet.

If some of your DOS computer games refuse to run (saying that they need more memory), put your System disk in drive A, choose Shut down from the Windows 95 Start menu and choose Restart the computer from the menu. That action can placate a cantankerous game into running.

Don't copy your AUTOEXEC.BAT or CONFIG.SYS files to your new floppy disk. Those are the files that your System disk is designed to bypass.

Upgrade Do's and Donuts

Whenever you need to do any of the following things, they are be mentioned in the appropriate chapter next to a description of what kind of screwdriver you need. But all the upgrade do's and do not's have been collected and placed here for quick retrieval.

Do upgrade one thing at a time

Even if you've just returned from the computer store with a new hard drive, modem, and monitor, don't try to install them at the same time. Install one part and make sure that it works before going on to the next part.

If you install all three parts at the same time and your computer doesn't work when you turn it on, you won't be able to figure out which one is gagging your computer.

Do watch out for static

You hear this warning several times because it's that important. Static electricity can destroy computer parts. That's why computer parts come packaged in those weird, silvery bags that reflect light like the visor on an astronaut's helmet. That high-tech plastic stuff absorbs any stray static before it zaps the part inside.

To make sure that you don't zap a computer part with static electricity, you need to discharge yourself — no matter how gross it sounds — before starting to work on your computer. Just touch a piece of bare metal, like the metal edge of your desk, to ground yourself. You also must ground yourself each time you move your feet, especially when standing on carpet or after you've moved the cat back out of the way.

Do hang onto your old boxes, manuals, warranties, and receipts

When you're wrapping up your computer for a move down the street, nothing works better than its old boxes. I keep mine on the top shelf in the garage, just in case I'll be moving. Don't bother hanging onto the smaller boxes, though, like the ones that come with a video card or mouse.

Hang on to *all* your old manuals, even if you don't understand a word they say. Sometimes a new part starts arguing with an older part, and the manuals often have hints on which switch to flip to break up the fight. (You can find even more hints in Chapter 18.)

Don't force parts together

Everything in your PC is designed to fit into place smoothly and without too much of a fight. If something doesn't fit right, stop, scratch your head, and try again using a slightly different tactic.

When trying to plug your monitor's cord into the back of your computer, for example, look closely at the end of the cord and then scrutinize the plug where it's supposed to fit. See how the pins are shaped a certain way? See how the plug's shape differs on one side? Turn the plug until it lines up with its socket and push slowly but firmly. Sometimes it helps if you jiggle it back and forth slightly. Ask your spouse to tickle you gently.

Things that plug directly onto your motherboard seem to need the most force. Things that plug onto the outside of your PC, by contrast, slip on pretty easily. They also slip off pretty easily, so most of the cables have little screws to hold everything in place firmly.

Don't bend stuff that comes on cards

Many of your computer's internal organs are mounted on fiberglass boards. That's the reason there's a warning coming up right now.

Don't bend these boards, no matter how tempting. Bending the board can break the circuits subtly enough to damage the card. Worse yet, the cracks can be too small to see, so you may not know what went wrong.

If you hear little crackling sounds while you're doing something with a board — plugging it into a socket or plugging something into it — you're pushing the wrong way.

Don't use head-cleaning disks

Many new computer owners get head-cleaning disks from well-meaning relatives the following Christmas. Head-cleaning disks look like a regular floppy disk with rice paper inside. Head-cleaning disks are supposed to clean any dirt and oxide deposits from the heads on your floppy drives.

Unfortunately, they often do more harm than good. If your floppy drive isn't working, try a head-cleaning disk to see whether it fixes the problem. But don't use head-cleaning disks on a regular basis.

Don't rush yourself

Give yourself plenty of time. If you rush yourself or get nervous, you're much more likely to break something, which can cause even more nervousness.

Don't open up monitors or power supplies

There's nothing inside monitors or power supplies that you can repair. Also, the power supply stores up voltage, even when it's not plugged in.

Don't open your power supply or monitor. They can store electricity inside that may really zap you.

How to Fish Out Dropped Screws

When a screw falls into the inner reaches of your PC, it usually lands in a spot inaccessible to human fingers. The following should call it back home:

- ✔ Is it in plain sight? Try grabbing it with some long tweezers. If that doesn't work, wrap some tape, sticky-side out, around the end of a pencil or chopstick. With a few deft pokes, you may be able to snag it. A magnetized screwdriver can come in handy here, as well. (Don't leave the magnetized screwdriver near your floppy disks, though; the magnets can wipe out the information on them.)

- ✔ If you don't see the runaway screw, gently tilt the computer to one side and then the other. Hopefully, the screw will roll out in plain sight. If you can hear it roll, you can often discover what it's hiding behind.

- ✔ Still can't find it? Pick up the computer's case with both hands, gently turn it upside down, and tilt it from side to side. The screw should fall out.

- ✔ If you still can't find the screw and it's not making any noise, check the floor beneath the computer. Sometimes screws hide in the carpet, where only bare feet can find them.

Do not power up your computer until you can account for every screw!

Chapter 3

Where Does This Piece Go? (Basic Computer Anatomy)

● ●

In This Chapter

▶ The types of PCs

▶ Your PC: the case, keyboards, mice, scanners, modems, monitors, and printer

▶ Where all the cables plug in

▶ Your PC's innards: the motherboard, CPU, memory, disk drives, cards, and the power supply

● ●

*T*his chapter merely points out where your PC's parts live and what they're supposed to do. There's nothing "hands on" in here and nothing thought-provoking enough to share with your spouse over dinner. Instead, treat this chapter like a map to Disneyland — something to keep handy in your back pocket but to pull out only for reference when you're looking for the nearest drinking fountain.

Oh, and just like when you visit Disneyland, you may find yourself visiting different sections of this chapter after you start reading it: If you see a confusing word that's presented in ***bold italics,*** like ***CPU*** or ***motherboard,*** the term is more fully explained somewhere else in the chapter.

The Types of PCs

You've probably heard the term ***PC*** or ***IBM compatible.*** You've also probably heard computers called by numbers such as 286, 386, or 486, to name a few. This naming system can confuse newcomers because several models of PCs exist.

Unlike in the car industry, where new models get fun, imaginative names like *Charisma* or *Entourage,* in the computer industry PCs usually just get slapped with a number — the number of the main chip or ***Central Processing Unit***

(CPU) that makes them run. (The newest CPUs have names like Pentium and Pentium Pro, but even those names sound more ancient than trendy.)

Here's a rundown of the different PC models so you know which one you've been tapping on and whether you can give it a little more zip.

Original IBM PC (1981)

The PC that started the whole craze more than a decade ago isn't worth much today, even to antique dealers (see Figure 3-1). A Model T Ford still gets a raised eyebrow of respect in Sunday parades, but the original IBM PC is worth less than a Brady Bunch lunch box.

Identifying characteristics: The original IBM PC has big, black *floppy disk drives,* which are almost four inches tall. It has no reset button and has the letters *IBM* across the front. It's heavy — and probably dusty, too. The original IBM PC has space for no more than five *cards.* It has an 8088 *CPU.*

Why you should care: This computer is way too old for any serious upgrading. Some new parts simply won't fit inside its *case;* other new parts balk at interacting with the machine's older parts. You can repair its broken parts but only with parts that are just as slow. This one may be able to balance your checkbook if you already have the right type of software. Most of today's software won't run on an old IBM original.

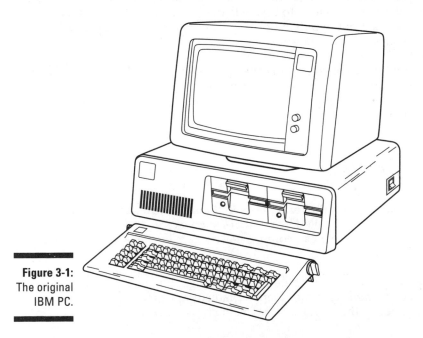

Figure 3-1:
The original
IBM PC.

Upgradability: One guy made a lamp out of his.

IBM XT (early 1980s)

IBM dumped its original IBM PC for the flashier XT model, which introduced the **hard disk** (also known as **hard drive**). Instead of storing all their programs and files on little floppy disks, people could simply copy their information to the huge hard disk inside the computer. Well, the hard disk was huge for those days, holding 10MB of information — the equivalent of seven 3.5-inch floppy disks, by today's standards.

Identifying characteristics: It has an 8086 or 8088 **CPU** and **slots** for eight 8-bit **cards.** But who wants to get technical? Just call the XT model a real slug.

Why you should care: Like its prototype, the original IBM PC, this computer is still a weakling. It can't run Windows, and it's too old to accept most of today's new parts. Like the original PC, it's repairable, but don't bother trying to upgrade it. Buy a new computer.

Upgradability: You can't even reuse the case from this model; the case is the wrong size for most of today's parts. Make this computer into a lamp for the *other* side of the couch.

IBM AT (mid-1980s)

The IBM AT is the **XT**'s replacement. This one finally added a little oomph to the desktop. In fact, all future computers copied this model. Today's computers are sometimes called AT-class computers, to separate them from the anemic XTs and PCs they replace.

Identifying characteristics: The IBM AT is up to five times faster than the XT; this computer's 286 **CPU** set the standard for computers to come. Plus, it has 16-bit **slots** for more powerful 16-bit **cards.**

Why you should care: This computer can do many of the things that today's powerhouse computers can do but with one big exception: It can't run Windows or any Windows software. That means it's living mostly on the shelves at Salvation Army.

Upgradability: If you're ready to spend a lot of money and time fiddling around inside the case, you may be able to bring this computer up to speed. Add a new **motherboard,** a new **power supply,** a larger **hard drive,** and lots of **RAM,** as well as a new **monitor** and **video card.** Yep — buying a completely new computer is almost always cheaper than upgrading an old AT computer, unfortunately.

386 class (late 1980s to present)

The 386 class of computer (see Figure 3-2) includes the 486 (1989) and 586 (1993, also known as the *Pentium*) and the Pentium Pro (1995).

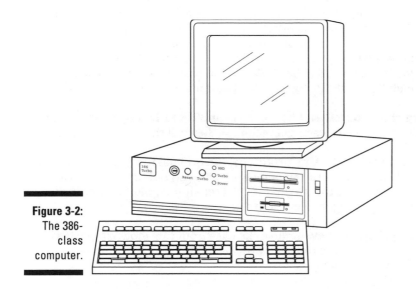

Figure 3-2:
The 386-
class
computer.

The chip designers finally got it right with the 386 chip used for these *CPU*s. In fact, that *CPU* spawned a whole new class of computers, simply called the *386 class*. This group includes the 386, the 486, and even the Pentium.

These 386-class computers don't squirm as much when you try to upgrade them. You can stick new parts into them without causing a huge chain reaction of replacements.

Identifying characteristics: If your computer is an oldster that can run Windows, it's probably a 386 or faster.

Why you should care: A vintage 386 computer owner is riding a dwindling wave; most people have upgraded to a 486 or Pentium by now. Owners of the 386 class of chips have an advantage of older chips, though: You can often upgrade the chips with replacement CPUs like the *OverDrive* chip.

Upgradability: These machines are the easiest to upgrade and can handle almost anything you throw at them. Most common upgrades include bigger **hard drives,** more **memory,** and faster video **cards.** The latest craze is to plug in faster CPU chips, which let the computer run software more quickly.

PS/2 (1987)

IBM, upset that so many other companies were making bucks off its computer design, decided to change the design. IBM added something called Micro Channel Architecture (also known as MCA for the nerds who like to sling letters around). I cover this stuff more fully in the Expansion Cards section a little later in the chapter.

Why you should care: Watch out because these guys differ from *normal* computers. Most important, they use special MCA versions of **cards,** like video cards or internal **modems.** Also, PS/2s have smaller **mouse ports** that can't use the plug on some mice cables (although you can buy a cable adapter for most mice). When it comes to finding replacement parts for your PS/2, your best bet is to haul your old part to the shop and say, "I need another one of these."

Upgradability: Here's the bad news: PS/2-compatible parts not only cost more than their generic counterparts, they're increasingly harder to find at local computer stores.

IBM pulled a fast one; not all PS/2s use that MCA stuff anymore. The only way you can know for sure is to pull out the manual and peek: Does it say MCA or *ISA?*

A look at laptops

Like a spouse, laptops are quite resistant to change. Upgrades are not only difficult but expensive — almost every part must come directly from the laptop manufacturer. Nothing else fits. Extra **memory,** internal **modems,** and bigger **hard drives** are available, but only if you want to pay the price.

To make these things even more expensive (and portable), many laptop manufacturers built little credit-card-sized slots into the laptops and let people stick little credit-card-sized gizmos called PC Cards inside those slots. Today, you can buy extra memory or even modems on those little PC cards. They slide right into the side of the laptop like an ATM card (see Figure 3-3). A modem that comes inside a PC Card still costs more than a regular-sized modem, but the prices are dropping quickly.

PC Cards used to be called PCMCIA cards, which stands for *Personal Computer Memory Card International Association.*

Keep your laptop's lid closed if you take it bungee jumping; otherwise, the screen can snap off at the hinge during the crucial bounce-back point.

Figure 3-3:
A PC card
inserted into
a laptop
computer.

PCjr

Many, many years ago, IBM tried to make a *home-sized* computer for the home market, but nobody bought it. Rumor has it that several thousand PCjrs are sitting in a warehouse somewhere back east. The PCjr is not standard with a *real* PC. Leave any PCjrs (yours included) sitting on the shelf with the 8-track players at the Salvation Army.

The Case

The guts of your PC live inside the case, which is almost always beige. However, some executives buy stylish black cases to match their leather chairs. Like everything else about PCs, cases come in several styles.

Big

The lumbering, old *XT* computers came in a big case to house all their big parts. Now, just as television sets have shrunk to fit in the dashboards of taxi cabs, computers have shrunk, too. Some newer parts don't fit in them. If you're stuck with an XT or AT, you shouldn't try to upgrade it, anyway. Buying a new computer is cheaper.

Little (also called small footprint)

These newer, smaller cases don't eat up as much room on your desktop as the big, *XT*-style cases. But they still hold as many computer parts because today's parts have shrunk along with the cases. Many AT and 386-class computers live in these cases.

Tower

Macho young men like to put big tires on their pickup trucks and stand around with their arms folded. Macho young computer nerds like to put their PCs in a *tower case* — a regular computer case that's been mounted on its side (take a look at Figure 3-4). Tower cases take up less space on your desk. They're often a little roomier so you can jam a few extra goodies inside. These cases are popular for the 386, 486, and Pentium-level computers.

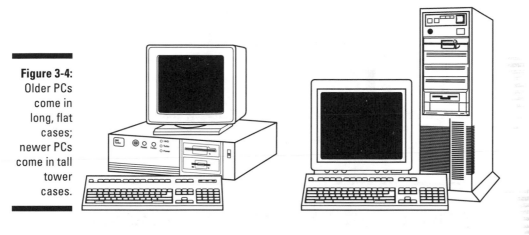

Figure 3-4: Older PCs come in long, flat cases; newer PCs come in tall tower cases.

Case Lights and Buttons

Like a car's dashboard, the front of your computer's case comes with lights and buttons (but no coffee cup holder, unfortunately). Figure 3-5 shows the various lights and buttons.

Power light

Some power lights have a picture of a little light bulb next to them; others simply say *Power*. Either way, the light comes on when you turn on your PC. (And the light is off when the computer is off.)

Power switch

The power switch used to be mounted on the back of a PC's case, where nobody could reach it. A few years later, some savvy engineers moved the power switch to the PC's side, which was one step better. After three more years had past, a core group of designers broke new ground by mounting

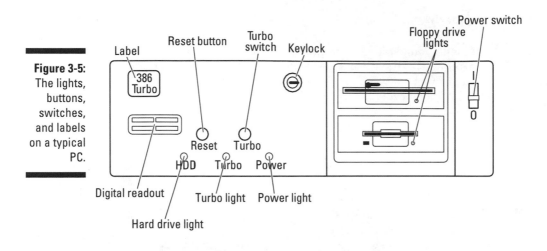

Figure 3-5: The lights, buttons, switches, and labels on a typical PC.

the switch on the computer's front, within easy reach. (However, some people still prefer the rear-mounted switch where three-year-old Larissa can't flip it back and forth while her father's trying to pay the bills.)

Can I just turn my regular case on its side?

Most computers can be propped up sideways. Some stores even sell cheap little *tower props* to keep your PC pointing skyward. But some of the older computers don't like working sideways.

Older hard drives never knew that people would try such weirdness, so they sometimes have trouble spitting your data back out if kept on their sides. If you're really keen on the sideways idea, give it a try. But back up your hard drive first and be on the lookout for any error messages in the weeks ahead.

In fact, some people recommend that you do the following steps if you're going to try the sideways thing:

1. **Back up all your data.**

2. **With the PC on its side, reformat your hard drive.**

3. **Copy all your data back to your hard drive.**

Finally, some CD-ROM drives also object to living sideways. Here's the general rule: CD-ROM drives that use *caddies* — little trays that hold your CDs — don't mind being mounted sideways. Other types of CD-ROM drives need to stay horizontal. (Feel free to root through your particular CD-ROM drive's manual, however, to see if your particular model can withstand living on edge.)

Warning: If your PC has cooling vents on its sides, make sure that the vents aren't covered when you turn it on its side.

The power switch is rarely labeled On or Off. Instead, the little line means On, and the little circle means Off. The most savvy users just listen to their PCs: The humming sound means on, and silence means off.

Reset button

The reset button is one of the most often used buttons and gets the attention of a PC that's frozen solid. Unfortunately, when your PC comes back to life, it drops everything it was working on. That means you can lose any work you didn't saved to a file. Only push the reset button as a last resort. Stuck with a PC that *doesn't* have a reset button? Then you have to turn your PC off, wait 30 seconds, and turn it back on again.

Floppy drive lights

Floppy drives are those slots in front of your computer that eat floppy disks. Almost all floppy drives have a little green or yellow light on the front. The little light turns on when your computer reads or writes any information to the disk, making it easier to tell whether the drive's working.

Don't ever remove a floppy disk from its drive while the little light is still on, or some of your data may vanish.

Turbo buttons and exhaust emission trivia

Fast computers are a good thing. That is, until you start losing to Rashtar because his ship can shoot faster than yours. So, frustrated computer engineers added a Turbo "toggle" switch to let their computers run slowly for games. Normally, your PC runs as fast as possible. But when you push the Turbo button, the little light goes off and the computer slows down.

Some computers don't have a mechanical Turbo switch. Instead, you press some awkward key combination, like Ctrl and Alt and a hyphen. You may have to pull out your manual to see which direction you'll need to contort your fingers.

If your computer seems to be running slowly, make sure that the Turbo switch is set to the normal, fast speed.

As game design advanced in the 1980s, programmers made games that ran on any speed of computer, so the Turbo toggles ceased to be an issue.

Hard drive light

Like their floppy cousins, **hard drives** also flip on their little light when sending information to or from your computer's brain. Sometimes that light is labeled with letters like *HDD;* other computers use a little picture that looks like a can of beans.

If your hard drive's light isn't working, it's an easy fix. Head for Chapter 13 to learn which wires fell off and need to be reattached. (Floppy drive lights can't be repaired as easily, if at all.)

Digital readout

The fanciest computers can flash little numbers and letters in a display on the front of the computer's case. Sometimes the display says how fast the computer's running, and other times it shows a user-written message, like "Ookie is Good." Digital readout is simply a frill, though, just like the fancy red bookmarks that come stitched into the Book Classics of the Month Club titles. A digital readout doesn't make your computer work any better, and they're slowly losing popularity.

Key and lock

The key doesn't start the computer. It doesn't even open a secret storage area in the case where you can find stashed snack foods. The key just disables the keyboard so nobody can poke through your computer while you're at lunch. Don't feel bad if your key disappears a few months after you buy your computer. Most people lose their keys. Some keys merely lock the case, and many newer PCs have abandoned the "locking PC" concept altogether.

Those Port Things

The front of a computer is pleasant and clean. A few sculptured air vents may add to the motif. The rear of a computer is an ugly conglomeration of twisted cables, plugs, and dust. You'll probably have to pull the PC away from the wall before you can see which cable protrudes from which hole.

Some people call these holes *ports.* Others call them *connectors* or even *jacks.* Either way, your PC's rear should look something like the one in Figure 3-6.

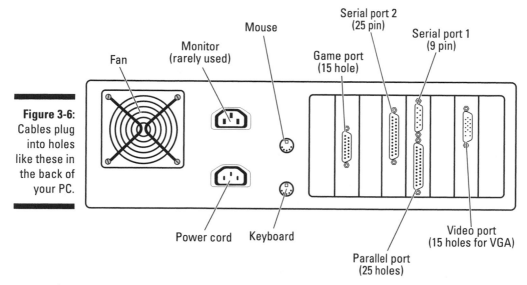

Figure 3-6:
Cables plug
into holes
like these in
the back of
your PC.

Most computers have a few empty ports on the back. They don't all need cables in them for your computer to work.

All the cables that plug into the back of your PC only fit one way. If a cable doesn't seem to fit right, try turning it gently back and forth until it slips in.

The following sections show you what these plugs look like and examine what they're *doing* back there, anyway.

Power cord

The power cord goes into one of the biggest holes in the back of your computer. (The power cord is usually the thickest cord coming out of your computer.) It looks like the picture in Figure 3-7.

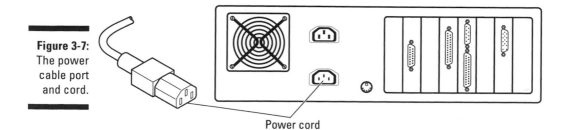

Figure 3-7:
The power
cable port
and cord.

Power cord

What's the other inverted power connector for? Many older computers have a second connector next to the power jack that looks the same — only with three holes, like the one in Figure 3-8. Years ago, that's where monitors used to plug in to get their power. Today, almost all monitors plug into the wall, but the little connector remains to befuddle the curious.

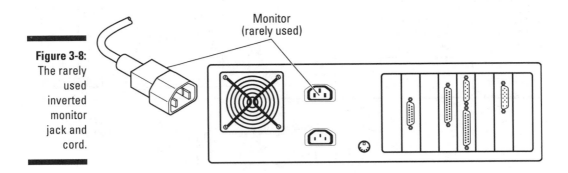

Monitor
(rarely used)

Figure 3-8:
The rarely used inverted monitor jack and cord.

Keyboard and mouse ports

Your *keyboard's* curly cord plugs into a little round hole in the back of your computer The keyboard's connector hole is usually located near the middle and about an inch up from the bottom. (An occasional renegade computer has the keyboard hole on the side or even the front.) Your *mouse* cord plugs into a similar-looking port, which is usually located right next to the keyboard port (see Figure 3-9). There's a lot of variation in mouse cords, though, so jump to the section entitled "Mice, Scanners, and Modems" for more on mice.

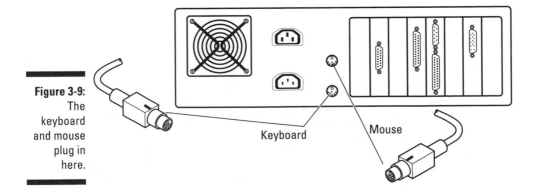

Figure 3-9:
The keyboard and mouse plug in here.

Keyboard   Mouse

Most of today's new computers use identical-looking ports for both the keyboard and the mouse. Look carefully for labels or pictures before plugging the keyboard or mouse connector into those two ports. Plugging them in the wrong way won't just keep your computer from working, it can fry sensitive parts.

Look carefully for a little raised plastic line or bump on one side of the keyboard and mouse plugs. That little bump faces up, toward the top of the case when you're plugging in the keyboard or the mouse.

Serial port

Here's where things get a little wacko. See a little port on the back of your computer that has little pins poking up from inside it? That's a serial port. If your computer has just one serial port, it's almost always shaped like the one in Figure 3-10.

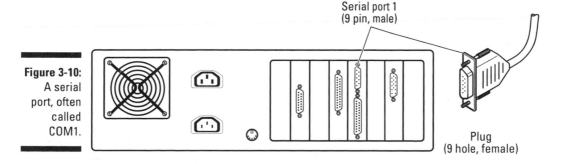

Serial port 1
(9 pin, male)

Plug
(9 hole, female)

Figure 3-10: A serial port, often called COM1.

If your computer has a second serial port, it usually looks the same as COM1.

Older computers often have a second serial port shaped like the one in Figure 3-11.

Serial ports are where you plug in cables connected to gizmos that feed the computer information — gizmos like modems, scanners, and even mice. Serial ports are extremely popular; dozens of gizmos want to use them. (Your computer can only listen to two serial ports at the same time, however, creating a bit of madness that's covered in Chapter 18.)

Some manuals refer to serial ports as COM ports. Manuals over the deep end call them RS-232 ports or even RS-232c ports. Nobody will guffaw if you just call yours a serial port, though.

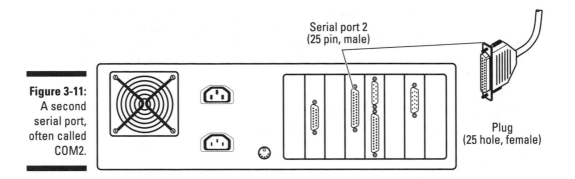

**Serial port 2
(25 pin, male)**

Figure 3-11:
A second
serial port,
often called
COM2.

**Plug
(25 hole, female)**

Some gizmos living inside your computer can use a serial port without physically plugging into one. Internal modems are notorious for this practice and, therefore, cause much confusion and gnashing of teeth. In fact, to receive an American Dental Association endorsement, this book added a special "COM port" section in Chapter 18.

The larger serial ports, seen in Figure 3-11, are losing favor; most new computers come with two of the smaller-sized ports already built in. Luckily, you can find inexpensive adapters at Radio Shack and most computer stores that can convert your small serial port to the larger type.

Parallel port

Plug the cable from your ***printer*** into the thing that looks like Figure 3-12. The end of the cable that looks like a grim robot's mouth plugs into your printer, and the end with little protruding pins plugs into your parallel port.

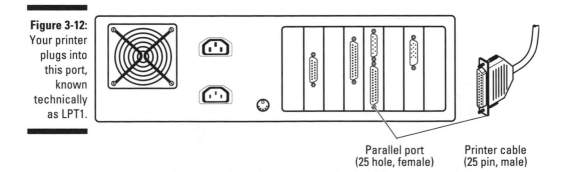

Figure 3-12:
Your printer
plugs into
this port,
known
technically
as LPT1.

**Parallel port
(25 hole, female)**

**Printer cable
(25 pin, male)**

Is your parallel port bi?

For years, parallel ports simply shoveled information to the printer. But now, *bidirectional parallel ports* are the rage. For example, Kingston Technologies sells a portable hard drive. It plugs into your parallel port and appears as drive D on your screen. You can copy information back and forth from it like a regular hard drive. Some little palmtop and laptop computers can send information back and forth through a parallel port, too.

Some computers don't have bidirectional parallel ports. If you're only going to be using your parallel port for sending information to your printer, that's no problem. But if you plug something into your parallel port that's supposed to send information to your computer, it may not work. Unfortunately, you have no sure way to tell whether the port is bidirectional before you try it out. Be forewarned.

Game port

Sized midway between a parallel port and a serial port, a game port is where you plug in the joystick (see Figure 3-13). The card that houses your serial and parallel port often has a game port tossed in as well.

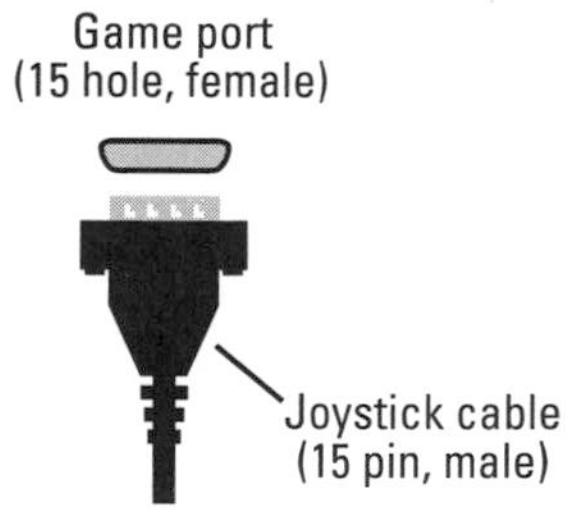

Figure 3-13:
Joysticks
plug into
this port,
which can
be found on
most sound
cards.

Game port
(15 hole, female)

Joystick cable
(15 pin, male)

You don't need two game ports to plug in two joysticks. Just buy a cheap Y adapter cable, usually sold at the same place you've been buying computer games.

Be aware that many **sound cards** come with game ports as well. In fact, the two game ports will probably argue over who gets priority until you disable one of them. (Jump to the "Jumpers" section in Chapter 18.)

Also, most sound cards let your game port double as a *MIDI* port. By plugging a weird boxy thing into your game port, you can plug in music synthesizers, drum machines, and other things that let you sound like Brian Eno.

Not even Brian Eno cares that MIDI stands for Musical Instrument Digital Interface.

Video port

Although it looks like a fat serial port, a video port is a connector for your *monitor.* Nothing but your monitor fits (unless you use a hammer). The most popular video ports, called *VGA* or *SuperVGA (SVGA),* look like the one in Figure 3-14. Older monitors may plug into ports like the one in Figure 3-15.

Figure 3-14:
VGA
monitors
plug into a
port with 15
holes.

15-hole female
(fatter)

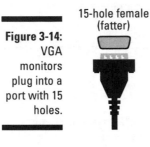

Figure 3-15:
Older
monitors
sometimes
plug into a
port with
nine holes.

9-hole female
EGA port

Other ports

Other unidentified ports may peek out from the back of your computer. Some may be for networks, letting your computer socialize with other computers. Other ports may be attached to *sound cards, video capture cards,* or special cards that control *compact disc drives.* You may even spot a plain old phone jack that is resting on the end of an internal *modem.*

The old IBM PCs had a second port identical to the keyboard port: Computer nerds would plug a tape recorder cord in there to store their files because floppy drives were too expensive.

Keyboards

Keyboards come in zillions of different brands but three basic flavors:

The old XT-style keyboard: One of the oldest keyboards, this 83-key antique doesn't have any little lights on it, making it hard to tell whether you've pressed your Caps Lock key.

The AT-style (standard) keyboard: The designers at IBM added little lights to this newer keyboard, as shown in Figure 3-16. They also tossed in a separate numeric keypad on the right side. Some eccentric engineer also added an 84th key, called SysRq, that has never done anything but confuse people. IBM meant to use it for something revolutionary but then forgot which department had come up with the idea. Nobody has used the key since.

The 101-key (enhanced) keyboard: Also known as the extended keyboard, the keyboard in Figure 3-17 not only has a separate numeric keypad, but it also has a second set of cursor-control keys sitting between the keypad and the rest of the letters. It's the most popular of the three keyboard styles.

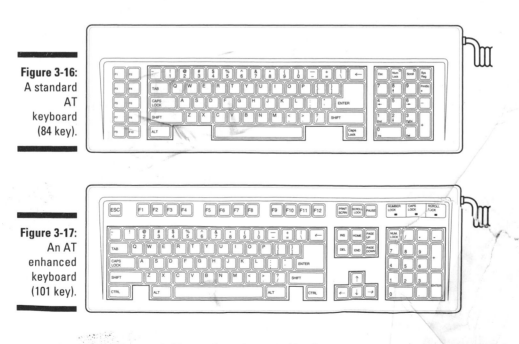

Figure 3-16:
A standard
AT
keyboard
(84 key).

Figure 3-17:
An AT
enhanced
keyboard
(101 key).

The Microsoft Natural Keyboard: Also known as an *ergonomic* keyboard, the keyboard in Figure 3-18 adds a few twists — literally — on the 101-key keyboard. First, the keyboard is bent into a shape that some people find more comfortable for typing. Second, it comes with new function keys for special keystrokes in Windows 95.

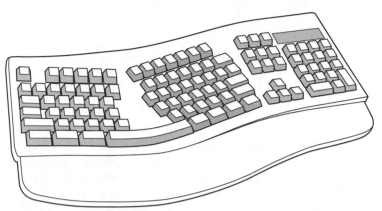

Figure 3-18:
A Microsoft
Natural
Keyboard.

✔ You can use either an AT-style keyboard or an enhanced keyboard with your AT or 386-class computer. But don't try to reuse your old XT keyboard — those guys used different types of wiring.

✔ The old XT-style keyboards don't work with anything but XTs. But here's a secret: Many manufacturers sell one keyboard that can work with both types of computers. Check the bottom of your keyboard, and you may find a little switch. Flip the switch to the X side to use it with an XT computer, or flip the switch to the A side to use it with the AT-style computer.

✔ Some expensive keyboards have a *trackball* built in: By whirling around the little ball, you can make an arrow scoot across your screen. When the arrow points to the right button on the screen, click the little button next to the trackball. The button on the screen is selected, just as if you'd pushed it with an electronic finger. It's quick, sanitary, and saves you the cost of a mouse.

Don't bang on your keyboard. You're not using an old typewriter anymore. Just a tap will do the trick and your keyboard will last a little longer.

That weird little ridge along the top of most keyboards isn't just there to look sporty. It's designed so you can prop a book against it, leaning it back toward your monitor. That makes copying stuff out of books a lot easier.

Looking for more ridges? Check out the F and J keys. You'll find little lumps on them, which makes it easier to reposition your fingers if you're typing in the dark. (By contrast, the Apple Macintosh places its keyboard ridges on the D and K keys, if you're playing a game of Stump the Nerd.)

Mice, Scanners, and Modems

Referred to as *input devices* by computer scientists, gizmos like mice, scanners, and modems feed information to your computer. For example, a mouse feeds the computer information about the movements of your hand, and a scanner feeds copies of images to your computer.

Mice

Like all things attached to PCs, mice come in several different breeds, described next:

PS/2 style: Originally found on IBM's PS/2 series of computers, the tail on this popular mouse plugs into a tiny round port with seven holes. Because this breed of mice doesn't need a serial port or a special ***bus mouse*** card, it's the most popular mouse — *if* your particular brand of computer comes with a built-in PS/2 mouse port. (Most do.)

Serial mouse: The tail from a serial mouse plugs into one of your ***serial ports.***

Bus mouse: The tail from a bus mouse, in contrast, plugs onto the mouse's own ***card.*** You need to take the ***case*** off your computer to stick the bus mouse's card inside. (These types of mice are losing popularity.)

Exotic species: A few other types of mice have hit the scene. For example, cordless mice come in handy for people who are tired of knocking papers off their desk with their mouse cord. Cordless mice are not only more expensive than their tailed counterparts, but they eat up batteries, too.

- ✔ The latest breed of mice uses feet rather than balls. When a normal mouse ball rolls around, it gathers dust, which rolls up into the mouse's guts. The little optomechanical feet on Honeywell's footed mouse don't roll, so they don't flip dust and hairs into any vital organs.

- ✔ A few people use optical mice, which use light beams to track their movement. Unfortunately, these mice use special, expensive mouse pads. Those fun mouse pads shaped like cows won't work.

- ✔ Some people prefer ***trackballs,*** which I describe in the "Keyboards" section of this chapter. Others think that trackballs are as awkward as dental floss, especially the tiny ones that clip to the sides of laptops.

- ✔ Microsoft's taking a bet with its new IntelliMouse — a PS/2-style mouse that has a little spinning wheel mounted between the two buttons. Spinning the wheel with the index finger performs various on-screen acrobatics: Your viewpoint into a picture zooms in and out, for instance, or a page moves up or down the screen.

Scanners

Handheld scanners look like *mice* with anvil heads, as you see in Figure 3-19.

Figure 3-19:
A handheld
scanner.

When you slide a scanner over letters or pictures, the scanner sends a copy of the image onto your computer screen, where it can be saved as a file (much to the consternation of copyright attorneys around the world). The latest, full-page scanners look a little bit like copy machines: You put your paper on top of the glass, shut the door over it, and push the button to send a copy into the depths of your computer.

Like *bus mice,* scanners usually come with their own *cards.* The expensive scanners can reproduce color pictures. The cheap ones can only produce black-and-white pictures — even if the original was color. Handheld scanners often fight against *modems* for available *serial ports;* full-page scanners often use *SCSI* cards, instead.

TIP

Who really cares how many buttons a mouse has?

Although mice come in two- and three-button models, few software packages require a three-button mouse. The old version of Windows, Windows 3.1, mostly used one button. Windows 95 and Windows NT use both mouse buttons extensively.

The three-button mouse seems to be a dying breed, so don't feel cheated if your mouse has only two buttons. (Just don't try to use a Macintosh mouse. It only has one button, and it won't work with *any* version of Windows.)

The latest breed of scanners often come with *Optical Character Recognition* (OCR) software. That fancy name simply means that the software examines the picture of the scanned-in page and "types" the text into your computer as letters and words.

Modems

These little boxes let your computer connect to the telephone line, so you can call up other computers, meet friends from around the world, and swap biscuit recipes. You can also grab the news, weather, stock reports, and weird stories about weird people doing weird things. Modems are the '90s equivalent of the '50s shortwave radio, but you don't need a towering network of nerdy antennas that embarrass your neighbors.

Like **mice** and **scanners,** external modems plug into **serial ports,** where they're easy to reach and use. An external modem is shown in Figure 3-20.

Figure 3-20:
An external
modem.

Internal modems live inside your computer on little **cards,** where they're hidden from view, but they cause more trouble. Actually, internal modems are easy to install but notoriously difficult to set up, especially if your computer's already hooked up to a mouse or a scanner. (Chapter 18 is waiting for you.)

When shopping for a fast internal modem to use with Windows, make sure the modem uses a 16550AFN UART chip. Slower chips often can't keep up with the heavy-duty data flow.

The newest modems can send faxes of information that's already inside your computer. That makes it easy to fax party fliers you've created in your word processor, but impossible to send that newspaper clipping that you know Jerry would get a kick out of. (You need a **scanner** for that.)

Monitors

A computer monitor may look like a TV, but it's nowhere near as repairable. In fact, you'll probably buy a new monitor after you hear how much money the shop wants to fix the old one. Monitors come in several styles, with the most expensive being the biggest, clearest, and most colorful.

Here are the basic types of monitors:

Hercules, Color Graphics Adapter (CGA), Enhanced Graphics Adapter (EGA): These are the older types of monitors and graphics cards you want to upgrade because everything on them looks so grainy. Plus, the colors are pretty awful, especially after you've seen a better quality monitor in the store.

Video Graphics Array (VGA): The industry workhorse of the early '90s, this type of monitor still works well with Windows. It often needs a *16-bit card* that requires a *16-bit slot,* so this type won't always work in an *XT.*

Super Video Graphics Array (SVGA): This type of monitor packs more colors and images onto the same size screen and has replaced VGA as the norm. If you want to watch movies in Windows, you want an SVGA card and monitor.

Extended Graphics Adapter (XGA), 8514/A: This expensive monitor is mostly for high-end (expensive) graphics work.

Beware: Your monitor only displays what your computer's *video card* has sent. The two work as a team. That's why it's best to buy your monitor and video card at the same time to make sure that they work well together.

No, a TV set won't work as a monitor anymore. They both use different technology, as you can see for yourself if you press your nose against the TV screen and then against your monitor. Some fancy cards let you watch TV on a computer monitor, though. However, the bad news is that monitors cost more than a real TV set of the same size.

Some gadgets *will* let you use a TV set as a monitor. Known as *VGA to NTSC adapters,* they're used mostly for corporate presentations or rabid video gamers. These adapters work well for displaying graphics, but most of the text will be illegible. Chapter 7 dishes up more information.

Because today's software slings a lot of graphics onto the screen, accelerator cards are the rage. The computer's brain, the CPU, was designed to crunch numbers, not to create on-screen cartoon worlds of tennis-playing bananas. To ease the workload, accelerator cards come with built-in graphics chips that help the CPU sling pictures around. Graphics software — including Windows — runs much faster with an accelerator card.

Printers

Printers take the information from your screen and stick it on paper. They accomplish this feat in a wide variety of ways. Several types of printers use different methods, as described next:

Dot-matrix: One of the noisiest printers, dot-matrix printers create images by pressing tiny dots against the paper. They're inexpensive, and it shows. Many people are dumping dot-matrix printers when they break and buying an inkjet or laser printer instead.

Daisywheel: The noisiest by far, these printers work like a typewriter, pushing little letters and numbers against a ribbon to leave images on the page. A dying breed, they're found most often in thrift shops. Upgrades? You can just replace the ribbon and add little *wheels* to get different styles of letters. Forget about graphics, though; these can only work like robot-driven typewriters.

Inkjet: Popular for their low price and high quality, inkjet printers squirt ink onto a page, which leads to a surprisingly high-quality image — often in color (see Figure 3-21). You need to replace the ink cartridges every once in a while, which can drain the wallet. However, these printers can be the best buy for the buck.

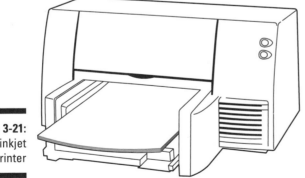

Figure 3-21:
An inkjet
printer

Laser: Laser printers, like the one in Figure 3-22, may be the most popular. They use the same technology as copy machines — *good* copy machines. You won't find much to upgrade here, although some laser printers let you put more memory into them. With more memory, they can print more graphics on a single page. Eventually, you have to replace their toner cartridge, a job easily handled on your desktop.

You can find tips for changing ribbons and cartridges in Chapter 8.

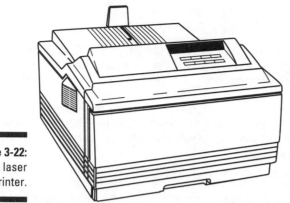

Figure 3-22:
A laser
printer.

The Kauffman Machine Shop in Olathe, Kansas, sells an expensive printer that transfers pictures from your computer's screen into colored icing on a cake. It can also decorate cookies and cupcakes.

The Motherboard

Some people call a motherboard a *system board,* but they're the same thing — a sheet of olive green or brown fiberglass that lines the inside bottom of your computer's **case.** A typical motherboard with its parts labeled is shown in Figure 3-23.

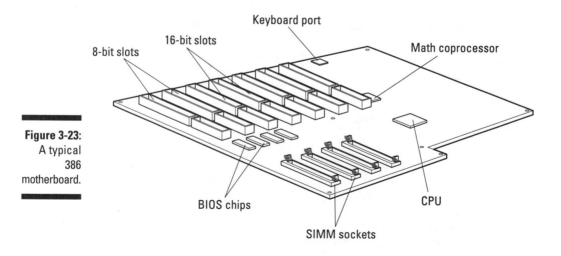

Figure 3-23:
A typical
386
motherboard.

Keyboard port

16-bit slots

8-bit slots

Math coprocessor

BIOS chips

CPU

SIMM sockets

By itself, a motherboard is like an empty plate. The important stuff lives on top of the motherboard. The motherboard then acts as a roadway of sorts, pushing information back and forth between all the following residents.

Central processing unit (CPU)

Your computer's brain is its CPU (pronounced *See Pee You*) — a little chip that shovels information back and forth among all your computer's parts. Like the one in Figure 3-24, a CPU is a small thing, ranging from the size of a Wheat Thin to a Triscuit.

Even though CPUs are tiny, they're one of the most expensive parts of your computer, often costing hundreds of dollars. That's why computers are named after the type of CPU they contain: a 286, 386, 486, Pentium (sometimes called the 586), or Pentium Pro.

TECHNICAL STUFF

PCL and PostScript perplexity

For years, the Cadillac of laser printers was called a *PostScript* printer. That meant the printer used the PostScript page description language — a special way for printers to stick graphics and letters onto a page. With PostScript, printers can shrink or enlarge graphics and fonts without creating the jagged edges left by cheaper printers. Desktop publishers quickly embraced the high quality, as did most software programmers.

Plus, a file saved in "PostScript format" can be taken to most professional typesetters, who also use PostScript technology on their mucho-expensive printers. Presto! The Gardening Club Newsletter suddenly looks like a magazine.

Unfortunately, such high class comes at a high price. PostScript printers can cost hundreds of dollars more than their competition.

To accommodate the budget-minded crowd, Hewlett-Packard's LaserJet series of printers provide an alternative dubbed *PCL: Printer Control Language*. Because not every computer user needed PostScript's versatility, PCL has grabbed an ever-increasing niche. Today, most laser printers are either "PostScript compatible" or "LaserJet/PCL compatible."

So, which one should you buy? If you do a lot of high-end graphics work or desktop publishing, spend the extra money for PostScript. It's more versatile, and the pages look better. If you print mostly text or charts, with a few graphics on the side, PCL printers work fine. Or, if you can't make up your mind, do what I did: Buy a laser printer that can switch between both PostScript *and* PCL modes. The big problem is making sure you've flipped the switch to the right "mode" before telling the software to print.

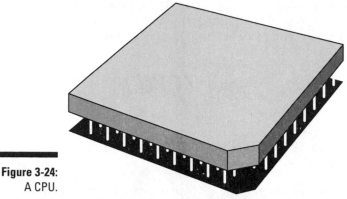

Figure 3-24:
A CPU.

68-pin package (80286 microprocessor)

Actually, CPUs get two numbers. The first is the design number (386, 486, and so on), which measures power or how big a shovelful of information the CPU can move around. The second number is the chip's megahertz (25 MHz, 33 MHz, 166MHz, and so on), which measures its speed or how fast it can sling information around. The design number is more important, though. For example, a 25 MHz 486 is faster than a 33 MHz 386.

- ✔ Some CPUs even get letters: A 386SX is a slower (and much cheaper) version of the 386DX (or a plain old 386). A 486SX is a slower version of a plain old 486. And a chip ending in SL means that it has some power-saving features, usually cherished by laptop users.

- ✔ With early computers, CPUs come bundled with the motherboard. You can't upgrade your XT or 286 computer by sticking a 486 CPU into it. The chip won't fit in the little hole, and the motherboard can't handle the chip's extra power.

- ✔ Some specially designed chips can upgrade a 386 to a 486 chip and a 486 to a Pentium, however, and I cover those chips in Chapter 10.

- ✔ Other chips, known as *clock-doubling* or *Overdrive* chips, can also speed up your older CPU. Some of these new chips replace your old chip; others plug into an additional socket on the motherboard. Clock-doubled chips end with "DX2" or "DX4," like the 486DX2. (They're also covered in Chapter 10.)

- ✔ The oldest PCs, like IBM's original PC and XT, came with an 8088 or 8086 CPU. These toddlers will never grow up. Leave them on the doorstep of a thrift shop and take a tax deduction. You can't upgrade them, and nobody wants to buy them.

Don't know what type of CPU your computer has? If you're using Windows 95, click the My Computer icon with your right mouse button and choose Properties from the menu. The computer's CPU number or name appears near the bottom of the pop-up window.

Not using Windows? Then save your work, exit any programs and press the computer's *reset* button. As the computer comes back to life, watch the screen closely for any listed chip numbers. Hidden in the malarkey, you should spot a chip number like Phoenix 80486 ROM BIOS or something similar. In this case, the 80486 means that you have a 486 CPU. No reset button? Turn the computer off, wait 30 seconds for it to catch its breath, turn it back on again, and watch the screen credits.

If you're using DOS version 6.0 or Windows 3.1, type **MSD** at the C:\> prompt thing. A program leaps to life, listing your computer's vital statistics. The CPU number is listed under the "Computer" category.

The definitive way to verify your computer's CPU is to pop open the case and look at the numbers or words stamped on top of the chip.

Here are some trivial CPU death facts: Most chips are rated by the number of "million hours" they're supposed to last. (One million hours is about 114 years, by the way.) When chips die, it's often because of dust particles that fell into the chip while it was being cooked up on the manufacturing line. With so many tiny wires and electrical passages packed into a little chip, a single dust particle is like a tree falling across a freeway. There's no highway patrolman to stop traffic and pull the tree off the road, so the chip just stops working.

Math coprocessor

The math coprocessor, a chip like the *CPU,* acts as a calculator of sorts. It pipes up with quick answers to math questions like that wiseguy in Mrs. Jackson's class. By listening to the math coprocessor's answers, the CPU can work more quickly.

For years, coprocessors were optional because they only sped up math problems: Most people don't calculate logarithms too often. Today, though, most CPUs come with built-in math coprocessor circuitry, so you don't have to worry about whether you need it or not.

486DX, Pentium, and Pentium Pro chips already have math coprocessors built in to the chip. The 486SX and earlier chips like the 386 lack the coprocessor, so you have to add one if you want to speed up your math homework. (Motherboards for both the 386 and 486SX usually come with special sockets for plugging in coprocessors.)

BIOS

If the *CPU* can be described as the computer's brain, then the BIOS can be called its nervous system. Short for Basic Input/Output System, the BIOS handles computing chores in the background, kind of like our nervous system keeps us breathing, even when we forget to.

The BIOS handles the bare grunt work of a PC: how **floppy disks** grab data or what happens when you press a key on the **keyboard.**

- ✔ The BIOS comes written on special little chips called *ROM* chips that live on the motherboard of all IBM-compatible computers. When you first turn on your computer, you see which company's bunch of nerds wrote your computer's BIOS and in what year. For example, one of my computers says, "386-BIOS (C)1988 American Megatrends Inc." when it starts. That means the American Megatrends company wrote my computer's BIOS in 1988. (It also means the computer uses a 386 *CPU*.)

- ✔ Why should you care? Well, an older BIOS sometimes can't handle a newer product (or vice versa). That means you need to buy new BIOS chips (often difficult to locate), or you can bite the bullet and buy a new motherboard, complete with already upgraded BIOS chips.

- ✔ Some newer computers come with upgradeable BIOS chips. Just pop in the new BIOS software, and the program copies the new BIOS to the old chips.

Expansion slots and cards

A motherboard has a little row of parking spaces called *slots*. The slots are for little computer gadgets that come on *cards*. Together, they make up-grades a breeze: Pop off the computer's case, push a card into an empty slot, fasten down the card with a single screw, and stick the case back on.

Cards look like miniature motherboards — daughterboards, so to speak. Such a simple design has to have a problem, however: Those slots and cards come in several different sizes and styles. The right-sized card needs to be matched up with the right-sized slot. Here's the rundown:

An **8-bit** card has *one* little tab protruding from its bottom that matches up with the single slot it fits into, as shown in Figure 3-25.

A **16-bit** card has *two* little tabs protruding from its bottom that match up with the two little slots it fits into, as shown in Figure 3-26. (Any card that says *16* in its name — SoundBlaster 16, for example — probably needs a 16-bit slot.)

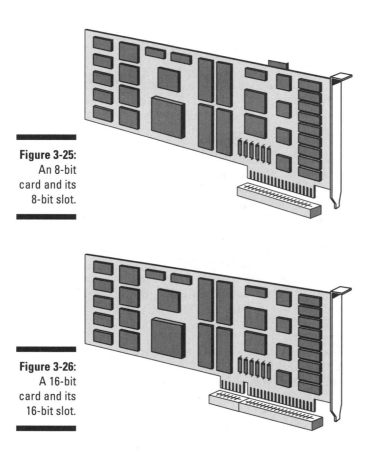

Figure 3-25:
An 8-bit
card and its
8-bit slot.

Figure 3-26:
A 16-bit
card and its
16-bit slot.

A ***local bus*** card has *three* little tabs protruding from its bottom that match up with the three little slots it fits into. These three slots, known as *VESA local bus* or *VL-Bus,* let your computer grab information more quickly than it could from an 8- or 16-bit card.

For example, a VL-Bus ***video card*** speeds up the way Windows slaps stuff on your monitor. This video card makes it easier to watch those little postage-stamp-sized movies that are all the rage in Video for Windows.

Finally, many Pentiums use a ***PCI,*** or peripheral component interconnect card. Using a PCI is yet another way of flinging information onto the screen as quickly as possible.

✔ Computer gurus refer to the row of slots as your computer's *expansion bus.*

✔ Some people refer to cards as *boards,* but they're both the same thing: little goodies that slide inside your computer to make it more fun.

✔ Before shopping for cards, peek inside your computer's case (or its manual) to see what sort of slots live on its expansion bus. Not all cards work in all types of slots.

✔ For example, *XTs* come with only 8-bit slots; *AT/286* and *386* computers usually have a mixture of 8- and 16-bit slots. Most *486 motherboards* usually come with a mixture of 16-bit and VL-Bus slots. Finally, Pentiums usually have a combination of 16-bit and PCI slots.

Occasionally, you *can* plug a long card into a short slot. Look at Figures 3-25 and 3-26 and squint: If you plug a 16-bit card into Figure 3-25's 8-bit slot, one of that 16-bit card's little tabs will dangle, with no slot to fit into. That 16-bit card *may* still work; however, that 16-bit card will trudge along slowly in 8-bit mode. Plus, some 16-bit cards won't work in 8-bit mode *at all*.

Some 386 computers have slots in odd places, and nothing seems to fit into them. Those are *32-bit* slots, custom-made for that computer manufacturer's *own* brand of card. For example, some manufacturers sell custom-made memory or CPU upgrade cards designed specifically for that slot. Those custom-made cards are always expensive, however, so most users just ignore those slots.

Your computer's *expansion bus* shuttles information between the cards and your computer's CPU. A *16-bit* slot can send information along a bigger roadway than an *8-bit* slot, so it's faster. *VL-Bus* slots are *32-bits,* so they're even *faster*.

Remembering all this card stuff can be as tough as remembering whether a straight flush beats a full house at poker. So, Table 3-1 explains the name of the cards and their slots, the pros and cons of each variety, as well as its compatibility level and identifying characteristics.

Table 3-1	Cards and Slots Used in PCs		
Name of the Card and Its Slot	**Pros/Cons**	**Compatibility**	**Identifying Characteristics**
ISA 8-bit (Industry Standard Architecture)	The original design, these cards and slots have been around for years. Most computers use these slots, so ISA cards are easy to find. Because they're an older design, ISA cards and slots aren't as fast or powerful as the others in this table.	An 8-bit ISA *card* fits into any slot except MCA and PCI. An 8-bit ISA *slot* accepts only 8-bit ISA cards. (Sometimes a 16-bit card works in an 8-bit slot, but not at full capacity.)	Look for a single protruding tab on the card which plugs into a single slot. See Figure 3-27 for an illustration.

Name of the Card and Its Slot	Pros/Cons	Compatibility	Identifying Characteristics
ISA 16-bit	These newer 16-bit slots can move information around twice as quickly as the older 8-bit cards. If a card says 16 somewhere in its name, it probably requires a 16-bit slot. The 16-bit slots started to show up on 286 computers.	A 16-bit ISA *card* fits into any slot but 8-bit ISA, MCA, and PCI. (A few 16-bit cards still work in an 8-bit slot, but not as quickly.) A 16-bit *slot* accepts any card but MCA, VESA Local-Bus, EISA, and PCI.	These cards have two protruding tabs right next to each other; the first tab slides into the ISA 8-bit slot, the other slides into a smaller slot right next to it. (See Figure 3-28.)
EISA (Enhanced Industry Standard Architecture)	These slots can run ISA cards as well as EISA cards — they're a faster and more powerful breed of cards. EISA slots never really caught on, so EISA cards are hard to find and work with.	An EISA *card* only works in an EISA slot. An EISA *slot* accepts any card but MCA, VESA Local Bus, and PCI.	These have two protruding tabs, like the previously described 16-bit cards, but the tabs have funny notches in them, as seen in Figure 3-29.
MCA (Micro Channel Architecture)	IBM tried to upgrade the old ISA design, but IBM's new card never caught on. MCA slots are only on old "genuine" IBM computers and a few esoteric computers. MCA cards are faster than regular ISA cards, but they're harder to find.	An MCA *card* only works in an MCA slot. An MCA *slot* only accepts MCA cards.	If you're having trouble finding cards that fit your slots — and your computer says IBM on the case — you probably have MCA slots. An MCA card's protruding tabs start a little farther back on the card than the other types. Some MCA cards have two tabs; others have three. (See Figure 3-30.)

(continued)

Table 3-1 *(continued)*

Name of the Card and Its Slot	Pros/Cons	Compatibility	Identifying Characteristics
VESA Local BUS (Known as VLB, or the Video Electronics Standards Association's Local Bus)	These cards make video hop onto the screen more quickly. Longer than normal, these cards bend a little more easily than the others, so be careful not to break them.	A VESA Local Bus *card* only works in a VESA Local Bus slot. A VESA Local Bus *slot* accepts any card except EISA, MCA, and PCI.	This card looks just like a 16-bit ISA card, but it has another notched tab protruding near its back end, as shown in Figure 3-31.
PCI (Peripheral Component Interconnect)	The newest design, these splash graphics onto the screen quickly with Pentium computers.	A PCI *card* only works in a PCI slot. A PCI *slot* only accepts PCI cards.	These cards look much like MCA cards, but with some subtle sizing differences. (See Figure 3-32.)

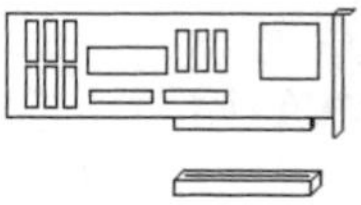

Figure 3-27:
The ISA
8-bit card
and slot.

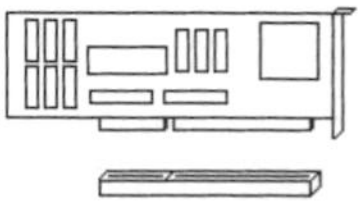

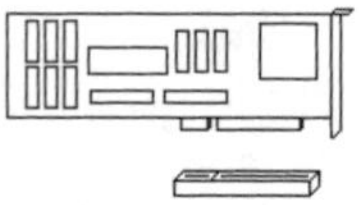

Figure 3-30:
The MCA
card and
slot.

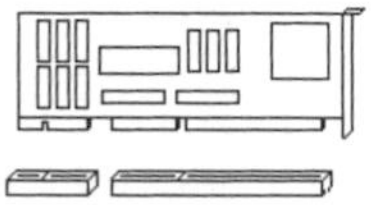

Figure 3-28:
The ISA
16-bit card
and slot.

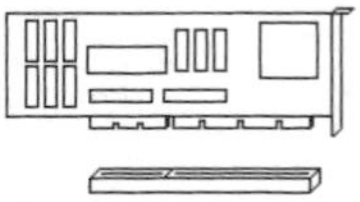

Figure 3-31:
The VESA
Local Bus
card and
slot.

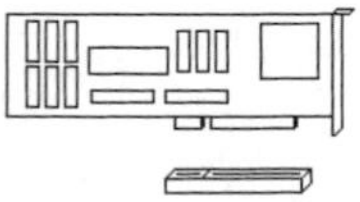

Figure 3-29:
The EISA
card and
slot.

Figure 3-32:
The PCI
card and
slot.

Does MCA or EISA sound vaguely familiar?

Your computer's little slots not only come in several different sizes, but they also come in the following types:

ISA: Chances are, your computer uses ISA (Industry Standard Architecture) cards. Just about every card you can find works in an ISA type of computer.

MCA: If you bought an IBM PS/2, you probably have MCA (Micro Channel Architecture) slots. These slots aren't compatible with the ISA cards everybody else is using, and they cost more. Don't feel bad, though: MCA cards have a better design, are easier to install, and usually work faster.

EISA: Finally, some people shelled out extra bucks for EISA (Enhanced Industry-Standard Architecture) slots. Designed by jealous computer companies after IBM came out with its MCA stuff, EISA hasn't really caught on.

Like MCA cards, EISA cards are better designed, easier to install, and usually faster. But very few companies make them, and they're mostly for boring network stuff. The good news? Unlike MCA, EISA cards can still run ISA cards, so EISA computer buyers aren't angry.

What cards does your computer have?

Get this: Several of those *ports* you plug cables into at the back of your computer are *really* cards. They're the *tail ends* of cards, as you'll see when you open your computer case for the first time.

In fact, your computer probably came with these three cards inside:

Video card: Your monitor plugs into this one. This card tells it what to put on the screen.

I/O card: This is a fancy name for the card with your *serial port* and *parallel port.* Some companies toss in a *game port,* as well.

Controller card: You may not know that you have this one because it's hidden inside the *case.* Cables from this card connect to your *floppy drives* and your *hard drive.*

Other cards: Any other cards you spot may be for internal *modems, compact disc players, sound cards, scanners,* and a variety of other toys.

Some cards are starting to do double duty. For example, Intel's SatisFAXtion 400 internal modem lets you plug a scanner into it, too. Orchid's Fahrenheit video card comes with built-in sound card circuitry that lets you record sounds. Sometimes these double-duty cards can be a lifesaver when you've run out of slots for all your cards.

All that VL-Bus, local bus, and PCI stuff

Powerhouse computer fans complained that the card-and-slot system was too slow. Those little slots couldn't send information to the computer's CPU fast enough, and they slowed down everything, especially video.

To speed things up, the industry came up with the idea of a *local bus*, a speedy technology that changes just as quickly. First, some manufacturers built a video card right onto the motherboard and called it *local bus video*. Sure, it sped up the video, but the built-in video circuitry was too hard to replace or upgrade.

Next, the industry came up with a *local bus slot*. With a special *local bus card* plugged into a special *local bus slot,* the computer could grab its video quickly. But different slot designers had different ideas: Not all local bus

cards and slots were compatible with each other.

Finally, the designers hunkered down and came up with a standard that everybody agreed on: *VESA Local Bus*, shortened to *VL-Bus*.

However, yet another standard quickly entered the race. Intel's *Peripheral Component Interconnect (PCI)* technology speeds things up, just like VL-Bus, and has other advantages, as well.

Which bus is the best? So far, a 486 works best with VL-Bus video, and Pentiums and Pentium Pros are quickly sucking up the PCI video cards.

Finally, an increasing number of computers are skipping the cards and building the ports directly onto the **motherboard** itself. That leaves more open slots for plugging in other goodies, like sound cards. The ports simply stick out of the back of the computer's case, ready for their cables.

Battery

Believe it or not, your PC has a battery, just like your smoke detector. The battery sits on the **motherboard** and usually lasts about three years. Most batteries are easy to replace. You'll know that yours has died if your computer keeps asking you what time it is or if it forgets what type of **hard drive** you own and subsequently won't let you use it. You can find out the sorry symptoms (and battery replacement instructions) in Chapter 10.

Memory (random-access memory, or RAM)

If you've talked to people about your computer problems, you've probably seen them rub their jaws, narrow their eyes, and say, "Sounds like you might need more memory." Adding more memory is one of the most popular upgrades today. It's also one of the cheapest and easiest upgrades, depending on the friendliness of your computer.

When your computer's **CPU** is telling all your computer's parts what to do, it doesn't have a scratch pad for taking notes. So the CPU stores its information in your computer's memory. The more memory the computer has to work with, the more complicated stuff it can do. And the faster that memory can move information around, the less time you'll spend waiting for your computer to catch up with your work.

If you're using Windows — and just about everybody is these days — you can probably use more memory. (If you haven't upgraded your older computer from DOS, upgrading your memory probably won't do you much good.)

Memory comes on *chips,* just like your CPU. Just as CPUs are rated by their power and speed, memory chips are rated by their storage and speed. You can find more about this in Chapter 11, however.

Although all the memory serves the same purpose, it comes in three different packages:

DIP: This is the old-style chip. DIP stands for dual in-line package, but everybody just calls it DIP. (This DIP is no relation to DIP switches, which are little rows of switches you can flip on or off.) DIPs look like antennaless cockroaches, as shown in Figure 3-33. These chips plug into sockets on the motherboard, where they lie down in neat little rows like graves.

SIMM: DIPs worked fine for years, except for two things: People kept breaking off the DIPs' little legs when trying to push them into their sockets. Plus, because they lie flat, DIPs hogged up too much room. So some spry engineer took a leftover strip of fiberglass from a motherboard, fastened the little DIPs onto it, and called it a SIMM (single in-line memory module). You can see both types of memory in Figure 3-33.

SIMMs come in two sizes: The older, smaller ones have 30 pins and can hold comparatively small amounts of memory: 1MB, 2MB, or 4MB. The newer, larger SIMMs have 72 pins. They can hold larger capacities of RAM, like 1MB, 2MB, 4MB, 8MB, 16MB, 32MB, 64MB, and more.

Confused between a SIMM's slots and **expansion slots?** They're actually very different: The SIMM's slots are tiny things; expansion slots are huge in comparison, as shown in Figure 3-23. There's no way to get slapped by accidentally putting the wrong one in the wrong place.

SIMMs come in several varieties. Some have three DIP chips on them; others have nine. Don't mix varieties if you can help it. In fact, many computers won't run if you try it.

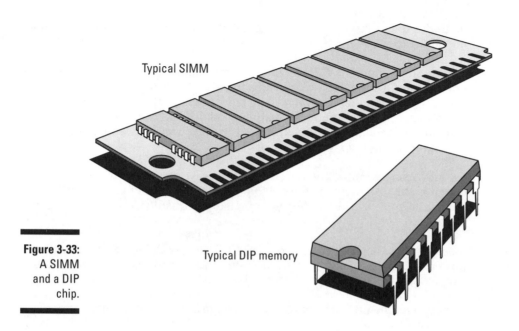

Typical SIMM

Figure 3-33:
A SIMM
and a DIP
chip.

Typical DIP memory

Some programs, notably IBM's OS/2, run into problems when a computer's SIMMs aren't all the same type. If your SIMMs don't all run at the same speed, OS/2 can burp indiscriminately and cause sporadic crashes that can't be traced to anything in particular. Also, OS/2 tends to have problems if some of your SIMMs use nine chips and others use three. To be on the safe side, try to keep your SIMMs running at the same speed and with the same number of DIP chips (three or nine).

DIMM: DIMMs are the biggest and the best. Resembling long SIMMs, many of today's Pentiums can take advantage of their special features. (That's why DIMMs cost the most, and only work in special, custom-designed DIMM slots; regular SIMM slots won't do.)

SIMMs and DIMMs slide or snap into their own tiny slots.

SIP: A SIP is pretty much like a SIMM: a tiny little card with a bunch of DIPs on it. But whereas a SIMM has a long flat edge that pushes into a slot, a SIP has a bunch of little prongs that push into a bunch of little holes. It looks kind of like a cat's flea comb. Most newer computers use SIMMs, but the chip dealers can often sell you SIP-to-SIMM converters that let you reuse your old SIPs in a newer motherboard — *if* those old SIPs are fast enough to keep up with your new CPU. (They usually aren't as I explain in Chapter 11.)

If you're not sure what kind of memory you have, pluck out a chip, put it in a Ziploc baggie, and bring it to the memory chip store. The person in the T-shirt behind the counter can then sell you some more of the same kind.

The price of chips moves up and down faster than pork belly futures. You'd be surprised how much money you can save by watching the prices and waiting for the right moment.

What's an owner of an older computer supposed to do if their computer's motherboard can't hold any more memory? Some people add a *memory expansion card.* Packed with memory chips, this card pops into a *slot* just like a *video card.*

The computer can grab for its memory there just as if the memory chips were sitting on the traditional spot in the motherboard. Unfortunately, memory on expansion cards won't work as quickly as memory sitting on the motherboard.

Here's yet more memory stuff to remember: The memory chips on your *motherboard* have life goals that are different from the ones on your *printer* or *video card.* You can't swap memory chips from your printer to your video card or from your computer to your printer. The chips won't fit.

Rambling about DRAM, SRAM, RAM, and ROM

For the most part, you're not breaking any computer etiquette rules when you say, "I need some more RAM for my computer." But here are the nerdy distinctions:

✔ SRAM (static random-access memory) is very fast and very expensive. Little snippets of SRAM live in a special place on your motherboard. Whenever the CPU dishes out information to a computer part, it sends a copy of that information to the SRAM. If any computer parts ask for the same information, the CPU just grabs it from the SRAM and dishes it out again, saving time.

✔ DRAM (dynamic random-access memory) is a little slower than SRAM but a little cheaper. When people say that you need more RAM, they're talking about DRAM.

✔ RAM, mentioned by itself, almost always means DRAM, described in the preceding paragraph.

✔ ROM (read-only memory) differs from all the preceding types of memory. Normally, a computer moves information in and out of RAM as it works. But a ROM chip holds onto information and doesn't ever let go. For example, your computer's *BIOS* comes on ROM. Because your computer's BIOS doesn't normally change, it's stored permanently on a ROM chip. ROM chips are not only a convenient way to store information, but they're a safer way, too: Your computer can't accidentally erase the information.

All those other little parts on the motherboard

Who cares about all those other little chips sitting on the motherboard, like the 8253 Programmable Interval Timer (U34)? Very few people, that's for sure. So ignore the rest of the little lumpy things sitting on your motherboard.

Even if those other little chips break, you won't be able to fix them or even tell which one's broken. Leave that job to the folks in the shop, who hook them up to expensive instruments with flashing lights and probe around while wolfing down mouthfuls of Atomic Fire Ball candies.

Disk Drives

Computers use memory chips for doing immediate work: running programs or putting pictures on the screen. But when you're done working and want to save the fruits of your labors, you put your data on disks. They come in three basic flavors: floppy disks, hard disks, and compact discs. Floppy disks fit into floppy drives, which read the information off them. A hard disk, often called hard drive, lives hidden inside your computer. And a compact disc moves in and out of your computer's CD-ROM drive. Your computer sucks and slurps information from the drives through a special controller that either lives on the motherboard, inside the drive itself, or on a card.

Floppy drives

Remember back in the old days of wide-spaced parking lots when you could easily back a car in and out of your parking space? Unfortunately, shop owners figured that they could cram a *lot* more cars into the same-sized lot by making each parking space a little smaller.

Computer engineers did the same thing with floppy disks and floppy drives.

The older floppy drives, like the one shown in Figure 3-34, are called *full-height drives*.

The newer one, shown in Figure 3-35, is half the size, so it's called a *half-height drive*.

But, although half-height drives take up half the space, they're more than twice as filling — they're *high-density drives*. That means they can pack your data onto disks more tightly, allowing the disks to hold more information.

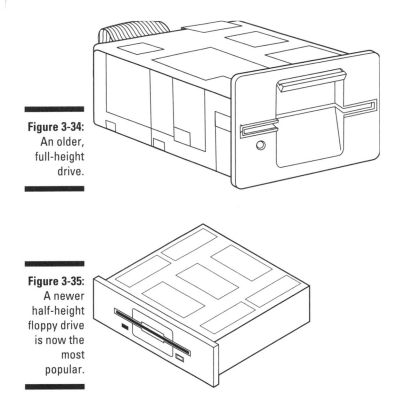

Figure 3-34:
An older,
full-height
drive.

Figure 3-35:
A newer
half-height
floppy drive
is now the
most
popular.

(Luckily, if you've stored any information on low-density floppies, the high-density drives can still read them.)

Table 3-2 shows the amount of information the low- and high-density drives can hold.

Table 3-2	Floppy Drive Sizes and Capacities
Drive Size	*Storage Room*
5$\frac{1}{4}$-inch, low-density	360K
3$\frac{1}{2}$-inch, low-density	720K
5$\frac{1}{4}$-inch, high-density	1.2MB
3$\frac{1}{2}$-inch, high-density	1.44MB (Most common)
3$\frac{1}{2}$-inch, extended-density	2.88MB

I don't wanna read about dead floppy drives!

Floppy drives die the quickest when people smoke around them or use the cheapest disks they can find. You know how bad your jacket smells the morning after you've had a night out at the Blue Bayou? Those same smoke particles coat the disk drive's little heads, which read information off the disks. The cheapest floppy disks are made of cheap materials, which can coat the disk drive's heads with a substance known technically as *gunk.*

Keep your computer in the nonsmoking section and don't feel so bad about spending an extra dollar or two for a box of disks. Your floppy drive will thank you for it.

Combo drives

The latest drives, like the one shown in Figure 3-36, pack two high-density floppy drives into a single package.

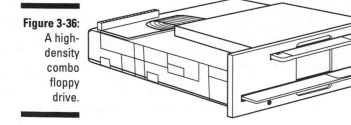

Figure 3-36:
A high-density combo floppy drive.

Instead of buying two drives, you can buy a single combo drive. Most people drool over them because they're so much smaller. The space where that second drive lived can now be rented out to another toy, like a **CD-ROM drive, tape backup unit,** or computerized yogurt maker.

Hard drives (hard disks)

Hard drives live inside your computer where they can't fall in the crack behind the wall and your desk. Hard drives can hold hundreds of floppy disks' worth of information, making them quite annoying when they finally wear out (often in about three years). Whether it's called a *hard disk* or a *hard drive,* it's just that big can of information that becomes your C:\> drive.

The hard drive has a friend inside your computer: a ***drive controller card.*** Like any other card, it plugs into a ***slot.*** The card grabs information from your computer's ***CPU*** and routes it through cables to your drives.

Hard drives not only come in several varieties, they're controlled by different devices, all described next:

EIDE: Currently the most popular type of drive in new PCs, EIDE stands for *Enhanced Integrated Drive Electronics*. Engineers figured out a way to hot-rod the previous standard, the IDE drives, so they'd work in sizes greater than 540MB. (They're also a few times faster at reading and writing information.) These drives still work in older PCs when connected to yesteryear's IDE controller cards, but not nearly as quickly.

IDE: The most popular type of drive in the early 90s, these drives are called *integrated drive electronics* because they also have a lot of the electronics that used to live on the controller card. In fact, many IDE drives don't need a controller: They can plug right into special connectors built in to the latest motherboards.

If your motherboard doesn't have a special slot, you can still use an IDE drive by buying an IDE controller card. It's cheaper than the average controller. Unfortunately, the IDE controller card is not as compatible with older hard drives.

MFM and RLL: These older hard drives, known as Modified Frequency Modulation and Run-Length Limited drives, are probably the ones you'll replace with the sexier new IDE drives.

The problem? Well, you can't mix IDE drives with these older drives: The two drives don't get along because they each like different kinds of controllers.

So you can use all IDE drives or use all MFM/RLL drives. Just don't try to mix the two.

ST-506, ST-412, and ESDI: These old-school drives and controllers are what you'll replace with the newer IDE or SCSI drives. Why mention them at all? So you know that the stores don't sell those same types of drive anymore. Go for the EIDE or SCSI drives instead, and make sure you pick up a new controller as well. (You can find a lot more information in Chapter 13.)

SCSI: Pronounced *scuzzy,* SCSI stands for Small Computer System Interface. SCSI drives, like MFM and RLL drives, use a controller card. And they're the most expensive option right now. But people like SCSI drives because they can chain stuff together.

For example, after installing the SCSI *card,* you can run its cable to your SCSI hard drive. From there, you can run the cable to your compact disc player, where it can head over to a tape backup unit or yet another SCSI toy, provided that all the parts get along with each other. By chaining all the doodads together, you can control them all through one card, which only grabs one slot — often a scarce resource on PCs.

Many *compact disc drives* use some form of SCSI cards. (The SCSI standard keeps changing. Sigh.)

Other ways to store data

The following sections describe data storage methods that have strayed from the traditional hard drive path but mostly for good reasons.

Compact disc drives

Compact disc drives are fun because compact discs are so versatile: They hold great gobs of information, so compact disc drives let you listen to music CDs, watch movies, read encyclopedias, or watch special multimedia CDs, which combine sound and pictures to create multifun.

- The vast majority of compact disc (CD) drives can only *play* stuff — not record stuff. You can't store your own information on them; compact discs come with the information already in place.

- Okay, you can store information on them. After all, somebody has to put the trombone sounds on there. But the technology is still expensive, and CD-ROM drives that can record cost from 500 dollars to a couple thousand dollars.

- CD drives, like modems, can be mounted inside your computer like a floppy drive or outside your computer in their own little case. If your computer doesn't have room for the internal CD drive, the external drive works just as well. (You'll need a spare power outlet to plug its power cord into the wall, though, unlike with the internal drive.)

- Most CD drives come with audio jacks in the back. You can't just plug in speakers, though; the sound needs to run through an amplifier before you can hear it. To combat this nonsense, some people hook their players up to *sound cards;* others hook their players to their home stereo system. Others forget about the speakers and simply use headphones, which don't need amplifiers.

- Many compact disc drives require a SCSI *card.* Some drives come with the card, and sometimes you have to pay extra for the card. You'd better check the side of the box to find out.

✔ Many sound cards come with a built-in SCSI port. Make sure that the SCSI port is compatible with the drive you're after, though. (A few sound cards aren't 100 percent compatible with all drives.)

✔ Compact disc players can move data around faster than a floppy drive but slower than a hard drive. When shopping, look for something called *access time*. A drive rated at 8X is faster than one rated at 4X.

Detachable hard drives

Detachable hard drives don't fit inside your computer. Instead, they come inside a little box. The box's cable then plugs into your computer's **parallel port** (the same place your printer cable lives). After you install a software driver (described in Chapter 18), you see your new drive D on the screen. It works just like any old hard drive after that, but you can carry it around from computer to computer, making it great for backups.

Don't forget to check out Chapter 13 for information on Zip drives (shown in Figure 3-37), the latest, greatest way to back up your information.

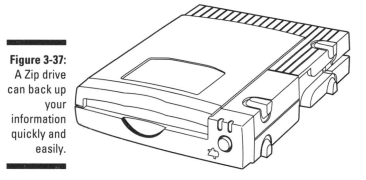

Figure 3-37:
A Zip drive can back up your information quickly and easily.

Tape backup units

Back in the 1970s, computer users recorded their files on a plain old tape recorder using a plain old audio cassette — a time-consuming process. Today, specialized tape backup units can store gobs of files. Some internal tape backup units slide into a computer's front, just like a floppy drive; external backup units live in a box next to your computer. Tape backup units have been around for more than 20 years, so you can find two decades worth of standards on the market. For best results, make sure the standard contains the words QIC (Quarter-Inch Cartridge).

Weird technical words on the CD drive box

Compact disc manufacturers all started sticking information on discs in different, incompatible ways. Instead of reaching a consensus, they just made compact disc players that support all the different standards. Here's a rundown of the weird words you might see:

MPC: Drives with this label can handle multimedia discs with pictures and sound. Almost all compact disc drives can handle these.

ISO-9660/High Sierra: Almost all CDs adhere to this standard, which makes sure that they store information in ways that DOS computers can recognize.

Kodak Photo CD: When you take your pictures to be developed, some developers can stick the pictures on a compact disc, too. Kodak Photo CD-compatible drives can display these pictures on your computer's monitor. Look for a multisession drive, which lets you stick all your pictures on the same disc; single session drives make you use a new disc for each roll of film.

Compact disc technology changes so fast that you probably need to read the newsstand computer magazines to keep up with the latest formats and details.

When shopping, look for a tape backup unit that can store as much information as you have on your hard drive. Then buy a bunch of tape cartridges that support your tape backup unit's particular format.

The Power Supply

PCs would be whisper-quiet if it weren't for their power supplies. Power supplies suck in the 110 volts from the standard American wall outlet and turn the 110 volts into the 5 or 12 volts that your computer prefers. This simple task heats up the power supplies, however, so they cool off with a noisy, whirling fan.

The fan also sucks any hot air out of your computer's case and blows it out the hole in the back. In fact, if you keep your computer too close to the wall and don't move it for several years, the fan will leave a round black dust-mark on the wall.

Extra fans are available as add-ons. They can be a lifesaver if your computer is failing due to heat buildup, which can happen if your motherboard uses a speedy **Pentium** chip.

For some reason, power supplies seem to die faster than most computer parts. Luckily, they're one of the easiest parts to replace. They vary in size, but a typical power supply and its wires appear in Figure 3-38.

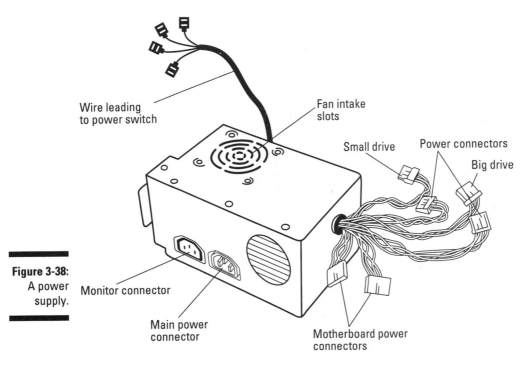

Wire leading
to power switch

Fan intake
slots

Small drive

Power connectors

Big drive

Figure 3-38:
A power
supply.

Monitor connector

Main power
connector

Motherboard power
connectors

Power supplies vary in size. Your best bet is to remove your old power supply and take it to the store so you can get another one that's the same size.

Don't ever open up the power supply to try to fix it. Doing so can cause serious bodily harm, even if the computer's turned off and unplugged.

✔ After finding a power supply that's the right size, check its wattage. Older XT computers can get away with the cheaper 130-watt models. If you're using a 386, 486, Pentium or faster computer, buy a 200-watt model. That's especially true if your computer also supplies power to a lot of internal toys: internal modems, tape backup drives, compact disc players, and other power-eating devices.

✔ If you live in an older area where the power fluctuates a lot, consider buying a *surge suppressor*. Basically, it plugs into the wall and conditions the power before it enters your computer. Many power strips come with a surge suppressor built in. They wear out, though, so for extra protection, replace power strips every six months or so. But most higher priced power strips have indicator lights to let you know when the suppressor has worn out.

✔ An uninterrupted power supply (UPS) goes one step further: If the power dies suddenly, it kicks in, keeping your computer up and running. Most uninterrupted power supplies only last for 5 to 15 minutes, but that's usually plenty of time to shut down your computer, grab a soda, and feel good about your foresight while waiting for the lights to come back on. The drawback? A UPS wears a huge price tag compared to a surge suppressor.

How Do I Know Which Parts I Have?

It's not always easy to figure out which parts are inside your computer. Computers really *do* look the same. Your best bet is to look around for your old manuals. They often have a hint as to which parts live inside your PC's case.

Sometimes your sales receipt can be a better gauge, however. Dealers occasionally hand out the wrong manual, but they're usually a little better about putting the right part on the receipt.

If you picked up your computer at a garage sale, or it's a hand-me-down from the office, you may have to do a little exploring on your own.

Still using DOS? Then type the following at any prompt and press Enter:

```
C:\> MSD
```

MSD stands for Microsoft Diagnostics, and it's a program Microsoft has been tossing in with some of its products for free. When you type **MSD,** the program probes the depths of your computer and reveals any pertinent information, including the amount of memory, ports, disk drives, claws, and tongue length. On my computer, MSD brings up the screen shown in Figure 3-39.

Figure 3-39: MSD brings this information about your computer to the screen.

```
 File  Utilities  Help

   Computer...      Dell/Phoenix        Disk Drives...    A: B: C: D:
                    486DX                                 E: F:

   Memory...        640K, 11264K Ext,   LPT Ports...      1
                    8919K XMS

   Video...         VGA, Orchid         COM Ports...      3

   Network...       No Network          IRQ Status...

   OS Version...    MS-DOS Version 5.00 TSR Programs...

   Mouse...         PS/2 Style Mouse    Device Drivers...
                    8.20

   Other Adapters...  Game Adapter

 Press ALT for menu, or press highlighted letter, or F3 to quit MSD.
```

For example, MSD found my computer's three COM ports as well as the printer port. For more detailed information about any subject, click its box. Some of the information will be technical glop that doesn't make any sense, but you may find some worthwhile information poking up from the swamp.

Still confused? Take off the computer's case (an occasionally laborious process described in the Cheat Sheet at the front of the book) and start looking at the parts described and pictured in this chapter. You find a product name and number stamped on the most important ones.

Computers often boast of their CPU when first turned on. Watch carefully when any words start flashing by. Your computer usually displays the name of its video card first and then its BIOS, which often contains the CPU number.

Some computers come with a diagnostic disk. If you haven't lost yours yet, put it into your floppy drive and run the program. The diagnostic disk can often identify what stuff's hiding inside your computer's case.

Windows 95 users can easily figure out what parts live inside their computer. Click the My Computer icon with your right mouse button and choose Properties from the pop-up menu. Windows lists the computer's CPU and amount of RAM on that page. Click the Device Manager tab along the top, and Windows 95 opens the closet doors, as seen in Figure 3-40. Chapter 17 explains more about how Windows 95 lets you fiddle with the parts inside your computer.

Figure 3-40: The Device Manager tab in Windows 95 can usually identify all of the parts living inside your computer.

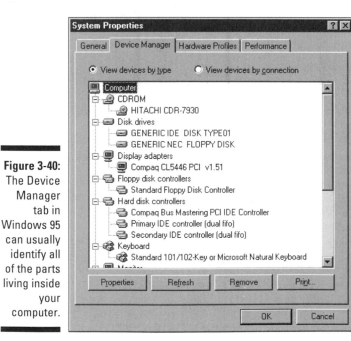

Chapter 4

Figuring Out What's Broken

● ●

In This Chapter

▶ Figuring out what's wrong with a computer

▶ Finding any recent changes

▶ Spotting clues when your PC is first turned on

▶ Listening for warning signals

▶ Using diagnostics programs

▶ Using Windows 95's Troubleshooting programs

▶ Buying replacement parts

▶ Calling technical support

● ●

*W*hen PCs aren't casting you in the role of the anguished user, they're making you play the detective in The Case of the Broken Part. Your computer's dead: Who dunnit?

At the PC repair shop, nerdy technodetectives wield expensive curly-wired probes that make accusatory blip sounds when they uncover the guilty part. You're merely armed with a cheap screwdriver.

If you already know what your computer needs — a bigger hard drive, for example, or a better monitor — head for that particular chapter. No need to stop here.

But if you're still searching for the culprit, this chapter can help you figure out which computer part has gone bad. After you finger the culprit, head for the chapter that describes the part in more detail.

It Doesn't Work Anymore!

PCs don't die very often. Unlike a car, PCs don't have many moving parts, leaving much less to wear out. When computers do start to cause problems, usually just one small piece has gone bad, spoiling the rest of the experience. (Kind of like finding gum under the table at a fancy restaurant.)

The hardest part isn't fixing the problem. It's simply *finding* the problem. Is the software acting up? Your disk drive? Both? Or is it some complicated mystery part you've never heard of before?

Before you whip out your screwdriver, give the tricks in the following sections one final shot.

Make sure that the computer is plugged in and turned on

This one sounds so obvious that many people overlook it. However, a vacuum cleaner or stray foot can inadvertently knock a power cord out of place. Give it one last check for the Gipper.

Make sure that the cables are fastened securely

Make sure that the PC's power cord nestles snugly between the back of your computer and the wall outlet. While you're rummaging around beneath the desk on your hands and knees, check the monitor's power cord as well. Finally, check the monitor's second cord — the one that runs to the back of your PC. Some monitor cords can come loose on both ends — from the back of the monitor as well as from the back of your PC.

Turn the computer off, wait 30 seconds, and turn it back on again

This sounds odd, but if it works, who cares? Turning the computer off and waiting a few seconds before turning it back on has solved many of my PC problems — although it always wipes out any information sitting on the screen at the time. This trick has even fixed my laser printer a couple of times, too. Be sure to wait 30 seconds before turning the computer back on, though.

Flipping a computer off and on quickly can send damaging shocks to its sensitive internal organs.

Does your monitor say something like

```
Non-System disk or disk error
Replace and press any key when ready
```

TECHNICAL STUFF

Dealing with your AUTOEXEC.BAT and CONFIG.SYS files

This tip's more important for old DOS users than for Windows 95 users, but here goes: When you flick your PC's power switch on, it immediately looks for two important files. They're called AUTOEXEC.BAT and CONFIG.SYS. Many programs add their own stuff to these files — things like the program's location on your hard drive and how the program should be treated. Sometimes, however, one program's additions upset those left by another program.

How do you combat the problem? Well, the best way is to copy those two important files to a floppy disk before installing a new program. Then if something goes dreadfully wrong, you can delete the new program and copy AUTOEXEC.BAT and CONFIG.SYS back onto your hard drive.

Of course, this advice comes after the fact, so it probably isn't helpful. But it will be next time.

Note that some programs save your old AUTOEXEC.BAT and CONFIG.SYS by renaming them when the program is installed. Check your manual.

This message usually means you've turned on your computer with a floppy disk sitting in drive A. Push the disk drive's eject button, press your spacebar (or any other handy key), and wish that all your problems were this easy to fix.

If none of these quick fixes works, move on to the next section.

Narrowing Down the Problem

Technogeeks talk up a storm in the locker room, but it's just talk. There *isn't* an easy way to figure out why your computer has gone kaput. It doesn't take much at all to send a PC running in circles. Maybe your software can't find a crucial piece of itself. Or maybe some tiny computer part buried deep inside the case simply gave up under pressure.

The only way to find a cure is to keep narrowing down the problem. Does the computer only act weird when a certain program is running? Or does it just act up when trying to print the eighth page? Do you hear a funny whine from inside the case?

When confronted with a real head-scratcher, ask yourself the following questions or try the following suggestions.

Have you added new software lately?

Sometimes new software not only doesn't work right, but it keeps everything else on your computer from working right, too. No easy solutions here. Your best bet is to reinstall the suspect software. This time, however, answer some of the installation questions differently.

Did you discover a weird file that didn't do anything and then delete it?

Some of the most important files on your PC have the weirdest names. Unfortunately, there's no easy way to tell the truly important files from the truly technoid trash.

If an adventurous urge caused you to delete a useless file and now your software doesn't work, you have two choices:

Choice 1: Beg a computer guru to figure out what you've done wrong.

Choice 2: Reinstall the software that's not working right.

Using Windows 95? Whew! You're lucky enough to have a third choice. You can probably retrieve that deleted file that you thought was useless. You see, Windows 95 hangs on to files for a little while after you've deleted from your hard drive. (Files from floppies get the axe immediately. No same luck.) Here's how to reclaim that file:

1. **Double-click the Recycle Bin icon.**

   The Recycle Bin window appears, listing all of your most recently deleted files.

2. **Choose <u>V</u>iew from the Recycle Bin menu, then choose <u>A</u>rrange Icons by Delete Date.**

   The Recycle Bin sorts your files in the order that you deleted them, with your most recently deleted file either at the top or bottom of the list.

3. **Choose <u>V</u>iew and then choose Details to see more information about the files.**

4. **Right-click the deleted file and choose Restore from the pop-up menu.**

   Windows 95 pulls the file back from the dead and places it back in its original home.

Have you moved any files or directories around? Changed any of their names?

When a program installs itself, it often tells the computer where it's living on your hard drive. If you subsequently move that program from one Windows 95 folder to another (or from C:\FISH to C:\FISH\TUNA), for example, your computer may not be able to find it again.

Windows 95 programs are notorious for this, leading to big trouble if you move files around, change a folder's location, or simply change some names. The fix? Try to remember which files or folders you moved and move them back. Change the filenames back to their originals, too. If the program still doesn't work, your best bet is to delete the programs that aren't working and reinstall them.

It's bad luck to delete unidentified files because they often turn out to be important. Don't delete a file unless you have a compelling reason. If in doubt, grab a computer guru the next time one shuffles down the hall. A guru can usually spot a wolf in sheep's clothing.

Have you changed the computer's location on your desktop?

Did you pull your computer out from the wall a few inches to plug in the joystick? Did the janitor move the desk slightly to clean beneath it? Cables often fall off or loosen themselves when the computer's case is moved, even just a few inches here and there.

If a *swivel-mounted* monitor swivels too far in one direction, the monitor's cables often come loose. Leave a little slack in the cables so they won't get yanked around. Often, loose cables don't dangle or give other visible warning signs. When in doubt, give them all a little push inward for good measure.

Try a different part

Here's where repair shops have you beat. If you don't think that your hard drive is working right, you can only flap your neck wattles in exasperation. At the repair shop, the nerds will pull out your computer's hard drive and stick it inside another computer to see whether it works.

If it works in that other computer, your hard drive must be okay. Something else inside your computer is making it act weird. Or, if your hard drive *doesn't* work, the nerds will sell you a new hard drive.

Even if you don't have a "test-drive" computer, you can try some of the same tricks. If your floppy drive is acting up, try using a different floppy disk. (Maybe the disk was bad.) Computer doesn't get any power? Try another wall socket.

By combining part swapping with other clues, you can continue to narrow down your PC's problem.

Watch the screen when your PC wakes up

Whenever you turn on your PC, it sits still for a while, flashes some words and numbers on the screen, and then belches out a beep or two before letting you get some work out of it.

Those aren't idle yawns and stretches. Your computer's using that time to examine itself and is trying to figure out what you've been able to afford to attach to it and whether everything is working up to snuff.

This series of wake-up checks is called the *power-on self test,* dubbed POST by the acronym-happy engineers. By watching and listening to your computer during its POST, you can often pick up a clue as to what's bothering it.

✔ When you find a cockroach in your slippers, you shriek. When the computer finds something it doesn't like, it beeps. This may sound like something straight out of a Captain Crunch commercial, but it's true. Listen to the number of beeps when you turn on your computer, and you'll know which of your computer's parts are acting up. (You hear more on this musical weirdness in the next section.)

✔ Sometimes your PC displays a cryptic code on your screen when it's first turned on. It never says anything really helpful, like `The mouse doesn't work`. Instead, it says something like `Error Code 1105`, forcing you to flip to Chapter 23 to find out what your computer is complaining about this time.

✔ Most POST errors happen after you've installed something on a card that the computer didn't like. (If the word *card* has you stumped, head for Chapter 3 for a quick refresher.)

✔ When your computer's battery dies, your exhausted computer probably won't be able to find your hard drive. The POST message may say, `ERROR Code 161`. That's usually a pretty simple fix. You can find the explanation in Chapter 10.

✔ The POST makes sure that your keyboard is plugged in — that's the reason that your keyboard's lights flash when you first turn on your computer. The lights on your disk drives flash, too, as your computer checks to see whether they're *really* there.

CHAIN REACTION

Cures for quarreling cards

If you have recently replaced or added a new card, then your POST may alert you to a potential problem or, worse yet, a chain reaction of replacements. Card problems leave four possible fixes:

🖝 Fiddle with the buttons on the new card so it won't interfere with the old card (see Chapter 18).

🖝 Fiddle with the buttons on the *old* card so it won't interfere with the new card.

🖝 Buy a different brand of card.

🖝 Replace the older card that's conflicting with your new card. (Unfortunately, doing so leads to the chain reaction talked about in the book's Introduction.)

🖝 The most visible part of the POST comes with the *memory check.* Your PC first counts all its memory and then checks to make sure that all the memory works. If you have a *lot* of memory, you'll be drumming your fingers on the table as your computer adds it all up on the screen for you.

Listen to the beeps, Luke!

That single beep you hear just after you turn on your computer is a happy beep. It means that the computer has found all its parts, given them a little kick, and decided that they're all working as they should.

If you hear more than a single beep, though, your computer is often trying to tell you some bad news. See, the PC designers figure that if PCs are so smart, they should be able to tell their users what's wrong with them. But because computers speak a bizarre language of numbers, the beep is the best they can do.

By counting the number of beeps and looking them up in Chapter 24, you can figure out what your computer is trying to tell you. Here's a summary:

🖝 POST messages and beeps sound serious and look befuddling. But they're not always that bad. Sometimes just a loose cable can start your PC beeping and weeping.

🖝 Even if you've bought a sound card, don't expect more elaborate beeps. Your PC's beeps will sound the same, no matter how much your sound card costs.

🖝 By combining your computer's beep clues with any accompanying error message, you can figure out which chapter to scurry toward for more information.

> ✔ Some computers, especially the ones made by Compaq, make two
> beeps when they're happy, not one. So much for standards.

Call in Doctor Software

In the old days, people bought software for PCs that *worked*. Then some sly
programmer made millions by designing software for computers that *didn't*
work. Today, some of the most popular software merely helps you figure out
why your PC has suddenly stopped walking the dog.

For example, many new PCs come bundled with a disk that says *diagnostic*
or *DIAG* somewhere on its label. If you're lucky, that disk contains a helpful
program designed to help you figure out what's wrong with your PC.

If you can find your PC's diagnostic disk, stick it into drive A and push your
computer's reset button. The diagnostic program will try to take over,
scrutinizing your system and offering clues as to what's ailing the beast. If
you can't find any kind of disk like this, try the following:

> ✔ Microsoft tossed in a helpful diagnostic program with Windows 3.1 and
> MS-DOS 6. Type **MSD** at any C:\> prompt and the program leaps into
> action, letting you know what parts are attached to your computer. For
> example, the program lets you know whether your computer knows
> that you've just added a new mouse. Best yet, the program is free.
>
> ✔ If you didn't get a diagnostic disk with your computer, head for the
> Utilities aisle of your local software store. The Norton Utilities program,
> for example, offers stealth-like information similar to Microsoft's MSD
> program. Other Norton programs can salvage the wreckage from
> damaged hard disks and other disasters.
>
> ✔ Some utility and diagnostic programs are better left for the computer
> gurus, however. Some of these programs dish out information that's
> detailed down to your PC's bare ribs. Then they delve into complicated
> technical specifics, like bone composition, blood type, and DNA compo-
> sition. A lot of the information these programs dish out won't make
> much sense at all. Still, the programs may be worth a try in some
> desperate cases.
>
> ✔ Windows 95 comes with some troubleshooting software that's de-
> scribed in Chapter 17, although you find a tidbit of advice in the next
> section.

Use Windows 95's built-in Troubleshooter

Windows 95 makes an effort to be friendly by supplying software that tries
to play doctor on itself. By using one of these "Troubleshooter" programs,

you can sometimes make Windows 95 do the dirty work of figuring out what's wrong and fixing it without charge. Follow these steps to put a wrench into Windows 95's hands:

1. **Click Windows 95's Start menu and choose Help.**

   The Help dialog box appears.

2. **Select the Contents tab, then double-click the Troubleshooting topic.**

   The information in Figure 4-1 appears.

Help Topics: Windows Help
Contents	Index	Find

Click a topic, and then click Display. Or click another tab, such as Index.

- Introducing Windows
- How To...
- Tips and Tricks
- Troubleshooting
  - ? If you have trouble printing
  - ? If you run out of memory
  - ? If you need more disk space
  - ? If you have a hardware conflict
  - ? If you have trouble running MS-DOS programs
  - ? If you have trouble using the Internet
  - ? If you have trouble using the network
  - ? If you have trouble using your modem
  - ? If you have trouble using Dial-Up Networking
  - ? If you have trouble using Direct Cable Connection
  - ? If you have trouble using a PC card (PCMCIA)

[Close] [Print...] [Cancel]

Figure 4-1: Windows 95 can sometimes troubleshoot and fix its own problems.

3. **Double-click on the problem that plagues you and follow the instructions.**

   For example, double-click the If you have trouble printing selection to see the window in Figure 4-2 that offers suggestions on fixing printers.

Windows 95 offers a more advanced method of self-diagnosis through its System Properties area. Right-click My Computer and choose Properties from the pop-up menu. Then, click the Device Manager tab to see a list of all your computer's parts.

A red X or a yellow exclamation point next to a computer part's name on the Device Manager list means that particular part isn't working right.

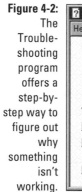

Figure 4-2:
The
Trouble-
shooting
program
offers a
step-by-
step way to
figure out
why
something
isn't
working.

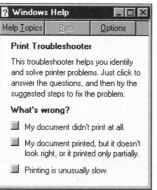

Buying Replacement Parts

After you finger the bad part, you have to decide how to replace it. Should you replace the bad part with a part of the same brand and model? Or should you buy something a little better? Only you can decide. Keep the following points in mind, though:

✔ Avoid the cheapest parts. They're made of shoddy material and are put together cheaply. Feel free to avoid some of the most expensive stuff, too. You'll pay for the name, the advertising, and the fancy package. Shoot for somewhere in between.

✔ Try to buy from friendly dealers. If your new part doesn't work, can you take it back? If you're having trouble installing it or getting it to work, can somebody tell you over the phone which buttons to push?

✔ Mail-order parts work well for computer geeks who know exactly what they want and how to put the parts together after they get them. If that's not you, you're probably best off shopping at the friendly local computer store.

✔ Most parts come with a standard one-year warranty covering parts and labor. Watch out for the ones that don't.

✔ Some places charge a 15 percent restocking fee if you return a product because you didn't like it or it didn't work right in your computer. Avoid these places.

✔ Check out some of the newer, upgradeable computer parts. For example, U.S. Robotics' latest modem comes with a special socket inside. When modems become faster, you can plug the new, speedy miracle chip into that socket. Voilà! Your six-month-old modem is instantly transformed into state-of-the-art stuff.

Calling Technical Support

There comes a time when you should just plain give up. You've installed a new part, and it won't work. You've fiddled with the part's switches, you've fiddled with the software, and still the part just sits there looking expensive.

Stay calm. Think of a flock of brilliant-green parrots flying toward you, bringing luscious chunks of pineapple and the latest hot movie rental.

Then start rooting through the part's packaging for a little piece of paper with the technical support number. It's often on the same paper with the warranty information. Found the number? Then collect the following information before you call.

The part's serial number

Usually printed on a small sticker, the serial number often lurks on the side of the box or somewhere on the product itself.

Information about your computer

The nerds on the phone will try to blame the part's failure on some other company. So write down the names of all the other gizmos installed in your computer.

The version of the operating system

Do you know what version of DOS or Windows you're using?

For DOS, type **VER** at the C:\> prompt and press Enter.

Using any version of Windows but Windows 95? Then open Windows Program Manager, press Alt+H and then A. A little box appears, listing the version number near the top. Windows 95 users can right-click the My Computer icon and choose Properties from the pop-up menu.

A printout of your important files

Make a copy of these files before anything goes wrong; technical support people love reading them. The following three sections show what to do whether you're using Windows 95, an earlier version of Windows, or plain old DOS.

Windows 95

Like many other things in Windows 95, this is pretty easy.

1. **Right-click the My Computer icon and choose P<u>r</u>operties.**

2. **Click the Device Manager tab.**

3. **Click the Pri<u>n</u>t button.**

4. **Click <u>A</u>ll devices and system summary option and click OK.**

Earlier Windows versions

These two files contain lines of gibberish that your computer likes to wallow in. If you're in the Windows Program Manager, press Alt+F and then R. When the little box comes up, type **SYSEDIT** and press Enter. A little program appears, looking like Notepad with four heads. See those two files — CONFIG.SYS and AUTOEXEC.BAT — lurking in there? Send them to your printer with the <u>P</u>rint command, just like you would in any other Windows program.

DOS users

Type these two lines at the C:\> prompt:

```
PRINT C:\AUTOEXEC.BAT
PRINT C:\CONFIG.SYS
```

You have to press Enter twice after typing the first line; then just press Enter once after the second line. In a few minutes, your printer spits those two files onto a piece of paper.

Gathered all the information listed above? Now load a favorite computer game and call the technical support number. You'll probably be on hold for many moons and be routed through several departments.

Hopefully, a helpful person will answer and explain why the part's not working or tell you where to send the part for a refund.

Whenever you find helpful people on technical support lines, *ask for their names and write them in a safe place.* Ask whether they have their own phone numbers as well. Sometimes, using this information will keep you from waiting on hold the next time you need to call.

If your modem's working, rummage around in the box's paperwork for the modem company's technical support BBS or World Wide Web site on the Internet. You can call the BBS or Web Site and type in your questions. Chances are that either a techie or a passing stranger will leave you an answer. Modem people are mysteriously helpful sometimes.

Part II
The PC Parts You Can See (Peripherals)

The 5th Wave   By Rich Tennant

"Now, when someone rings my doorbell, the current goes to a scanner that digitizes the audio impulses and sends the image to the PC where it's converted to a Pict file. The image is then animated, compressed, and sent via high-speed modem to an automated phone service that sends an e-mail message back to tell me someone was at my door 40 minutes ago."

In this part . . .

This part of the book deals with the parts of the PC you can see — the parts that aren't hiding from you inside the computer's case.

Here, keyboards, mice, modems, monitors, and printers all get their due. In each chapter, you'll find a list of the part's symptoms. Next to each symptom, you'll find the fix — be it a software tweak, a flip of a switch, or a gentle, fatherly discussion.

And, if none of those fixes does the trick, you can find explicit instructions for ripping the darn thing out, throwing it away, and installing a replacement that'll work twice as well.

Chapter 5
The Sticky Keyboard

· ·

In This Chapter

▶ Helping your computer find your keyboard

▶ Removing a spilled beverage from the keys

▶ Stopping arrow keys from making numbers

▶ Working with the F11 and F12 keys

▶ Fixing keyboards that just beep

▶ Changing to a Dvorak keyboard

▶ Using an ergonomic or "natural" keyboard

▶ Using the "Windows 95" key

▶ Installing a new keyboard

▶ Using keyboards with different plugs

· ·

*T*alk about moving parts — most keyboards have more than 100 of 'em, each moving up and down hundreds of times during the day.

Keyboards don't die very often, but when they start to go, they're easy to diagnose. A few keys start to stickkkk or stop working altogether. And when a water glass hits the keyboard, every key stops working at the same time.

This chapter starts with a list of sick keyboard symptoms that are followed by a quick fix. If you discover that your tired, old keyboard is ready for retirement, however, head for the "How Do I Install a New Keyboard?" section at the end of the chapter.

When I Turn On My Computer, the Screen Says "Keyboard Not Found, Press <F1> to Continue" or Something Equally Depressing!

Chances are that your keyboard's cord isn't plugged all the way into its socket. (And pressing F1 won't do anything, no matter what your computer says.) Fumble around in the back of your computer until you find the keyboard's cable. Push it into its socket a little harder.

 After you fasten the keyboard's cable more securely, you probably have to push your computer's reset button. Some computers only look for their keyboards once — and that's when they're first turned on. The reset button forces the computer to take a second look. Or, if there's no reset button, then turn off your computer, wait 30 seconds, and turn it back on again.

Also, make sure that nothing's sitting on any of the keys, like the corner of a book or magazine. If any of your keys are pressed when you first turn the computer on, the computer thinks that the keyboard is broken.

Still doesn't work? Look for a tiny switch on the bottom of your keyboard and try flicking it the other way. Maybe some nerdy jokester flipped the switch while you weren't looking. (Not all keyboards have this switch, though, so just shrug your shoulders in bewilderment if yours doesn't.)

If your keyboard still doesn't work, check to see whether something gross may have been spilled on it (see the following section).

Some of the Keys Stick After I Spilled a Hansen's Natural Raspberry Soda over Them!

Your keyboard is probably a goner. But here's the Emergency Keyboard Preservation Procedure: Save your work if possible, turn off your computer, and unplug the keyboard.

With a sponge, wipe off all the spilled stuff you can find. Then sit there and feel foolish for the 24 hours or so that it takes for the keyboard to dry.

If you only spill water, your keyboard may still work the next day. But if you spill anything containing sugar — soda pop, coffee, margaritas, Tang — you'll probably coat the inside of your keyboard with sticky gunk. This gunk then attracts dust and grime — your keyboard starts a slow decline within a few months and dies sooner or later, depending on the tragedy level of the spill.

- ✔ If you have a lot of spare time, pry off all the keycaps one by one. Start in one corner and work your way across. (Don't bother trying to take off the spacebar because it has too many gizmos holding it on.) When the keys are off, sponge off any stray gunk, dry off the moisture, and try to put all the keycaps back in their right locations. (Figures 3-16, 3-17, and 3-18 in Chapter 3 may help.)

- ✔ Some people report success and, sometimes, odd stares by immediately taking their wet keyboard to the gas station and squirting it with air from the tire pump to loosen debris. Other people (including me) have cautiously — and successfully — used a hair dryer.

- ✔ Wait at least 24 hours before giving up on your keyboard. You can salvage many wet keyboards but only after they are completely dry.

If you spill something more gross than water on your laptop's keyboard, don't take it apart. If you're emotionally attached to your keyboard, take it to the nearest repair shop to be cleaned professionally and keep your fingers crossed. You won't be typing with them again for a few days anyway. For the most part, however, the cost of cleaning a keyboard is more than the cost of a new one.

Don't ever give up hope. Erik writes in from Portugal with an old college story about a basketball player who borrowed his computer for video games. Unfortunately, the sportster knocked a cup of spit and tobacco juice into the keyboard. Figuring he had nothing to lose, Erik rinsed off the keyboard at the nearby gym's shower and toweled it off. A few hours later, Erik plugged in the keyboard and it came back from the dead.

My Arrow Keys Don't Move the Cursor — They Make Numbers!

Look for a key labeled Num Lock or something similar. Press it once. The little Num Lock light on your keyboard should go out, and your arrow keys should go back to normal.

WELL-WORN

My keyboard doesn't have F11 and F12 keys, and Microsoft Word for Windows uses those!

If your keyboard doesn't have F11 and F12 keys, you're using an older 83- or 84-key keyboard. Microsoft Word for Windows and some other Windows programs prefer the more expensive (naturally) 101-key keyboard. Buy a 101-key keyboard and try to find a place in the garage to store your old keyboard. (Very few stores take trade-ins.)

Windows still works with an older keyboard, however, and the programs that do use the F11 and F12 keys usually don't make those keys do anything very exciting.

Besides, a mouse almost always works faster than function keys.

All the Letters and Numbers Wore Off from My Keys!

If your rapidly moving fingers wear the letters off, you probably already memorized all the locations. Still want labels? Then either buy a new keyboard, salvage the keycaps from a friend's dead keyboard, or look in the back pages of computer magazines for a mail-order company that sells new keycaps. Magic markers don't work. They just turn your fingertips black.

Every Time I Press a Key, the Computer Beeps at Me!

Are you in a program possibly filling out some boring form? Some computers beep frantically if they want *letters* and you're typing *numbers* or vice versa. Other times, they'll beep if you're trying to squeeze some more letters or numbers into a box that's already full.

Can your computer be frozen solid? A frozen computer beeps every time you press a key.

The reason is that your keyboard stores about 20 characters in a special place called a *keyboard buffer*. If the computer doesn't wake up from its icy slumber, the buffer fills up as you pound the keyboard in exasperation. When the buffer's finally full, each character that didn't make it inside beeps in protest.

That's bad news. Your only solution is to hold down your Ctrl, Alt, and Delete keys at the same time. If you're using Windows 95, often you can close down the bottleneck program and continue work. (Chapter 17 explores ways to fix Windows 95 problems.)

With other versions of Windows or DOS, unfortunately, pressing Ctrl+Alt+Del destroys all the work you haven't had time to save. It restarts your computer from scratch.

If the Ctrl+Alt+Delete thing doesn't work, push the reset button on your computer's front or just turn the thing off. You still lose all your unsaved work that way, but at least you can get your computer's attention when it starts up again.

How Can I Change to a Dvorak Keyboard?

The *Dvorak* keyboard strays from the standard key arrangement — the one that spells *QWERTY* along the top row. Instead, the Dvorak keyboard uses a layout that engineers have calibrated especially for speed and finger efficiency.

Very few people want the agony of learning how to type all over again. So only a few diehards use the Dvorak keyboard. If you want to be a diehard, head for the software stores and ask for a *Dvorak keyboard layout program.*

Windows comes with a built-in Dvorak keyboard option. If you're using Windows 95, click the Start button, choose Settings then choose Control Panel and double-click the Keyboard icon. Click the Language tab and then click the Properties button. From the Language Properties dialog box choose United States-Dvorak from the drop-down list. (See Figure 5-1.) Click OK, then OK again and be prepared to insert your Windows 95 disks or CD.

In Windows 3.1, head for the Control Panel and double-click the International icon. There, buried under the Keyboard Layout drop-down list (shown in Figure 5-2) is the US-Dvorak option. You still have to move around all your keycaps yourself, though. (You can pry off and reseat the keycaps pretty easily.)

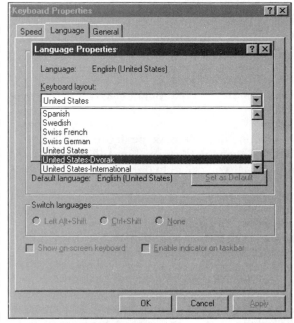

Figure 5-1:
To switch to the Dvorak keyboard layout in Windows 95, double-click on the Keyboard icon in the Windows 95 Control Panel, click the Language tab, and choose Properties.

Figure 5-2:
Double-click the International icon in the Windows 3.1 Control Panel to switch to the Dvorak keyboard layout.

TIP

Windows NT users can choose the Keyboard icon from the Control Panel, and click the General tab. Click the Change button and Windows NT shows the keyboard models currently compatible with your computer. If the new keyboard came with a disk, put the disk in your floppy drive, click the Have Disk button, and follow the instructions. (They vary with different keyboards.) No disk? Then click the Show all devices button and choose your keyboard's brand from the master list.

✔ Although the Dvorak layout sounds as promising as solar energy, keep your QWERTY layout memorized, as well. Otherwise, you'll be hunting and pecking at typewriters and terminals in airports, libraries, offices, and just about every other place in the civilized world.

✔ Also, if you're interested in more comfortable keyboards, check out the section on Ergonomic keyboards coming up next.

Do Ergonomic Keyboards Feel as Natural as Soybeans?

In the past 50 years, computers have advanced from awkward, room-sized primitive calculators into sleek powerhouses that let executives play three-dimensional flight simulation games during business trips.

The typewriter, by contrast, hasn't changed from its straight, three-row lineup of keys in more than 100 years.

That same typewriter-key layout still lives on most computers, often leading to sore fingers and wrists for people who keep their fingers attached to their keyboards all day.

The solution? First, try several keyboards before buying a new one. The engineers gave more thought to comfort in some models. For instance, "ergonomic" keyboards like Microsoft's Natural Keyboard are sculpted in nontraditional ways so your fingers approach the keys from different angles.

Ergonomic keyboards don't appeal to everybody, but their users often worship them.

A wrist-pad — a piece of foam that your wrists rest upon as you type — sometimes helps deter typing soreness. To see if you can benefit from one, make a test model from a thin, rolled-up magazine taped shut. Put it along the front of the keyboard and see if your arms feel better when the magazine lifts your wrists slightly.

What's That Special "Windows" Key on a Microsoft Natural Keyboard?

As a business, Microsoft stays almost exclusively within the software market. Computer programs are relatively inexpensive to make and distribute because they can be sold months before creation, and they can be fixed by adding more software when something screws up.

Microsoft trots out a piece of hardware every few years, and the relaxed-looking Microsoft Natural Keyboard is one of the most popular, moving a step beyond the past century's awkward keyboard design. Shaped with angled rows of keys that aim toward a typist's elbows, the Natural Keyboard does something besides comfort the user's limbs: It comes with a special "Windows" key (shown in the margin) that can perform the mystical tricks listed in Table 5-1.

Table 5-1 The "Windows" Key on the Microsoft Natural Keyboard	
Press this...	*to do this.*
Win+F1	Help
Win+E	Starts Windows Explorer
Win+F	Brings up the Find program
Ctrl+Win+F	Finds a computer on a network
Win+Tab	Cycles through taskbar options
Win+R	Brings up the Run program
Win+M	Minimizes everything on the screen
Shift+Win+M	Undoes the minimize all

(Other keyboards now come with the special Windows key, if you think the fuss is worth it.)

How Do I Install a New Keyboard?

IQ level: 70

Tools you need: One hand

Cost: From $25 to $150 or more for elaborate models with speakers or scanners

Things to watch out for:

If you don't know the difference between an XT's 84-key keyboard and an AT's 101-key Enhanced Keyboard, flip back to Chapter 3 to make sure you buy the right one. Other than that, you shouldn't have much trouble. Keyboards come with their own circuitry built in, so computers rarely reject them.

Most new keyboards come with small, "PS/2-style" connectors, as shown in Chapter 3. Older ones use larger connectors. Make sure that your new keyboard has the same type of cable connector as your old keyboard, or it won't plug into the same hole. It never hurts to bring along the old keyboard when shopping for the new one. You can buy an adapter at the store, if necessary. (***Tip:*** That same adapter often lets you plug an older keyboard into a laptop.)

Some expensive keyboards come with a built-in *trackball* that works like a built-in mouse. Others let you change the keys around to match your own keyboard tastes. Let your pocketbook be your guide.

Finally, don't buy a keyboard without taking it out of the box and typing nonsense words on it with your own fingers. You'll be working closely with that keyboard for years to come, so don't pick one that's too hard, spongy or just plain unfriendly.

To install a new keyboard, perform the following steps:

1. **Save any work you have on the screen, exit your program, and turn off your computer.**

    Don't ever unplug or plug in your keyboard cable while the PC is turned on. Something dreadful is supposed to happen. Besides, the computer only recognizes the keyboard when it's first turned on anyway.

2. **Remove your old keyboard by pulling the cable's plug from its socket on the back of your computer.**

    When unplugging a cord, pull on the plug, not the cord. The cord lasts a little longer that way.

3. **Carefully insert the new keyboard's plug into the socket.**

    The plug only fits one way. If the plug has a little plastic lump or ridge on its outside edge, that edge faces up. If there's no lump, try to match up the plug's little pins with the socket's little holes. Then gently push the plug into the socket and turn it back and forth slowly until it begins to slip into the holes. Got it? Then push firmly until it's all the way in.

    If that doesn't work, find out whether your keyboard has a PS/2 connector. It's a small little plug, about the size of a back molar. A PS/2 connector doesn't fit in the standard-sized hole, which is about the size of your thumb. You can buy a converter at most computer shops for about $5.

    Unlike most computer cables, a keyboard's cable doesn't have tiny screws to hold it tightly in place. Just push it in, and friction holds it in place.

Because there aren't any screws holding a keyboard's cable in place, the cable can sometimes work its way loose, especially during violent typing sessions. If the keyboard's acting up, make sure that the cable's plugged in securely.

4. Turn your computer back on.

One of the first things a computer does when waking up is reach for its keyboard. If the computer doesn't complain, it found the new keyboard and decided that it was appropriate. Hurrah!

If it does complain, however, head for the three chapters at the end of this book; they're designed to help diagnose strange and depressing startup sights and sounds.

If your computer makes it to Windows before complaining, head for Chapter 17 for some resuscitative medicines. Windows recognizes most new keyboards on touch, but sometimes Windows needs drivers or special cable connectors for weird models with speakers, calculators, or trackballs.

Chapter 6
Mice in the Pantry

· ·

· ·

Mice all tackle the same computing chore. When you move your mouse across your desk, you subsequently move a little arrow across your computer's screen. By pointing at buttons on the screen and pushing buttons on the mouse, you "push" the buttons on the screen.

Most mice even look pretty much alike. They all resemble a plastic bar of soap with two buttons and a long tail. The confusing part of the mouse kingdom comes when trying to figure out where that tail plugs into the back of your computer. In fact, sometimes several computer devices want to plug into the same place, causing much gnashing of mouse teeth.

This chapter tells you how to referee the fights and tend to the injured. And don't forget that I decipher weird words like *cards* and *serial ports* in Chapter 3.

My Mouse's Arrow or Cursor Is Starting to Jerk Around

If you haven't installed any new software or hardware recently, your mouse is probably just dirty. (If you *have* installed new software or hardware, head for the "How Do I Install or Replace a Serial or PS/2-Style Mouse?" section later in this chapter.) Mouse balls must be cleaned by hand every so often. It's a pretty simple procedure:

1. **Turn the mouse upside down and look at the little square or round plastic plate that holds the ball in place.**

   You usually find an arrow indicating which way to turn a round plate or which way to push a square plate.

2. **Remove the plastic plate holding the ball in place, turn the mouse right side up, and let the mouse ball fall into your hand.**

   Two things fall out: the plate holding the ball in place and the ball itself.

3. **Set the plate aside and pick all the hairs and crud off the mouse ball. Remove any other dirt and debris from the mouse's ball cavity, too.**

   If you have a Q-Tip and some rubbing alcohol handy, wipe any crud off the little rollers inside the mouse's ball cavity. The rollers are usually white or silver thingies that rub against the mouse ball. Roll the little rollers around with your finger to make sure that there's no stubborn crud that you can't see hiding on the sides. Make sure that the crud falls *outside* the mouse and not back into the mouse's guts.

   If there's some stubborn grunge on the mouse ball, some mild soap and warm water should melt it off. Never use alcohol on the mouse ball; that can damage the rubber. Also, make sure that the ball is dry before popping it back inside the mouse.

   Mouse balls give off a very disappointing bounce. Don't waste too much time trying to play with them.

4. **Drop the mouse ball back inside the mouse and put the plate back on. Turn or push the plate until the mouse ball is locked in place.**

   This cleaning chore cures most jerky mouse cursor problems. However, the mouse ball stays only as clean as your desk. Computer users with cats or shaggy beards may have to pluck stray hairs from their mouse ball every month or so.

My Computer Says That It Can't Find My Mouse

Are you sure that the mouse is plugged in? Grope around until you're sure that the plug on the end of its cable fits snugly into the little socket on the back of your computer. Plugged in tight? Then the problem could be something like the following.

Ever had a soggy bit of lettuce mulch stuck between your teeth after lunch, but you didn't know that it was there until you got home and looked in the mirror? Computers are the same way. Even though a mouse may be plugged into the case, the computer doesn't necessarily know that the mouse is there.

Before the computer can fiddle with your mouse, the computer needs to read a piece of software known as a *driver*. (Drivers are confusing enough to warrant their own section in Chapter 15.)

Here's what may be happening: When you turn on your computer, it finds the mouse's special *driver* software. The driver tells the computer where to look for the mouse. But when the computer turns its head and looks, the mouse isn't there.

So, make sure your mouse is plugged into the back of your computer, and try reloading the driver yourself by doing this: While you're at the DOS prompt (that C:\> thing), type the following line, followed by a press of the Enter key.

```
C:\>\DOS\MOUSE
```

Then load up your program again and see if the mouse works this time.

- A mouse often works in Windows programs, but not in DOS programs. That's because Windows comes with a mouse driver built in and DOS doesn't. The solution? Type **\DOS\MOUSE** or just plain **MOUSE** at the DOS prompt before loading your DOS program. That should load the driver so the mouse and computer can start talking to each other.

- If you want the mouse driver to be loaded all the time, head for Chapter 15. By putting the MOUSE line in a file called AUTOEXEC.BAT, your computer will load the mouse driver every time you restart your computer.

My Friend's Mouse Won't Work on My Computer

Chances are that the mouse needs different drivers — software that translates your mouse's movements into something the computer can relate to. Ask for the software that came with your friend's mouse and run its installation program.

Also, some mice are *optical*, which means that they don't have balls like normal mice; instead, they use little sensors that read a special reflective pad with little lines on it. Without that special pad, the mouse won't work. In fact, if you have an optical mouse, you're forever stuck with that special optical pad. You can't use the free one that a computer magazine sends you for subscribing.

Okay, so somebody already broke the rules. Honeywell's newfangled optomechanical mouse doesn't need a special reflective pad. In fact, it doesn't need any pad at all. Because there's no ball, there's nothing to clean. Finally, the mouse even works upside down, making it suitable for outer-space computing. (The laptop aboard the Space Shuttle Discovery uses Microsoft's Ballpoint *trackball.* The trackball clips to the laptop's edge so it doesn't float around in the aisles.)

I Installed a Modem (Or Scanner or Sound Card or Weird Network Thing), and Now My Mouse Cursor Jerks Around or Disappears

Mice and modems usually squirt information into the computer through something called a *serial port.* Unfortunately, sometimes a mouse and modem try to squirt through the same port at the same time. When stuck with two conflicting sources of information, your poor computer feels as lost as a character in a Franz Kafka novel.

It boils down to this: You need to make sure that all your devices get a serial port all to themselves. This stuff gets pretty grueling, so head for Chapter 18 to see how to break up fights over a serial port.

A serial port is sometimes called a COM port, which is short for *communications* port. Your computer uses the serial port to communicate with other computer parts by moving messages back and forth.

Sometimes, you install a serial modem and a mouse and suddenly you don't have a serial port left for your other gizmos. This problem is rough enough to send you to Chapters 17 and 18. Serial ports can quickly turn into a complicated, odorous problem. Your computer can only use two serial ports at the same time, and yet dozens of computer gadgets want to grab one of them.

One quick solution may be to buy a *bus* mouse, described in the section "Which Is Better: A Bus Mouse, PS/2 Mouse, or a Serial Mouse?"

My Cordless Mouse Sometimes Acts Weird

Cordless mice need fresh batteries every so often. If your cordless mouse is acting funny, try replacing the batteries. Some batteries fit in the mouse's receiving unit; others slip into the bottom of the mouse itself.

An *infrared* cordless mouse needs a clean line of sight between itself and its *receiving unit,* the thing that actually plugs into the back of your computer. But because that clean line of sight is going to be the only clean spot on your desk, that's the first place you may tend to set down books and junk mail. Try moving your books and junk mail out of the way, and the mouse will probably calm down.

My Mouse Doesn't Work Under Windows 95 When I Use DOS!

Windows 95 keeps a firm hold on your computer's parts. For example, it automatically keeps track of your mouse's movements, quickly turning them into on-screen movements of your mouse pointer.

But if you leave Windows 95 — through the Run command (under the Start button) or by using the Restart the computer in MS-DOS mode command — you enter an older, less efficient operating system. As an oldster that lacks Windows' savvy, DOS doesn't always recognize your mouse.

The solution? Turn your mouse back on by typing this at the command prompt and pressing Enter:

```
C:\> MOUSE
```

If that doesn't work, try typing this and pressing Enter:

```
C:\>\MOUSE\MOUSE
```

Hopefully that brings a mouse program to life that can serve as translator between your mouse and computer.

How Can I Get A Better Windows 95 Mouse Pointer?

To get a better mouse pointer in Windows 95, click the Start button, choose Settings, then choose Control Panel and double-click the Mouse icon. The Mouse Properties dialog box appears. Click the Pointers tab and Windows 95 displays your choice of available mouse pointers. The scheme drop-down menu is shown in Figure 6-1.

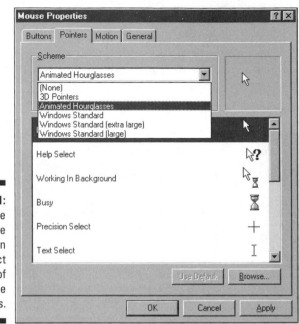

Figure 6-1:
Click the
<u>S</u>cheme
drop-down
list to select
a variety of
mouse
pointers.

Windows comes with a few different mouse pointer schemes; some programs toss their own in here, as well.

Laptop users should try the Windows Standard (large) scheme; sometimes that makes a small pointer easier to spot.

A friend of an editor at IDG Books switched to a dinosaur for his mouse pointer and then couldn't get his mouse to work. Why? He didn't realize the *head* of the dinosaur was the pointer. Be sure to try all parts of your new pointer before giving up hope.

Which Is Better: A Bus Mouse, PS/2 Mouse, or a Serial Mouse?

At first glance, none of the above. All three breeds of mice scoot the little arrow across the screen in the same way. You won't be able to tell any difference in the mouse's look or feel. So, your choice of mouse depends on your computer's needs.

PS/2 mouse: Most new computers come with a built-in PS/2 mouse port, so that's the best choice. That port — usually labeled "Mouse" — lets you plug in most of the mice on store shelves today, including Microsoft's new IntelliMouse.

Serial mouse: The cable from a serial mouse plugs into your computer's serial port — one of those protruding outlets along the back of your computer's case. Simple and easy — if you have an unused serial port on your computer's rear. Many PS/2 mice also work in a serial port — provided the mouse's cable can plug into the hole. Older computers may need an adapter that lets the PS/2 mouse's newfangled tail plug into an old-style serial port.

Bus mouse: Open the package of a bus mouse, and you find two things: the mouse and a special card to stick inside your computer. After you install the card, you see its little *mouse port* on the back of your computer. The cord from the bus mouse plugs in there.

Why bother with such hardship? The answer is that you may not have any serial ports left. For example, some computers have only one serial port, and the modem's cable may already be hogging it. Other computers have two serial ports, but the modem grabs one and some other toy hogs the other. By installing a bus mouse, you don't have to worry about filling up your coveted serial ports with a mouse. A bus mouse can cause problems if you're running out of slots, however. (I describe slots in Chapter 3.)

So, if your computer has a PS/2 mouse port, buy a PS/2-compatible mouse. No PS/2 port? Then plug a serial mouse into an empty serial port. Get a bus mouse only if your computer doesn't have a PS/2 port and all your serial ports are used up.

Why Is All This COM and Serial Port Stuff So Difficult?

All of this port stuff is a lot easier than it sounds — unless you already have a bunch of toys plugged into your computer. Like a nursing mother, a computer has a limited number of resources. If you try to install more than two gizmos, the extra gizmos have problems talking to your PC.

If you're only installing a mouse and a modem, you'll probably do fine. But if you try to install a third guy — a scanner, a network card, or even a sound card — the potential for problems will increase.

It all boils down to the fact that your PC was designed more than a decade ago when nobody could afford more than two toys. Now, with cheap toys everywhere, the PC's antique design is coming back to haunt people.

How Do I Install or Replace a Serial or PS/2-Style Mouse?

IQ level: 80 – 110, depending on your computer's setup

Tools you need: A screwdriver

Cost: Anywhere from $10 – $120

Things to watch out for:

If you are going to replace a serial or PS/2-style mouse, you need to look out for a few things. Make sure that your mouse box says *Microsoft mode, Microsoft compatible,* or just plain *Microsoft mouse* somewhere on the package. Most programs prefer that kind of mouse.

Some mice can work in two modes: Microsoft mode and some other weird mode. Increase your chances of success by installing them to work under Microsoft mode. Then whenever a new program asks what type of mouse you're using, answer Microsoft.

Mice come with their own software and attached cord. You don't have to buy any extras. You can buy serial mice dirt cheap — often as low as $10. The ones with the better warranties, better parts, and bigger ad campaigns can cost a lot more.

To replace or add a serial or PS/2-style mouse, follow these steps:

1. **Look at the back of your computer and look at the serial ports section of Chapter 3 to see where you're going to plug in your mouse. Then follow the instructions listed for that particular port.**

   Your old mouse: If you're just replacing a dead mouse, take its corpse to the software store and buy another one just like it. That way you can be sure to plug into the same hole and all will be well.

   Small, round PS/2-style port: You're in luck! The plug on the cable of just about every mouse sold today fits without a problem. You can buy a PS/2-style mouse and plug it right in.

   Small serial port: Many mice plug directly into this port; others require a PS/2-style mouse adapter that costs less than $10.

This smaller port is usually called COM1. The software will ask you about it later in the installation process.

Big serial port: Described in Chapter 3, this port is probably too big for the mouse cable plug, so ask the salesperson for a 9-pin to 25-pin adapter. Some people call it a DB25 female/DB9 male connector. Whatever it's called, it costs less than $10 and lets a serial mouse's small plug fit into a computer's big serial port.

This larger port is usually called COM2. The software will want to know later in the installation process.

If you have a PS/2-style mouse port, by all means use it. By using this port, you can free up one of your serial ports for other computer gadgets.

No empty port at all: If you don't have *any* visible serial ports at all, head to the computer store and ask for an *I/O card.* (Installation instructions are in Chapter 15.)

If your computer only has *one* serial port and your modem is using it, head back to the computer store and ask for a second serial port for your I/O card. The second serial port is probably one of the big serial ports, described earlier.

If you have *two* serial ports, but a modem is in one and a scanner or something is plugged into the other, sidestep this serial port stuff altogether by buying a *bus mouse.* It comes with a *card* that has its own port and is covered in Chapter 14.

2. **Turn off your computer.**

   Be sure to exit any of your currently running programs first.

3. **Push the plug that's on the end of the mouse's tail into the port on the back of your computer.**

   Push the plug until it fits tightly. If it doesn't fit correctly, you're probably trying to push it in the wrong port. (You may need one of the adapters that I describe in Step 1.) After you connect the cable firmly, use your tiny screwdriver to screw it in place. Some plugs have protruding thumb screws, making them easier to screw in; some mice plugs don't screw in at all.

4. **Run the mouse's installation program.**

   Somewhere in your mouse's box, you should find a floppy disk. Stick the floppy disk into drive A or drive B, close the latch, type **A:** or **B:**, and press Enter. Then type the word **INSTALL** or **SETUP** and press Enter to start things rolling.

   Some installation programs can figure out for themselves where you've plugged in your mouse — they handle everything automatically. Others interview you like a job applicant. Some programs make you tell them whether the mouse is connected to COM1 or COM2. If the program asks, answer with the COM port you remembered from Step 1.

The program probably wants to add some information to your
AUTOEXEC.BAT or CONFIG.SYS file, even if you don't care what those
files do. Feel free to let it continue. You can find more information on
those two files in Chapter 16. And if you're stuck at that weird COM
port stuff, head for Chapter 18.

You may need to reboot your computer before the mouse starts
working. When the installation program is through, press
Ctrl+Alt+Delete to give birth to your newly activated mouse.

Windows 95 recognizes your new mouse and immediately treats it as a
good friend. If problems arise, head for Chapter 17.

Chapter 7

Mucked-Up Modems

*A*dding a modem to your computer is probably the most dramatic upgrade you can make. Suddenly your computing horizons jump from *you + computer,* to *you + computer + entire universe.* After you install a modem, you can use the Internet to type a message to someone halfway around the world or fax someone halfway across town — all from the privacy of your worn old PJs.

Here's the chapter that gets you connected and checking your e-mail (electronic mail) along with the rest of humanity. Oh, and you don't have to call it a "fax-modem" anymore. Most modems come with built-in faxing capabilities, so just leave it at *modem.* (But don't buy a modem that can't fax!)

Who Can Understand All This Modem Stuff?

Nobody understands modems, really, but here's enough information so you can fake it, like everybody else.

The main thing that counts with modems is how fast they spew information back and forth over the telephone lines. Check out the rundown in Table 7-1.

Table 7-1	Funny Modem Words
This Funny Word	*Means This*
300 baud or bps	Slow relics to be avoided.
1200 baud or bps	Four times faster than the 300 bps models; rowboats among cruise ships.
2400 bps	Faster than 1200 bps models, but outdated and outpaced by faster modems.
9600 bps	These modems briefly served as 'speed demons' until the far more popular 14400 bps modems appeared.
14400 bps	Yesterday's best-seller, the 14400 bps model held favor with modem maniacs until the 28800 bps models became affordable. Unbearably slow on the portion of the Internet called the World Wide Web.
28800 bps	The current workhorses of today's modem-savvy public.
33600 bps	Modem makers added an edge to the 28800 bps models that pushes data transfer speeds up to 33600 bps — but mostly under ideal phone-line conditions and only when connected to a similarly speedy modem.
56000 bps	More often seen as *56K,* this new modem standard bears watching. Only works when calling some compatible services.
Cable modems, ISDN modems	They're not *real* modems, and they're still not widely supported today. Find out more about these new modes of data transfer in this chapter's "Fast, faster, fastest!" sidebar.

✔ Note that the higher the modem's bps number, the faster the modem can move data around — and the more it costs.

✔ Thanks to something known as *backwards compatibility,* the speediest modems can still talk to the slower ones. For example, a 9600 bps modem can still talk to a 2400 bps modem, a 1200 bps modem, and a 300 bps modem. The faster modem must slow down to the lower bps speed to do so, but it still works.

Don't bother with bps and baud banter

Modem speed is measured in *bps* (bits per second) — the number of bits of information a modem can throw across a telephone line in one second. Some people measure modem speed in *baud rate,* a term that only engineers really understand.

Here's where things get sticky. A 300 or 1200 bps modem is also a 300 or 1200 baud modem. But the terms *bps* and *baud* don't stay the same past speeds of 2,400 bps.

The point? If you casually mention that your modem works at 2400 baud or 9600 baud, the nerds will laugh at you.

Forget about the word *baud* and always use the term *bps.* Then you won't have to see the orange stuff between the nerds' teeth when they start laughing.

Also, if you see the term Kbps, they're using the metric system (remember when the U.S. was slated to switch over?) to say, "thousands (Kilo) of bits per second." So instead of taking the trouble to spell out 28800 bps, modem insiders frequently shorten it to *28.8 Kbps,* and *28.8K* when even more pressed for time.

What Are Modem Standards?

You've already glimpsed a few modem terms, but you're not off the hook yet. One important concept, *modem standards,* comes in handy whether you're upgrading to a better modem or trying to understand the one you have.

You may know that modems work at various speeds to rustle data through the phone lines. Well, each speed corresponds to a formal modem standard, decided by an actual standards committee. Your 28800 bps modem, for example, complies with the V.34 standard for modem speed. Your modem also complies with preceding speed standards, making it backwards compatible. Plus, most 28800 bps modems conform to standards that govern important functions like *error control* and *data compression,* ensuring that a particular bit of data arrives faster and unscathed even when traveling through the noisiest phone lines.

Who cares about standards? You do, because manufacturers often claim impossibly high *throughput,* or transmission speeds, by testing their modems when connected with identical models. Their claims may not be completely false, but how many times will you find yourself connecting with your modem's exact twin? On the other hand, no manufacturer can fake compliance with a modem standard. To make sure you're getting the best modem, shop *standards,* and not just speeds. A modem's package proclaims the modem's standards in the form of vee-dot numbers like V.34 (say *vee-dot thirty-four*) and others. For the scoop on those complicated-looking vee-dot numbers, check out Table 7-2.

Table 7-2	Keep your Eye on the Vee-dot Number
This Vee-dot Number	*Corresponds to This Feature*
V.34	28800 bps data transfer speeds; 14400 bps faxing
V.34 plus or enhanced	Touts 33600 bps data transfer speeds, but in reality, more a guarantee of 28.8 Kbps connections
V.42/MNP 2-4	Error control; modem detects and corrects missing bits during noisy connections or other less-than-ideal conditions; be sure you buy one with *hardware error control*
V.42*bis*/MNP5	Data compression, uses modem shorthand to squish data and boost the number of bits transferred; get *hardware data compression*
Class 1/Class 2, Group III	Fax standards that ensure the modem can talk to the broadest range of fax devices

Note that no standard can work unless it's supported by the modems on each end of the connection. (When you hear the modems wail upon connecting, they're negotiating what standards to use.) When a fast modem calls one that supports a slower standard, for example, they just agree to use the (slow) one they can both manage.

Upgrading to a better (upgradeable) modem

While you're gazing at modem packages, look for the term *Flash ROM, software upgradeable,* or *firmware upgradeable* plastered somewhere among all the vee-dot numbers. The best modems come ready for upgrades to future standards (like faster speeds) because their manufacturers distribute *firmware upgrades,* special files that update the modem when run on your computer.

Look for instructions on how to find and download the file from your modem's Web site or BBS (electronic Bulletin Board System). Avoid modem brands that expect you to mail them your modem for a hardware upgrade (usually involving a chip replacement, a hefty charge, and a long wait).

What You Need to Get on the Internet

Some modems include pre-fab "Internet Starter Kits," bursting with software and booklets to help you make your first Internet connection. Most modems assume that each of their users want to call different places, however, and so they leave out the software.

Getting an Internet account involves finding a company called an *Internet Service Provider (ISP)* and buying access through them, much like starting up phone service with the local phone company. Many people decide that it's easier to take the Internet plunge by going through an online service like America Online (AOL) or CompuServe. Other users look for national or local Internet providers. Either way, if your new modem failed to include any cool Internet software, peruse Table 7-3 to find out what to do next.

Table 7-3	Getting Started with the Internet
Using This Software	*Do This*
AOL or CompuServe	Obtain and install the free software; most modems include trial offers for both services. After you connect, click the Internet button to go there. (No software? Call and have some mailed to you: AOL, 800-827-6364; CompuServe, 800-848-8199.)
Windows 95 & Internet provider	Ask your Internet provider to send you explicit instructions on how to set up Windows 95's Dial-Up Networking program to call their computers. Your provider should also send you software called a *Web browser* so you can surf the Web and send and receive e-mail.
Windows 3.1*x* & Internet provider	Ask your Internet provider for a program called Trumpet Winsock and for instructions on setting up Winsock to dial their computers. Also ask for a Web browser (see above).

After you're connected, your modem can snag dozens of other Internet-related programs for you that can help you organize your e-mail, streamline your special-interest groups, block your kids' Internet access, and more. Try heading to a Web page called TUCOWS, my favorite site for Internet software, at www.tucows.com.

Will a Modem Replace a Fax Machine?

Ninety-nine percent of all modems can fax, but if you already have a fax machine, don't throw it away! You still need it to fax today's Dilbert strip, or that take-out menu from Adalberto's Tacos — and anything else you can't store on a computer file.

Actually, if you have a scanner, you can scan the Adalberto's Tacos take-out menu, save it as a computer file, and then fax it from your fax/modem. Everyone else will have to pop it in the mail, make their buddies drive to Adalberto's to get their own darn menus, or find a fax machine.

Sending/receiving faxes

Almost any modem can fax, but you still need special fax software to make it all work. Fortunately, most modems come with a fairly decent program called WinFax Lite. (Windows 95 comes with the MS-Fax program.) If you plan to do a lot of faxing from your computer, splurge for a good commercial-grade program like WinFax Pro, BitComm Pro, or Procomm Plus.

Sending a fax

Sending a fax works like this: When you install fax software, it adds a fax program to your list of printers. After you create a document you want to fax, you select your word processor or other software's Print command and choose the fax program instead of your usual printer. Your fax software pops up, asks you a couple of questions (such as the name and fax number of your recipient) and, with the touch of a Send key, your document chugs across the phone lines.

Receiving a fax

Unless you're sitting right in front of your computer awaiting a fax, it takes a bit of preparation before you can reliably receive a fax.

First, you must start your fax software or set it to work in the background, otherwise your fax won't hear the modem ring. Then, you need to fiddle with your modem and fax software so they can *auto-answer* an incoming phone call. Fortunately, your modem's manual explains how you can set the modem to pick up only after several rings so it doesn't beat you to the phone (eight or nine rings works well).

For these reasons, many business owners prefer to keep a fax machine around for receiving unexpected faxes. Then the only hassle comes with those Internet-generated "junk" faxes that are sent indiscriminately and use up all your fax paper!

Fixing the fax

One or more of these fixes may prod your computer to receive that crucial fax. For more fax troubleshooting tips, you may want to consult *More Modems For Dummies,* by Tina Rathbone (IDG Books Worldwide, Inc.).

- ✔ Try lowering the speed by dropping the fax software's *fax receive rate* to a lower bps number.

- ✔ Check to make sure the fax software's Class 1/Class 2 setting accurately reflects your modem's capabilities (the modem's manual gives you the scoop).

- ✔ Windows users should make sure their computers have a current 16550 UART chip on the serial port. (If you're using a newer internal modem, it's probably fine.)

Using a Modem on a Laptop or Palmtop

Depending on the age of your laptop, you can make it modem-ready in several ways. Most laptops come equipped with special PC Card slots where you slide a tiny, credit-card sized PC Card modem (as shown in Figure 7-1). (Older PC Card modems are called PCMCIA modems.) Very old laptops or laptops without slots can still accommodate a serial cable and an external modem. Often you can find smallish external modems designed for travelers.

A special Card & Socket Services program comes with your laptop. This program helps your computer recognize a number of PC Card devices — including modems — on the market. Before you hit the road, or a mission-critical situation, make sure you install your laptop's Card & Socket Services software and that you know how to access it. This is a grand occasion for visiting your laptop's Web site and downloading the latest version of the Card & Socket Services program.

If your Card & Socket Services program fails to recognize your modem, don't despair. Your PC Card modem came with a program to help your laptop recognize it. Look in your modem's manual for directions on how to install that; your reward should be a screen that indicates your laptop and modem are talking to one another.

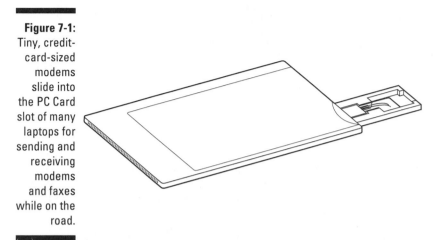

Note: If your laptop came with a built-in modem but you want to use a faster modem on a PC Card, you may need to go into your laptop's setup files and disable the built-in modem. Your manual should prove helpful here.

How Do I Call the Computer at My Work?

Some employers set up BBSs to help workers keep in touch. Other companies create their own, employee-only Internet site, called an *intranet.* Because so many on-ramps exist, it's best to ask your company's network guru or system administrator how to dial-in from home or while traveling. Cultivate this person: He or she can give you tips about the special software you need to connect, and you can even glean more modem tips!

My Modem Hangs Up Whenever Anybody Calls Me!

Some popular people have *call waiting* installed on their phone line. When the person is talking on the phone and somebody else calls, the phone makes a little *beep* sound. The person then interrupts the conversation to say, "Can you hold on a second? I have another call."

But your modem is even ruder than that. If your modem is talking to another modem and call waiting beep blasts into the discussion, your modem may simply hang up.

Fast, faster, fastest!

The newspapers are full of stories on cable modems and ISDN — two budding services that hope to speed the masses (that's you and me) onto the Internet.

Cable modems got their name because television cable companies everywhere are gearing up to sell you high-speed communications services. Downloading onto your computer through a cable modem takes place at speeds ranging from 10 Mbps (*Megabits* per second) to 30 Mbps — depending on the cable modem's press release. Uploading something from your computer to another takes place at normal modem speeds (about 2.5 Mbps). All this speed sounds grand, but very few cities offer cable modem service yet. Look for cable modem prices to level out at $250 or so soon. Your cable company will charge anywhere from $30 to $50 per month for unlimited Internet access; some cable outfits offer community programming and other special stuff to subscribers, as well.

ISDN stands for Integrated Services Digital Network, and it's here now. It took so long to get here, however, that many people for many years dubbed it, "It Still Does Nothing." ISDN uses all-digital signaling to send and receive data at a maximum speed of 128 Kbps over two channels. Prices for ISDN modems have dropped recently, but don't buy one that doesn't include an analog port, which is where you can plug in a phone, fax machine, or even a modem. One cool thing about ISDN is that you can talk on the phone on one channel while you're dialing up your Internet provider on another. Your phone company will send out a technician to wire your house with a special ISDN line; prices vary widely.

The bottom line? When listening to all the amazing speed claims, consider this: The Internet itself is the slowest part of the connection. The Internet's simply an umbrella term for a vast web of connected computers; few of these are equipped with these speedy services, or even 28.8 Kbps modems, for that matter.

The solution? Dial the four characters ***70,** (that's an asterisk, the number seven, the number zero, and a comma) before dialing the other modem's number if you have a push-button, tone dialing phone line. For example, instead of dialing **555-1212**, dial ***70,555-1212** in order to turn off your call waiting on a push-button line. That funky little code tells the phone company to turn off call waiting for your next call. Incoming callers get busy signals. Then when you finish that call, your call waiting is automatically turned back on.

If you have a pulse phone, dial **1170,** (that's the numbers 1170 followed by a comma).

It's hard to remember to turn off call waiting before each call, so you can tell your modem software to do it automatically. Look for a "dialing command" area in the software. The dialing command is usually set up to say ATDT. Change it to **ATDT*70,** (or change it to **ATDT 1170,** if you have a pulse phone) and call waiting is turned off automatically before each call.

How Do I Install or Replace an External Modem?

IQ level: 80 – 110, depending on your computer's setup

Tools you need: One hand

Cost: Anywhere from $25 – $400

Things to watch out for:

First, buy the fastest modem you can afford. You can find cheap, slow ones for under $30. The faster ones can cost more than ten times as much.

Modems are as easy as mice to install. The hard part is trying to make them do something useful. A mouse's software is pretty much automatic; it works in the background. A modem's software forces you to make all the complicated decisions, even when you're not in that kind of a mood.

Also, mice need special *drivers.* Modems don't. However, external modems need cables. Unlike mice, they don't come with any attached, and most modems don't include any cables in their boxes.

Finally, internal modems come on *cards,* so I cover them in Chapter 15.

To install an external modem, follow these steps:

1. **Locate where to plug in your modem.**

   Look at the back of your computer and then look at the serial ports section of Chapter 3 to find out the right place for your modem to plug into. Then follow the instructions for that port.

   If you're replacing your old modem: Pull the cable off the back of your old modem and plug it into the back of your new modem. Then jump to Step 3.

   Small serial port: A small serial port has 9 little pins in it. Most external modems have big female serial ports on them. The female ports have 25 little holes in them. So, to connect them, your cable needs to have a 9-pin female plug on one end and a 25-pin male plug on the other.

   This smaller port is usually called COM1. Your modem software will want to know that port's name in a few minutes.

   Big serial port: For this, you need a cable with a 25-pin female plug on one end and a 25-pin male plug on the other end.

   This larger serial port is usually called COM2. Modem software always wants to know these things so it can find the modem.

Having trouble remembering all that male/female pin adapter stuff? Grab a piece of paper and draw a picture of the port on the back of your modem and the one on the back of your computer. Then bring that paper to the computer store when shopping. (Don't bother counting all the pins or holes. The number is either 9 or 25.) This information helps when shopping for the right cable, as well.

No empty port at all: If you don't have any serial ports at all, head to the software store and ask for an *I/O card.* (You can find installation instructions in Chapter 15.)

If your computer only has *one* serial port and your mouse is already using it, head back to the computer store and ask for a second serial port for your I/O card. The I/O card will probably be one of the big serial ports that I described earlier. Or buy an internal modem, which I describe in the next paragraph.

If you have two serial ports and both are being used, sidestep this serial port stuff altogether by buying an *internal modem.* It comes on a *card,* so it's covered in Chapter 15.

2. **Connect your cable between the end of your modem and the port on the back of your computer.**

   The cable should fit perfectly at either end. If not, keep perusing Step 1 until you find a cable that fits right. Sometimes it helps to draw a picture. When you've finally plugged the cable in, use your little screw-driver to fasten the two little screws that hold it in place. The more expensive cables have thumb screws that make screwing them in easier.

3. **Plug the phone line into the back of the modem.**

   If your modem has a single phone jack in the back, plug one end of the phone cord into there and plug the cord's other end into the phone's wall jack.

   However, if your modem has two phone jacks, the procedure is a little harder. One phone jack is for the phone line cord, and the other is for you to plug a desk phone into. You must put the right cord into the right jack, or the modem won't work.

   If you're lucky, the two phone jacks are labeled. The one that says *phone* is where you plug your desk phone's cord. The one that's labeled *line* is for the cord that runs to the phone jack in your wall.

   If the two jacks *aren't* labeled, dig out the manual while cursing under your breath the whole while. Turn the modem upside down first, though. Sometimes you can find helpful pictures or labels on its bottom.

   If the two jacks aren't labeled and you can't find the manual, just guess at which line plugs into which jack. If the modem or your phone doesn't work, just swap the two plugs. (Having them wrong at first doesn't harm anything.)

4. **Plug the modem's AC adapter into the wall and plug the other end into the modem. Then turn the modem's power switch to on.**

    Modems aren't so self-contained. Almost all of them need an AC adapter. Then they need to be turned on. (These are two things that can go wrong.)

5. **Run your modem software.**

    Modems usually don't need complicated *drivers,* like mice do. No, a modem's communications software is complicated enough. You can find it on a disk somewhere inside the box.

    When you type SETUP or INSTALL, the software takes over and starts asking you questions. You did remember which COM port you plugged your modem into, didn't you?

    The software also asks your modem's speed, so keep that information handy as well. (It's listed on the box.)

    If your modem software complains about IRQ conflicts or COM port problems, sigh sadly. (Sigh.) Then troop to Chapter 18 for help with all the IRQ stuff.

    Finally, modems are notoriously cranky partners for computing. If you want to know how to force your modem into behaving, check out my wife's book *Modems For Dummies,* 3rd Edition, by Tina Rathbone (IDG Books Worldwide, Inc.). You can find a bunch of valuable tips and convincing weapons.

Fast external modems sometimes have a problem when installed in older computers, especially when used with Windows programs. That's because the chip used in the old computer's serial port can't keep up with the data flowing through the speedy new modem. If your modem seems to lose parts of transmissions, make sure your old computer's serial port uses a 16550AFN UART chip. (The MSD program described at the end of Chapter 3 lists the type of UART chip inside your computer under the "COM Ports" heading.) If the computer's chip is an oldster, either replace your I/O card or buy an internal modem — internal modems come with a speedy 16550AFN UART chip built in.

Chapter 8

Tweaking the Monitor

*M*ost computer terms sound dreadfully ho-hum: High density. Device driver. Video adapter. Yawn.

But the engineers had just returned from a horror flick when they started coming up with monitor terms: Electron gun! Cathode ray! Electromagnetic radiation! Zounds!

This chapter talks about the thing everybody stares at and puts sticky notes on — the computer monitor. Plus, you get to hear a few digestible tidbits about your *video card,* which is the gizmo inside your computer that bosses your monitor around.

The Screen Has Dust All over It

Monitors not only attract your attention, but they also attract dust. Thick, furry layers of dust. And that dust is attracted on a weekly basis.

Do not clean your monitor while it is turned on! The static charge that builds up on the surface can wipe out a few little parts in your computer. Wait three to five minutes after you shut the monitor off before you clean it.

Computer salespeople brush dust off quickly with a single swipe of their sleeves. Don't have a beige sport coat? A soft cloth and a little glass cleaner does the trick. You really have only one thing to remember:

Spray the Windex onto the *cloth,* not the monitor itself. A monitor won't blow up if its screen gets wet, but the Windex can drip down the screen's front and make the parts inside soggy. If you like fine print, check the manufacturer's recommendations regarding cleaning solutions for your particular monitor's screen.

And don't spray Windex into the monitor's top or side vents, even if you like the burning smell.

My Monitor Doesn't Turn On!

Are you *sure* that your monitor is plugged in? Actually, your monitor has four plugs you need to check:

- ✔ Check to make sure that you plugged the power cord securely into the wall or power strip.
- ✔ Wiggle the connection where the monitor's cord plugs into the back of your computer.
- ✔ Check the back of your monitor.

  Some cords aren't built-in to the monitor, leading to loose connections. Push the cord hard to make sure that it's plugged in tight.

- ✔ Check the back of your computer.

  On particularly old models, you plug the monitor's power cord into the back of the computer — not the wall.

You know how some outlets are wired to wall switches? For example, you flip a wall switch by the door, and a lamp turns on from across the room. Well, don't plug your monitor (or your computer) into one of those switched outlets. If you use one of those outlets, you may find yourself scratching your head, wondering why the monitor doesn't always work.

What Do All Those Funny Video Words Mean?

Video cards and monitors are full of technical buzzwords. But you don't need to know what the buzzwords mean. Instead, just trust your eyes.

Believe it or not, one of the best ways to buy a monitor and a card is to head for the computer store and play Windows Solitaire on a bunch of different monitors. When you decide which monitor looks best, buy it along with the video card that's powering it.

If you're looking for a monitor to watch multimedia movies, ask to see some on-screen videos — somebody sailing a 60-foot yacht or eating crackers while parachuting off the Eiffel Tower. Compare the videos on different screens, and trust your eyes.

 Some salespeople may gab about *dot pitch* this and *vertical sync* that. But don't buy a monitor and card unless you see it in action. All the technical specifications in the world don't mean anything compared with what you see with your own eyeballs.

If you're still curious about what those video buzzwords mean, check out Table 8-1.

Table 8-1		Awful Monitor Terms	
This word...	*describes this...*	*...and means this.*	*So?*
Pixel (PIX-el)	Monitor	A single little "dot" on your monitor.	Computer pictures are merely collections of thousands of little dots.
Resolution	Monitor, card	Pixel dots are stacked across your monitor in a grid, like tiny bottles in a wine rack. "Resolution" describes the number of rows and columns your monitor and card can display.	Common resolutions are 640 rows by 480 columns, 800 rows by 600 columns, or 1,024 rows by 768 columns. Bigger rows and columns mean you can pack more information onto the screen. (It also means a bigger price tag.)

(continued)

Table 8-1 *(continued)*

This word...	describes this...	...and means this.	So?
Color	Card	The number of colors you are be able to see on the screen.	Here, the card is the limiting factor. Most of the newer monitors can display *any* amount of colors.
Mode	Card, monitor	A combination of resolution and color.	Most cards and monitors can usually display several different "modes." For example, you could run Windows in 640 by 480 resolution with 65,000 colors. Or, you could switch to 800 by 600 resolution with 256 colors. There's no right or wrong mode. It all depends on personal preference.
Dot pitch	Monitor	The distance between the little "pixel" dots on the monitor. The smaller the dot pitch, the clearer the picture.	**Tip:** Don't buy any monitors with less than .28 dot pitch, or the picture looks hazy.
Digital	Monitor	**Tip:** An old-technology way to display pictures.	These monitors don't work with newer cards, like VGA, Super VGA, and other newcomers. **Tip:** Check to see if an old monitor has a "digital/analog" switch. If so, it may still work with some of the newer cards.
Analog	Monitor	The new-technology way of displaying pictures.	Today's video cards all require analog monitors.
Multiscan, Multi-frequency, or Multisync	Monitor	These friendly monitors can switch back and forth to work with a wide variety of video cards.	Being the easiest monitors to please, they're also the most expensive.

This word...	*describes this...*	*...and means this.*	*So?*
Bandwidth	Monitor, card	The speed at which your card can send information to your monitor. Faster is the better. It's measured in megahertz, and 70 MHz is easy on the eyes. (Bigger numbers are faster.)	A monitor has to be able to accept the information as fast as the card can send it. That's why those "multi-scanning" monitors are popular: They can accept information at a bunch of different "bandwidths."
Refresh rate	Monitor, card	How fast your monitor and card can "repaint" the picture.	The bigger the number, the less flicker on the screen.
3-D Accelerator	Card	These cards have a special chip that helps your computer put pictures on the screen more quickly.	**Tip:** For an easy way to work faster in Windows and other graphics programs, replace your old card with an accelerator card. (These work especially well with games.)
Memory	Card	The amount of RAM chips on your video card. Some cards can be upgraded by adding more memory chips. The higher the card's resolution, the more memory it needs. High-resolution images with lots of colors can require 1MB or more of memory.	Don't confuse video memory with your computer's memory. Video memory lives on the video card, computer's memory lives on the motherboard. They can never visit each other's houses. **Tip:** Don't buy a video card with a small amount of memory, thinking you can add more memory later. That only leads to problems.

(continued)

Table 8-1 *(continued)*

This word...	describes this...	...and means this.	So?
Driver	Card	A piece of software that translates a program's numbers into pictures that you can drool over.	If you're going to use Windows NT or OS/2, make sure the card has a Windows or OS/2 "driver." **Tip:** Windows 95 and earlier versions work with most popular video cards. OS/2 doesn't.
Interlaced, non-interlaced	Monitor	Technical stuff that's much too awful to bother with.	Just remember that a non-interlaced display has less flicker and is easier on your eyes.

I Bought an Expensive New Monitor, but My Screen Still Looks Ugly

A television merely displays pictures that come through the air waves, like the Movie of the Week. Even with cable television, you're stuck with whatever's coming over the wire.

The same goes for computer monitors. They only display what is being sent by your computer's video card, which lives inside your computer's case.

Upgrading your computer's display can get expensive — fast. The expense quickly adds up because you usually need a new video card as well as a new monitor.

Basically, card- and monitor-shopping boils down to these simple "make sures":

- ✔ Make sure that your video card and your monitor match in resolution — the number of little rows and columns they can display. The most popular resolutions are 640 by 480, 800 by 600, 1,024 by 768 and 1,280 by 1,024.

- ✔ VGA monitors rarely work with CGA or EGA cards. If you upgrade your old CGA or EGA monitor, make sure that you buy a new video card, too. Likewise,

- ✔ VGA cards rarely work with CGA or EGA monitors. If you upgrade your card to VGA, make sure that you buy a new monitor, too.

✔ A VGA monitor still works with a newer, SuperVGA card but only in VGA mode. A VGA monitor can't show any of the SuperVGA card's super-duper video modes.

✔ The term "spit roasted" sounds pretty unhygienic, if you stop to think about it.

The monitor's screen looks washed out

Just like a television set, a monitor comes with a row of fiddling knobs. Although most people just kind of spin 'em around and squint until things look better, there really is an official way to fine-tune your monitor's picture.

Here's the scoop:

1. **Locate your monitor's brightness and contrast knobs or buttons.**

   The knobs or buttons usually live along the monitor's right edge where they irritate left-handers. Or they are somewhere beneath the monitor's front edge where they are often concealed behind a little fold-down plate.

   The knobs and buttons aren't always labeled, unfortunately, but they almost always have little symbols next to them, like in Figure 8-1.

Figure 8-1:
These moon and sun symbols usually appear next to the contrast and brightness knobs.

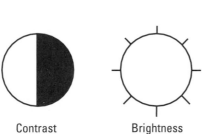

Contrast   Brightness

2. **Open your word processor and put some text on the screen.**

   With characters on-screen, turn the monitor's brightness knob all the way clockwise, which turns the brightness up all the way. A light-colored border glows along the edges of the screen.

3. **Turn the contrast knob back and forth until the letters on-screen look sharp.**

Look for a clear difference between the dim and bright areas. You may have to fiddle for a bit until it looks just right. Also, try moving your desk lamp around until you find the best picture.

4. **Turn down the brightness until the light-colored glow around the screen's border merges into the blackness.**

   Your screen should be at its best. You may need to repeat the trick after your monitor has warmed up or after a well-meaning coworker fiddles with the knobs.

The colors look awful in one of my programs

You can adjust a monitor's brightness and contrast. But, unlike with a television, you can't fiddle with the colors. You're spared from the bother of rectifying green newscasters.

Instead, you can change the colors from within your program. Look for the program's *setup screen* or *control panel*. Chances are that the setup screen or control panel will let you change the colors to something more pleasing.

If you're using an older laptop without a color screen, check to see whether the program supports *LCD* or *monochrome* settings.

Windows users — and color laptop users — can flip to Chapter 17 to see how to change your desktop's colors from the traditional boring blue to the Egyptian look of Carved Stone. (You can also find some settings particularly beneficial to laptop users.)

How Do I Know That My Old Monitor Will Work with My New Video Card?

New cards can nearly always work with older monitors. However, older monitors usually can't display all the new colors and resolutions the new card has to offer.

The only way to tell whether an old monitor and your new card can work together is to get technical. You have to find the old monitor's manual and make sure that your monitor can match your new card's *resolution* and *refresh rates*. You can find those weird words explained in Table 8-1.

Or you can just plug your monitor in, turn it on, and have a look-see.

WELL-WORN

My computer doesn't have a video card!

Some computers don't have a video card. The video stuff is built right onto the computer's motherboard. This was the rage in the first days of 486 *local bus video* — a way to speed up the flow of pictures on the monitor. Unfortunately, these "built-in" video computers have a problem when you want to upgrade: You need to turn off the built-in video before your computer can start using your newly installed card.

You may need to pull out the computer's manual for this one. Some computers want you to move a jumper, an act I describe in Chapter 18. Other computers make you run the setup program that came with the computer.

Finally, some computers are smart enough to know that you've plugged in a new card and that they should turn off their own card. Imagine that — a smart computer!

What's That Local Bus and PCI Video Stuff?

For years, people simply pushed video cards into the row of slots sitting inside their computers. Today, the process is a little more complicated. The concept is the same — push the card into the slot — but the slots are trickier.

Computer manufacturers figured that the old-style slots didn't let computers grab information from the cards quickly enough to do fancy things, such as show Alpine skiing movies on the monitor. Therefore, two newer, faster types of slots emerged: VL-Bus and PCI.

The old-style slots are still there, mind you. But PCI slots are standard equipment on today's Pentiums and Pentium Pros, and yesterday's 486's usually sport a VL-Bus.

Should I Buy an Accelerator Card?

For years, people bought new video cards to make their pictures look more realistic on-screen. That little green parrot would look more and more like it flew right out of *National Geographic*.

But as the video quality improved, the computer had to slow down. Tossing all those hundreds of thousands of colored dots onto the screen takes a lot of muscle.

So somebody invented a *graphics accelerator chip.* Instead of straining to toss dots onto the screen, the computer just tosses the chore to the graphics accelerator chip. The chip takes over all the rough graphics, and the computer goes back to doing more traditional computer-oriented stuff.

These accelerator cards come with the accelerator chip built in, so you merely have to install the card.

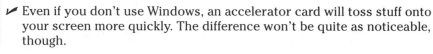

- ✔ If you use Windows and you're in the market for a new video card, buy an accelerator card. Windows will really zoom.

- ✔ Even if you don't use Windows, an accelerator card will toss stuff onto your screen more quickly. The difference won't be quite as noticeable, though.

Gamers should check out 3-D Accelerator cards that take advantage of the latest gaming technology. ATI's 3D XPRESSION+PC2TV card, for instance, not only speeds up the action on the screen but sends a copy to your television set, as well.

My Cursor Disappeared!

Some programs are not only rude but spiteful. When you give up on an awkward program and return to the C:\> thing, you discover that the program has left you a final insult. The program has stolen your little blinking cursor. There's simply nothing there.

Crashed programs often take the cursor down with them, too. Neither of these cursor kidnappings is your fault.

You can retrieve your cursor in two ways, depending on your mood. First, you can load another program and then immediately exit it. Your cursor will probably reappear when the program ends. (Windows 95's <u>R</u>estart the Computer option is almost always a surefire cure.)

DOS users can also cure the cursor kidnapping by just rebooting your computer. Save your work, then press the Ctrl, Alt, and Delete keys at the same time.

My Monitor Makes Weird Noises!

Almost all monitors make little *popping* sounds when first turned on or while warming up. That's nothing to worry about. But they're never supposed to whine, buzz, or make threatening sounds like they're about to blow up.

Monitors are normally one of the quietest parts of your PC. If your monitor ever starts making noise, something is wrong. If those noises are ever accompanied by an odd smell or even smoke, turn off your monitor immediately.

If your monitor is slowly turning into an old creaker, it may pick up a few odd sounds toward the end. Better start saving the cash for a new one.

If you install a new video card and the monitor's screams, the card's trying to make the monitor do something cruel and unnatural. Chances are that the two aren't compatible. Try fiddling with the card's software to make it run in a different video mode.

- Even if you've had the card and monitor for a great deal of time, changing the card's video mode can make the monitor squeal. Avoid the video mode that's causing the problem. Only power supply fans are allowed to squeal.

- If the monitor only squeals in one program, then that program is probably forcing the monitor to display a mode it just can't handle. Color televisions can cheerfully display old black-and-white movies, but monitors can burn themselves out if they're not built for the mode they're receiving. Head for that program's setup area and choose a different video mode or video resolution.

I Don't Want My Screen to Burn-In

Have you ever seen an old monitor that looks like it's running WordPerfect even when it's turned off? That permanent, leftover image is known as *screen burn-in.*

When constantly displaying the same program, older monochrome monitors develop screen burn-in. The program's lines permanently burn themselves into the monitor.

To prevent the burn-in, some wizened computer guru invented a *screen blanker.* After nobody touches a computer's keyboard for a few minutes, the computer assumes that the owner has wandered off and blanks the screen.

Color monitors don't have much of a burn-in problem. But some wizened, wacky, and now wealthy computer guru invented a colorful *screen saver.* Instead of blanking the screen while the owner is away, the computer displays a fish tank complete with animated fish (or flying toasters or other colorful images).

✔ Windows comes with a screen saver built in. It's rolled around in Chapter 17.

✔ Some people like screen savers because prying eyes can't read their screens when they're in the lunch room getting coffee.

✔ Most people just use screen savers because they're fun. Besides, you never have to scrub the algae off the insides of the on-screen aquarium.

My Laptop's Screen Looks Weird

Most laptop screens are temperature sensitive. Whenever I charge the battery in my laptop, for example, the battery heats up and warms the bottom corner of the screen. Then when I turn on my laptop, that bottom corner looks weird until it cools down.

Also, check your program's setup screen. Most programs let you change the colors. Keep cycling through them all until you find the one that is most readable.

Also, freezing temperatures can damage your display. Don't apply pressure to get that "mood ring" effect.

How Do I Install a New Monitor?

IQ level: 70

Tools you need: A screwdriver

Cost: Anywhere from $150 – $2,000

Things to watch out for:

Be sure to match your monitor with your video card. Like Bill and Hillary, your monitor and video card work as a team.

If you're installing a video card at the same time, flip to Chapter 15 first. There you find all the card-installing instructions. When the card is in, head back here.

Unless you're installing a new card while adding a new monitor, your new monitor's screen won't look much different from your old monitor's screen.

Finally, don't shudder too violently when looking at that $150 to $2,000 price range listed. The cheapest monitors are black and white, and the most expensive ones are huge, colorful appliances that can display two full-size pages on the screen at the same time. Chances are that your monitor will fall somewhere between $200 and $500, depending on its level of video oomph.

To install a new monitor, perform the following steps:

1. **Turn off your computer and unplug your old monitor.**

   Save your work and exit any programs. Then after turning off your computer, unplug your old monitor's power cord from the wall. Then unplug the monitor's video cable from its little port on the back of your computer's case. You may need a tiny screwdriver to loosen the tiny screws.

   Remember what little port the monitor cable plugged into. That's where you need to plug in your new monitor's cable.

2. **Remove the old monitor from your desktop.**

   You can either store the old monitor next to the electric wok in your garage's Old Appliance Graveyard or try to sell it to a friend or stranger.

3. **Remove the new monitor from the box.**

   Monitors are packaged pretty securely, so you have to remove a lot of Styrofoam balls and plastic wrap. The cable is wrapped up in its own little package as well.

4. **Place the monitor on your desk and plug it in the video port, as shown in Figure 8-2.**

Figure 8-2:
Most monitors plug into a port that looks like this.

15 - hole female (fatter)

5. **Plug the monitor's cable into the back of your computer. Make sure that the cable is fastened securely on the monitor's end as well.**

   If the cable is not fitting right, then you either bought the wrong monitor or are trying to plug it into the wrong card.

Do you have one of those cool *swivel* stands? Then be sure to leave a little slack on the cables. Otherwise, one little angle adjustment can pull the cables loose.

6. **Plug the monitor's power cord into the wall or a power strip.**

   Or if your monitor's power cord plugs in the back of your computer, plug it in there.

7. **Turn on your monitor and then turn on your computer.**

   Can you see words on the screen as the computer spews its opening remarks? If so, you're done. Hurrah! If it doesn't work, however, keep going through some of the fixes you skimmed in this chapter. The monitor should be pretty easy to fix.

If you bought a fancy monitor with speakers, cameras, or other goodies, you have to perform two more tricks: Plug the cords from the speakers and cameras to their spots in the back of your computer — usually on cards (covered in Chapter 15). Then if Windows 95 doesn't recognize your new monitor's special features, you probably have to install the drivers that came on the floppy disk that came with the monitor. (Your monitor *did* come with a floppy disk, didn't it?) Either way, Chapter 17 can help out.

Chapter 9

Printers (Those Paper Wasters)

* *

In This Chapter

▶ Troubleshooting the printer

▶ Curing blotchy pages

▶ Fixing spacing problems

▶ Understanding fonts

▶ Fixing paper jams

▶ Understanding printer terms

* *

*M*ost newly installed programs grovel around inside your computer. After some electronic poking and prodding, the programs can figure out for themselves what stuff is hiding in there. But even the smartest programs can't figure out what's on the end of your printer cable.

Windows makes this process a little easier. After you tell Windows your printer's brand name, Windows kindly spreads the printer's name to any Windows programs that ask.

Even without Windows, printers are getting easier to use every day. The only problem is those odd days. You know, when the margins just don't look right, the letter to the phone company looks like some weird weather map, or the printer won't even turn on.

When your printed pages look funny — or the paper won't even come out of the printer — this is the chapter to peruse.

I Dunno What All This Printer Stuff Means

Like monitors, printers have picked up some pretty weird terms over the years. There's nothing really violent sounding, unless *laser* counts. The terms are all just dreadfully boring — unless, of course, the terms are placed in a table that's pleasing to the eye, like Table 9-1.

Table 9-1	Boring Printer Words
The Boring Term	*What It Means*
Emulation or printer mode	Some printers pretend to be *other* printers so they can work with more varieties of software. The most commonly copied printers and designs include IBM, Hewlett Packard LaserJet, PostScript, and Epson.
Laser printer	The office workhorse for creating letters. These sound dangerous, but their lasers are tiny little things buried deep inside. In fact, laser printers are no more dangerous than copy machines. Nobody makes scary movies about deadly copy machines.
Hewlett-Packard LaserJet	One of the most popular laser printers. This printer is also copied a lot. *Tip:* For surefire results, set your laser printer to LaserJet mode and choose LaserJet from your program's printer menu.
Inkjet printer	Cheap, practical, well-supported printer that can print sharp color pictures.
Dot-matrix printer	A dying breed of printers. Avoid them unless the price at the thrift shop is too good to pass up. (Windows still supports them, but not all programs do. For example, the Fed Ex software for sending packages can't use some old dot matrix printers because they don't print sharp enough images to create bar codes.)
Epson	When in doubt about what kind of dot-matrix printer you have, choose Epson. Just about every dot matrix printer copies Epson, so just about every printer works in Epson mode.
PostScript	A weird *programming language* for printers. This expensive language excites artsy graphics people who put peacock feathers on their desks. PostScript printers can handle high-end, professional-quality graphics and great gobs of fancy fonts. *Tip:* If you have a PostScript printer, set it to PostScript mode. Choose PostScript from your program's printer menu.
Printer control language (pcl)	The way a program explains a page to the printer. (See pdl)

The Boring Term	What It Means
Page description language (pdl)	Another way a program explains a page to the printer. For example, PostScript and LaserJet use their own pdl.
Pages per minute (ppm)	The number of pages a laser printer can squirt out in one minute. That's the *same* page, though. If you print several different pages, the pages won't come out nearly as fast.
Dots per inch (dpi)	The number of dots a laser printer can pack into one square inch. The more dots per inch, the better your printed stuff will look.
Driver	This little piece of software translates the stuff on your screen into the stuff you see on the page. Windows 95 uses different drivers to talk to different brands of printers. Because most printers mimic the most popular printers, choose the driver for the printer that your printer mimics. It's probably Hewlett-Packard's LaserJet, PostScript, or Epson.
Point size	The size of a single letter. This word uses a bigger point size than this word.
Typeface	This describes a letter's distinctive style. Courier is a different typeface than TimesRoman.
Font	A typeface of a certain size and characteristic. For example, TimesRoman is a typeface, but **TimesRoman Bold** is a font within that typeface family.
Pitch	The amount of space between letters.
Line feed	Flip this switch only if everything is always double-spaced. Or flip this switch if everything is printing on the same line, over and over. Otherwise, ignore it. Note that some dot-matrix printers let you push this button to advance the paper one line at a time.
Form feed	On some printers, selecting this button brings up the top of the next piece of paper so it is ready for printing.
Toner cartridge	The plastic box inside a laser printer that holds black powder, known as *toner*. The toner is transferred to the paper electrostatically and melted on by the fuser rollers.

(continued)

Table 9-1 *(continued)*

The Boring Term	What It Means
Skip perforation	Does your dot-matrix printer keep printing over the perforation where you tear the paper into pieces? Or does your printer skip the perforation and leave an inch or so between each page? If so, this toggle switch lets you choose to skip or not skip. *Tip:* After changing a printer's settings, you often need to turn your printer off and then turn it on again. (Turn your printer on and off slowly, though. Electric stuff doesn't like quick flicks.)

My Printer Doesn't Print Anything

Are you *sure* that the printer is plugged in and turned on?

Check to see whether the printer's little *power* light is beaming merrily. If not, plug a lamp into the outlet to make sure that the outlet works. If the lamp works in the outlet where your printer doesn't, the printer is most likely suffering from a blown power supply. You have to take your printer to the repair shop and hope that the repair folks can fix it within two weeks. If the power light is on, though, keep reading.

✔ Does the printer have paper? Is the paper jammed somewhere? Some printers have a little readout that announces *paper jam* when the paper is stuck. With other printers, you have to ogle the paper supply yourself.

✔ Is the printer cable plugged firmly into its ports? Be sure that you check the port on the computer and the port on the printer.

✔ Do you have a *switch box* that lets two computers connect to one printer? Check to make sure that the switch box is switched to the right printer. While you're there, give the cables a tug to make sure that they're firmly attached.

✔ Also, try printing from a different program. Maybe your program is messing up, and the printer is perfectly innocent. If the program is messing up, it probably doesn't know what brand of printer you have bought. Head to the "When I try to print something, I get Greek" section.

Laser printers are *supposed* to heat up. That's why you shouldn't put pillowcases or covers on laser printers when they're running. If you don't allow for plenty of air ventilation, your laser printer may overheat. When you're not using your laser printer, however, put the cover on to keep dust and dead flies out of it.

When I Try to Print Something, I Get Greek!

When you see Greek rather than English (or, for you overseas readers, English rather than Greek), chances are that your printer is working right. It's your *software* that's messing up. The software thinks that you have a different kind of printer on the end of the cable. For example, Figure 9-1 shows what Microsoft Word for Windows prints when it thinks that there's a PostScript printer on the line but there's really a Hewlett-Packard LaserJet.

```
%!PS-Adobe-3.0
%%Creator: Windows PSCRIPT
%%Title: Microsoft Word - CHAP08.DOC
%%BoundingBox: 13 15 595 778
%%DocumentNeededResources: (atend)
%%DocumentSuppliedResources: (atend)
%%Pages: (atend)
%%BeginResource: procset Win35Dict 3 1
/Win35Dict 290 dict def Win35Dict begin/bd{bind def}bind def/in{72
mul}bd/ed{exch def}bd/ld{load def}bd/tr/translate ld/gs/gsave ld/gr
/grestore ld/M/moveto ld/L/lineto ld/rmt/rmoveto ld/rlt/rlineto ld
/rct/rcurveto ld/st/stroke ld/n/newpath ld/sm/setmatrix ld/cm/currentmatrix
ld/cp/closepath ld/ARC/arcn ld/TR{65536 div}bd/lj/setlinejoin ld/lc
/setlinecap ld/ml/setmiterlimit ld/sl/setlinewidth ld/scignore false
def/sc{scignore{pop pop pop}{0 index 2 index eq 2 index 4 index eq
and{pop pop 255 div setgray}{3{255 div 3 1 roll}repeat setrgbcolor}ifelse}ifelse
/FC{bR bG bB sc}bd/fC{/bB ed/bG ed/bR ed}bd/HC{hR hG hB sc}bd/hC{
/hB ed/hG ed/hR ed}bd/PC{pR pG pB sc}bd/pC{/pB ed/pG ed/pR ed}bd/sM
matrix def/PenW 1 def/iPen 5 def/mxF matrix def/mxE matrix def/mxUE
matrix def/mxUF matrix def/fBE false def/iDevRes 72 0 matrix defaultmatrix
dtransform dup mul exch dup mul add sqrt def/fPP false def/SS{fPP{
/SV save def}{gs}ifelse}bd/RS{fPP{SV restore}{gr}ifelse}bd/EJ{gsave
showpage grestore}bd/#C{userdict begin/#copies ed end}bd/FEbuf 2 string
def/FEglyph(G )def/FE{1 exch{dup 16 FEbuf cvrs FEglyph exch 1 exch
putinterval 1 index exch FEglyph cvn put}for}bd/SM{/iRes ed/cyP ed
/cxPg ed/cyM ed/cxM ed 72 100 div dup scale dup 0 ne{90 eq{cyM exch
0 eq{cxM exch tr -90 rotate -1 1 scale}{cxM cxPg add exch tr +90 rotate}ifelse}{
cyM sub exch 0 ne{cxM exch tr -90 rotate}{cxM cxPg add exch tr -90
rotate 1 -1 scale}ifelse}ifelse}{pop cyP cyM sub exch 0 ne{cxM cxPg
add exch tr 180 rotate}{cxM exch tr 1 -1 scale}ifelse}ifelse 100 iRes
div dup scale 0 0 transform .25 add round .25 sub exch .25 add round
.25 sub exch itransform translate}bd/SJ{1 index 0 eq{pop pop/fBE false
def}{1 index/Break ed div/dxBreak ed/fBE true def}ifelse}bd/ANSIVec{
16#0/grave 16#1/acute 16#2/circumflex 16#3/tilde 16#4/macron 16#5/breve
16#6/dotaccent 16#7/dieresis 16#8/ring 16#9/cedilla 16#A/hungarumlaut
16#B/ogonek 16#C/caron 16#D/dotlessi 16#27/quotesingle 16#60/grave
16#7C/bar 16#82/quotesinglbase 16#83/florin 16#84/quotedblbase 16#85
/ellipsis 16#86/dagger 16#87/daggerdbl 16#89/perthousand 16#8A/Scaron
16#8B/guilsinglleft 16#8C/OE 16#91/quoteleft 16#92/quoteright 16#93
/quotedblleft 16#94/quotedblright 16#95/bullet 16#96/endash 16#97
/emdash 16#99/trademark 16#9A/scaron 16#9B/guilsinglright 16#9C/oe
16#9F/Ydieresis 16#A0/space 16#A4/currency 16#A6/brokenbar 16#A7/section
16#A8/dieresis 16#A9/copyright 16#AA/ordfeminine 16#AB/guillemotleft
16#AC/logicalnot 16#AD/hyphen 16#AE/registered 16#AF/macron 16#B0/degree
16#B1/plusminus 16#B2/twosuperior 16#B3/threesuperior 16#B4/acute 16#B5
/mu 16#B6/paragraph 16#B7/periodcentered 16#B8/cedilla 16#B9/onesuperior
16#BA/ordmasculine 16#BB/guillemotright 16#BC/onequarter 16#BD/onehalf
16#BE/threequarters 16#BF/questiondown 16#C0/Agrave 16#C1/Aacute 16#C2
/Acircumflex 16#C3/Atilde 16#C4/Adieresis 16#C5/Aring 16#C6/AE 16#C7
/Ccedilla 16#C8/Egrave 16#C9/Eacute 16#CA/Ecircumflex 16#CB/Edieresis
16#CC/Igrave 16#CD/Iacute 16#CE/Icircumflex 16#CF/Idieresis 16#D0/Eth
16#D1/Ntilde 16#D2/Ograve 16#D3/Oacute 16#D4/Ocircumflex 16#D5/Otilde
16#D6/Odieresis 16#D7/multiply 16#D8/Oslash 16#D9/Ugrave 16#DA/Uacute
16#DB/Ucircumflex 16#DC/Udieresis 16#DD/Yacute 16#DE/Thorn 16#DF/germandbls
16#E0/agrave 16#E1/aacute 16#E2/acircumflex 16#E3/atilde 16#E4/adieresis
16#E5/aring 16#E6/ae 16#E7/ccedilla 16#E8/egrave 16#E9/eacute 16#EA
/ecircumflex 16#EB/edieresis 16#EC/igrave 16#ED/iacute 16#EE/icircumflex
16#EF/idieresis 16#F0/eth 16#F1/ntilde 16#F2/ograve 16#F3/oacute 16#F4
/ocircumflex 16#F5/otilde 16#F6/odieresis 16#F7/divide 16#F8/oslash
16#F9/ugrave 16#FA/uacute 16#FB/ucircumflex 16#FC/udieresis 16#FD/yacute
```

Figure 9-1: This garbage appears when Word for Windows prints in PostScript format to a LaserJet printer.

You can reuse your scrap paper. Turn it upside down before sticking it in your printer tray. You don't want to use scrap paper for important stuff but use it for stuff you're not going to show other people.

Instead of having Greek come out of your printer, the opposite — having nothing print — can be equally annoying. When Word for Windows prints in LaserJet format to PostScript, nothing comes out of the printer at all.

The problem is that the software is using the wrong *driver*. You need to head for the program's Print Setup menu and then choose the driver that's right for your printer.

- ✔ In Windows 95, open the My Computer program and double-click the Printers folder inside. Double-click the Add Printer icon, and follow the steps to introduce Windows to your computer. (You can find a more complete description of how to do this in Chapter 18.)

- ✔ If you're using a DOS program, you may need to reinstall the program but tell it the name of the right printer this time.

- ✔ Windows already comes with drivers for most printers.

- ✔ You can find more information about PostScript in Chapter 3.

If your printer can switch between PostScript or LaserJet emulation, try to make sure that it's set to the right mode before you start printing on it. Nobody can *always* remember, but you can at least try.

Paper Keeps Jamming in My Laser Printer!

Sounds like you need to get your printer cleaned by a professional. In the meantime, open the laser printer's top and carefully remove the offending sheet of paper.

Grab hold of the paper stack, hold it loosely with both hands, and flick the edges as if they were one of those little flip-page cartoons. This process loosens up the paper and makes it flow through the feeder easier. I also blow gently against the edge to separate the pages.

Keep cats away from laser printers. My friend's cat peed in hers, and the printer cost her $500 to repair.

Don't run labels through your laser printer — unless the label's box says specifically that it's okay. The heat inside the printer can make the labels fall off inside the printer. The labels gum up everything, which makes you feel just awful.

My Printer Says That it Has 35 Built-In Fonts — Where?

A printer company's marketing department often plays on the confusion between *typeface* and *font*.

A typeface is a family of letters. Helvetica is a typeface, for example. Courier is a typeface, too.

A font describes a particular *breed* of typeface. Helvetica Bold is a font and so is Helvetica Italic.

Your printer considers Helvetica, Helvetica Bold, and Helvetica Italic to be three different fonts. That's why the term "35 built-in fonts" is pretty boring after you see what the letters really look like.

How Can I Add PostScript to My Printer?

The easiest way to add PostScript to your LaserJet printer is to buy a PostScript cartridge and stick it inside. (Many Hewlett Packard printers can be upgraded.)

The hardest way to add PostScript to your printer is to buy a special card that sits inside your computer and translates your information into PostScript. (This addition adds speed to your printing; it is faster than the cartridge add-on.)

The in-between way is to buy a PostScript translation program. The program translates your pages back from PostScript to something a non-PostScript printer can handle. All that translating can take some time, however. Translating considerably slows down the printing process (and often requires a memory upgrade for the printer).

PostScript translation software may be the only way to use PostScript software with inkjet printers.

Everything's Double-Spaced or Everything's Printing on the Same Line

After a printer puts a single line of text on the paper, the printer needs to drop down a line and start printing the next line. But should the printer do so automatically? Or should the printer wait until the computer says so?

This awful bit of computerized politeness can really mess things up. If your printer and computer *both* drop down a line, everything turns out double-spaced. But, if neither of them speaks up, all your text prints out on the same line, over and over.

The solution? If your lines are always double-spaced or all the text prints on the same line, flip the printer's *line feed* switch.

- After flipping the line feed switch, you need to turn your printer off, wait ten seconds, and turn it back on again. Printers only look at their switches when they're first turned on.

- If only one of your programs has this problem, *don't* flip the printer's line feed switch. Flipping the switch makes the printer act weird with all your other programs. Instead, tell that renegade program to reverse its line feed setting. You find that setting in the program's setup area or installation program.

- Some printers change their line feeds with a *DIP* switch. A DIP switch is the size of two ants standing side by side. You need a little paper clip to flick the DIP switch the other way. (That delicate procedure is covered in Chapter 18.) The switch is usually near the back.

- If your stuff is printing okay, ignore the line feed switch. Otherwise, your stuff won't print okay.

- Some printers come with software to control line feeds. Instead of searching for little switches, you'll have to search for the right software.

The Page Looks Blotchy on My Laser Printer

Sometimes the page looks, well, blotchy. You see big patches of black here and there or big empty white spots. Those patches and spots usually mean that it's time for a trip to the repair shop. Your laser printer needs to be poked, prodded, cleaned, and billed by a professional.

Black streaks: These usually mean that you need a new drum — a big, expensive thingy inside the laser printer. Sometimes, the repair shop can just clean the drum to bring it back to normal, though. Or sometimes you need a new toner cartridge — an increasing number of printers now put the drum inside the cartridge.

Faded print: You probably need a new toner cartridge. But, before you buy a new one, try this tip:

When your print looks faded, your printer is probably running out of toner. Open the lid to the laser printer and look for a big, black plastic thing. Pull it straight out and then gently rock it back and forth. Don't turn the cartridge upside down unless you want to make an incredible mess. Then slide the cartridge back in the same way. This procedure sometimes lets your laser printer squeeze out a few dozen extra pages.

Creased paper: Keep paper stored in a dry place and not the bottom corner of the garage or under the coffee maker. Moist paper can crease as it runs through a laser printer.

Also, all that laser stuff really heats up a laser printer. If you're running some preprinted letterhead through it, the ink on the letterhead may smear.

How Do I Install a New Toner Cartridge?

Laser printers need black stuff to put on the page. That black stuff is called *toner,* and it comes inside *cartridges.* When your pages start to look blotchy or faint, you probably need a new cartridge.

Various printers work differently, but here's the general rundown:

1. **Turn off the printer and open its top.**

   Laser printers usually have a hood-release type of latch that lets their top pop up. You may need to remove the paper tray first.

   If your laser printer has been turned on, let it cool off for 15 minutes. Laser printers get hot enough inside to brand a pig. The parts that seem hot *are* hot, and they can hurt your fingers.

2. **Pull out the old cartridge.**

   The cartridge usually slides straight out. While the cartridge is out, wipe away any dust or dirt you see inside the printer. The printer's manual tells you the most appropriate places to clean. A little rubbing alcohol on a soft rag usually works well. Check your printer's manual to make sure that alcohol won't damage any parts inside.

3. **Slide in the new cartridge.**

   Before sliding in the new cartridge, gently rock it back and forth to evenly distribute the toner that lurks inside. Don't turn the cartridge upside down or completely on one end.

   Some toner cartridges have a protective plastic strip that you must remove before you install the cartridge. Better check the instruction book on this one.

4. **When the new cartridge snaps in place, close the printer's top and turn it back on.**

   You may need to put the paper cartridge back on.

   ✔ You should check your printer's manual for mention of any "fuser pads" or "corona wires" that need to changed at the same time.

   ✔ New toner cartridges are sometimes blotchy for the first few pages, so don't print any résumés right off the bat.

   ✔ If you run into trouble, take the printer to the repair shop. The printer probably needs a good cleaning anyway.

Can I Save Money by Refilling My Cartridges?

Some people say that recycling is a great way to save money and protect the environment. Other people say that a botched refill can ruin a printer. There's no clear-cut answer.

Let your own experience be your guide. If you do decide to refill your laser toner cartridge, however, don't try to do it yourself. Let the repair shop handle the job. A qualified repair person is a better judge of whether or not your cartridge should be refilled.

Inkjet cartridges can be refilled, as well. Check the backs of computer magazines for mail-order outfits that sell the kits. Make sure that you're using the specially formulated inkjet cartridge ink, though.

Can I Upgrade My Laser Printer?

Like computers, laser printers often have secret compartments where you can add gizmos. Here's the rundown:

Cartridges: Many printers work like Atari's old computer game systems: You can stick different cartridges in them to make them do different things. You can add different fonts, for example, or add PostScript if you're serious about printing high-quality stuff.

Memory: Text doesn't take much oomph to print. But, if you start adding graphics to a page — pictures, fancy borders, or pie charts — the printer is going to need a lot of memory to handle it all. Many printers let you stick little memory modules inside them so that they can print fancier pages faster.

The memory that goes inside your printer isn't the same kind of memory that goes inside your computer. You can't swap them back and forth. (You can't grab any of the memory off your video card, either.)

Unfortunately, you have to buy most of these *add-on* gizmos from the printer's company. They're rarely interchangeable among different brands of printers.

Why Is My Printer Cable So Short?

It's short because parallel ports are wimpy. They lack the tongue muscles to spit data over a long distance, so the cables are usually only six feet long. Expensive cables may add a few feet, but generally your printer needs to sit pretty close to your computer.

How Can Two Computers Share One Printer?

Most folks solve the problem of two computers and one printer with an *A/B switch box*. The printer plugs into the box's printer port. One computer plugs into the box's *A* port, and the other computer plugs into its *B* port.

When you want to print from one computer, flip the switch to A. When you want to print from the other computer, flip the switch to B.

It's a pretty simple arrangement, actually. The only problem occurs when you forget to switch the A/B switch box to your computer. Everybody does it. Some folks even brag about forgetting to switch the box.

The newer A/B switch boxes can automatically detect which printer is trying to print and route the incoming page to the appropriate printer. These boxes cost a little more (okay, a *lot* more), but they can prevent a lot of crankiness.

A *network* — an expensive, high-class version of an A/B switch — connects bunches of computers with cards and cables. If you're using a network in Windows, you can print to any active printer that's listed on the network. You still have to get up and walk over to get your printout, but hopefully the network's printer isn't too far away.

WELL-WORN

My laser printer smells funny

Laser printers contribute to the Earth's ozone layer. Unfortunately, laser printers release the ozone right next to your desk and not 12 to 15 miles into the Earth's atmosphere.

Laser printers come with an ozone filter to absorb the dangerous gas before it reaches your nostrils. The filter can wear out, however. Check your printer's manual to see how often you need to replace your filter. Sometimes you can replace the old one yourself; other printers make you head for a repair shop.

What's the Best Paper for a Color Inkjet Printer?

The latest and greatest variety of printer, the inexpensive and powerful color inkjet printers, can spit out some awfully pretty color pictures, provided you use the right paper. On ordinary office paper, the paper's fibers soak up the ink a little bit, letting it bleed and blur. On specially designed (and especially expensive) color inkjet paper, the colors stay put, creating a sharp image.

Check the labels on paper before shopping, and be sure to get some of each.

How Do I Install a New Printer?

IQ level: 70

Tools you need: One hand and a screwdriver

Cost: Anywhere from $150 – $2,500

Things to watch out for:

When shopping for a laser printer, compare printouts from several different printers. Laser printers use several different printing mechanisms, each with its own advantage and disadvantage. For example, one printer may be better for dark graphics but lousy for letters. Other printers may be just the opposite.

Be sure to compare the output from several inkjet printers before making a final decision. No matter what printer you choose, you may have to buy a printer cable; printers don't always come with a printer cable included. Just ask the salesperson for an IBM-compatible printer cable. All printer cables for PCs do the same thing (unless you have a serial printer, which I describe at the end of this chapter).

To install a printer, follow these steps:

1. **Turn off your computer.**

   Turning off you computer is a good idea when installing anything but software. Be sure to save your work and exit any programs before turning it off, however.

2. **Remove the new printer from the box.**

   Remove any stray bits of Styrofoam, tape, or plastic baggies. Check inside the box for any stray bits of stuffing. Grab all the manuals and disks; they can get lost amid all the packaging material.

3. **Find the printer cable, your computer's printer port, and the port on the back of your printer.**

   The printer port looks the same on a PC, an XT, an AT, a 386, or any other IBM-compatible computer. Look for the big port with 25 *holes* in it, as shown in Figure 9-2. (The big port with 25 *pins* is a serial port.)

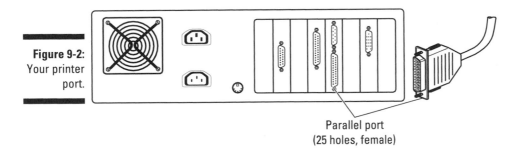

Figure 9-2:
Your printer
port.

Parallel port
(25 holes, female)

4. **Plug the cable into the printer and computer.**

   Plug the side of the cable that looks like a robot's mouth into the printer, and plug the other side into your computer's printer port.

   Different printers accept paper in different ways. Check the printer's manual for this one.

   Using a dot-matrix or inkjet printer? You'll probably need to slide in a ribbon or ink cartridges so the printer has some ink to smear on the pages.

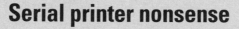

Testing your printer

If you still run DOS, you can test your printer with this neat trick. Type the following line at the DOS prompt:

```
C:\> DIR > LPT1:
```

That is, type DIR, a space, a greater-than sign, another space, and LPT1:.

If your printer says

```
Write fault error writing device
    LPT1
Abort, Retry, Ignore, Fail?
```

then press A. Make sure that your cables are connected and the printer is turned on. Of course, make sure that your printer has paper in it, too. If everything is working, your printer spits out a list of files on your computer's current directory.

Doesn't work? Maybe your printer is in PostScript mode. Try flicking it to LaserJet mode and try again. If it's not working, something is still wrong with your printer, cable, or printer port.

Printers usually come with a built-in *self-test* program. You run the self-test program by pushing buttons on the printer's control panel. The program squirts out a piece of paper showing alphabetical rows of letters. The test merely shows that the printer works by itself. The test doesn't prove that the printer is hooked up to the computer right. Chapter 17 shows how to tell Windows about your new printer — Windows gives you the option of printing a test page to make sure everything's connected to the computer correctly.

Serial printer nonsense

A few old printers want to be plugged into your computer's serial port. If you picked up one of these feisty old printers at a garage sale, here's the procedure:

First, flip the printer's switches until it works at 9600 baud, no parity, 8 data bits, and 1 stop bit.

Then type the following at your C:\> prompt:

```
C:\>MODE9600,n,8,1,p
```

When your computer is ready for more action, type the following:

```
C:\> MODE LPT1=COM1
```

If your printer is installed on your second serial port, type COM2 rather than COM1.

Last, you'll need to buy a special serial printer cable. The one attached to your modem won't work.

Part III
The Stuff Hiding
Inside Your PC

In this part . . .

You're probably pretty familiar with the stuff that lives outside your PC. You've shuffled the pieces around on your desk, pausing occasionally when a cable pops off the back of your PC.

This part of the book, however, describes the stuff you've never touched. Here, you'll find out about the unseen parts of your computer — the pieces that lurk deep inside its case, making ominous humming noises.

This part of the book uncovers what's beneath your PC's cover.

Chapter 10

The Motherboard (And Its CPU, Math Coprocessor, BIOS, and Even a Battery)

*I*f your computer is one big omelet, then your motherboard is the great mass of egg that holds together all the mushrooms, cheese, and occasional bits of sausage.

That's why replacing your computer's motherboard is such a colossal bother. You need to pick *everything* off your motherboard before you can remove it. You can't overlook a single bit of sausage.

Replacing a motherboard isn't a job for weekend chefs. The task is best left for the technocooks at the computer shop.

If you're *sure* that you want to replace your motherboard, you can find the recipe at the end of this chapter. A few easier projects are sprinkled in along the way, however. In fact, the first section explains how to replace something that nobody expects computers to have — a battery.

WELL-WORN

A *lot* of effort for a little time

The old PC and XT computers didn't come with batteries, so they couldn't remember the date.

So some time-conscious owners opened 'em up and put special *clock* cards inside. Those cards have a battery that can keep the clock ticking.

However, computers are too dumb to look at a card for the current time and date. Computers need a special *program* to tell them where to look. Without that program, the clock card is useless.

If you buy an old PC or XT at a garage sale, make the people root through their boxes of old floppy disks until they find that little program. It's usually called SETCLOCK or something equally clock oriented.

Savvy PC and XT users copy the special program to their hard drive and put the program's name on a line in their AUTOEXEC.BAT files. Then each time they turn on their computers, that program runs and fetches the time and date.

That AUTOEXEC.BAT file stuff is wrapped up in Chapter 16. Oh, and you can install clock cards just like any other card, which I describe in Chapter 15.

My Computer Forgot That It Has a Hard Drive, and It Doesn't Know What Day It Is!

Just like a cheap wristwatch, your computer relies on a battery to keep track of time. That constant flow of electricity lets the computer remember the current time and date, even when it's unplugged from the wall. The computer can also remember what parts have been stuffed inside since it left the shop.

But when the battery starts to peter out (after anywhere from one to ten years), the computer forgets two important things: the date and the type of hard drive it has been using all these years. Frightened, the computer sends out a scary message like the following:

```
Invalid Configuration Information
Hard Disk Failure
```

This is often your computer's friendly way of telling you that it needs a new battery.

I can't find my computer's battery!

Don't bother looking for a battery in most XTs and old PCs — they don't have one. That's why they beg you to type in the current time and date every time they're turned on.

Some people ignore the computer when it asks them to type in the current time and date. So their computer simply tacks the date January 1, 1980, on every file it creates that day. That makes it rough when you're looking for a file you created yesterday, though, because they'll *all* look nearly 20 years old.

If your computer constantly comes up with the correct date, it's harboring a battery inside somewhere. But where? Computer batteries rarely *look* like batteries.

If you have an XT or old PC, look on its cards for a round, silvery thing. The battery usually looks like a huge watch battery that is held in place by a little metal flap.

If you have a newer computer, its battery could hail from one of these five tribes:

- The friendliest computers use AA batteries in a little plastic pack that's taped to the power supply — that big, silver thing in the computer's back corner.

  Wires from the plastic pack connect to little pins on the motherboard. Those AA batteries last about three years.

- Some computers use a huge watch battery about the size of a quarter that pops into a little socket on the motherboard.

- Other computers use a little cube-shaped battery, which is also taped to the power supply.

  Like the AA cells, these guys have wires leading to pins on the motherboard. A cube-shaped battery's life span is about three years.

- Older computers often use little battery cylinders about the size of a cigar butt.

  Battery cylinders live between little prongs on the motherboard, like the one in Figure 10-1.

- The most elusive batteries hide inside a chip that looks nothing at all like a battery.

  The chip says *Dallas* and has a little picture of an alarm clock on it. (This chip is supposed to last about ten years.) When the chip dies, ask your local computer store for a *Dallas Real Time* chip. If the store's clerk stares at you funny, try bugging Dallas Semiconductor at 972-788-2197.

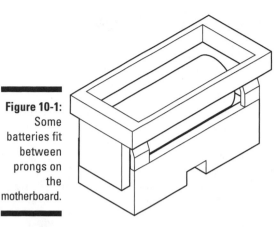

A newer computer's batteries usually live close to where the keyboard plugs into the motherboard.

How do I install a new battery?

IQ level: 80

Tools you need: Screwdriver, flashlight, and prying fingers

Cost: Anywhere from $5 – $20

Things to watch out for:

If your computer's battery looks especially unworldly, try Radio Shack. A salesperson there can special-order odd-sized batteries from a wide variety of planets.

Some manufacturers were especially vile and *soldered* the computer's battery onto the motherboard. Solder is like molten lead, so just give up. You can melt the solder with a *soldering iron,* but doing so can be both scary and dangerous. Take this one to the repair shop unless you soldered something before and enjoyed the experience. Melting solder even smells bad.

Don't forget what your computer is supposed to remember

When you remove the battery, your computer forgets a lot of information about itself. If your battery is dead, it has already forgotten, so this little tip comes too late.

WELL-WORN

To ignore this, press Enter

Even computers with a *working* clock occasionally query you for the time and date. Your computer picks up the current time and date from its internal clock, just like normal. But then your computer displays the date and time on-screen and asks you whether it's *really* okay.

Just press Enter to confirm that yes, indeed, the computer already knows the right time and date. This bit of weirdness pops up when a computer can't find an AUTOEXEC.BAT file. With that file missing, the computer gets suspicious and asks you whether it *really* knows the time and date.

Your computer is most likely to question its internal clock when you boot from floppy disks that don't have an AUTOEXEC.BAT file. Are you a little sketchy on what an AUTOEXEC.BAT file is supposed to do? Troop to Chapter 16 for a refresher.

But if your battery is still grasping at life, head for Chapter 18. In that chapter, you find out how to access your computer's CMOS and find out the type number of your hard drive.

After you install the new battery, you need to tell your computer the hard drive type number. If you didn't write down that information beforehand, you have to page through dusty manuals and search for the right number to type back in. Yuck.

To install a battery, follow these steps:

1. **Turn off your computer, unplug it, and remove its case.**

   This merry little chore is covered in the Cheat Sheet at the front of this book.

2. **Find and remove the computer's old battery.**

   Don't know what the battery looks like? Head for the "I can't find my computer's battery!" section earlier in this chapter.

   Be sure to draw a picture of the old battery's position. Each end has a + or – sign. The signs need to face the same way on the new battery as they did on the old battery.

   AA batteries simply snap out of their plastic case, just like in a small radio. The batteries shaped like a cigar butt slip out of their little prong sockets, but this can take some pressure.

   Don't force anything; some batteries may be *soldered* in, which means that you should stop immediately and take the computer to the shop.

If you have a Dallas clock chip, pry it out gently. If you don't have a chip-puller tool (and who does, anyway?), grab the chip between your thumb and forefinger and pull straight up with a gentle rocking motion. The chip is pretty big, so it's easy to grab. Keep track of which direction the chip faces; the new one needs to face the same way.

3. **Take the old battery to the computer store and buy a replacement battery.**

4. **Place the new battery where the old one lived.**

Make sure that the + and – ends of the new battery face the same direction as they did on the old battery.

If you accidentally yank any wires from their pins on the motherboard, all is not lost. Look for the pin with the number 1 written closest to it. *The red wire always connects to Pin 1.* Computer technicians have that on their bumper stickers. Once you've connected the red wire, the other wires usually fall into place logically.

5. **Put the computer's case back on and plug it back in.**

The battery problem should be solved, but the computer won't be grateful. When first turned on, your computer will probably send out a horrible-sounding error message about your *incorrect CMOS.*

You usually need to tell your computer's CMOS what type of hard drive you have. (You remembered to write down that information before you started, didn't you?) You can find that CMOS stuff hashed out in Chapter 18.

Can a Math Coprocessor Really Speed Up My Computer?

All the new computers come with math coprocessors built in, so this is really oldster stuff. But if you're using a 486 or older computer, here's the scoop: A *math coprocessor* is a little chip that plugs into your motherboard. With a math coprocessor, your PC is faster at statistics, engineering, and some graphics, which means that your computer is fastest and nerdiest at statistical graphics engineering.

Unless you're doing that kind of work, however, a math coprocessor won't speed up your computer at all.

Note that not any math coprocessor will do. Pick up the math coprocessor that matches your CPU, as listed in Table 10-1.

Table 10-1	Math Coprocessors
Your CPU	*The Appropriate Math Coprocessor*
8088, 8086, 80188, V20, V30	8087
286	287
386SX	387SX
386DX	387DX
486DX	Doesn't need one; the math coprocessor is already built in
486SX	487SX
586, Pentium, Pentium Pro	Doesn't need one; the math coprocessor is already built in

How can I add a math coprocessor to my older computer?

Even an ancient computer can do math a little more quickly with a math coprocessor. But if you're after speed, buy a new computer with a faster CPU. That will speed up *everything*, not just occasional spurts of math.

A 386 with a math coprocessor is still half as fast at math as a 486DX computer. If you're really looking for speed, think about biting the bullet and buying a completely new computer.

Utterly trivial math stuff about the 486SX

When Intel made the world's first 486 chip, it tried something new. Intel built all the math coprocessor stuff right inside the 486 chip. Because the math circuits were so close at hand, the CPU could do math faster than ever before.

But then a rival company started selling 486 chips *without* the coprocessor stuff inside. And they were cheaper! So Intel disabled the math coprocessor in some of its chips, called

the stripped-down version a 486SX and sold the 486SX for less money.

The result? If you buy a 486SX and want faster math stuff, you need to buy a 486DX chip. But if you have a 486DX chip, your math coprocessor already lives inside.

Don't be confused by DX stuff, either. A 386DX *doesn't* have a math coprocessor built in, but a 486DX *does*. It's more confusing that way.

As computers age, math coprocessors are becoming increasingly difficult to find. You may have to look around for these coprocessors in computer user groups or pull them out of older computers found in classified ads.

How do I install a math coprocessor?

IQ level: 90

Tools you need: Screwdriver and strong fingers

Cost: Anywhere from $50 – $100

Things to watch out for:

This one is basically easy — just push the math coprocessor chip into the empty little socket.

The problem? Well, the chip sometimes fits into that socket four different ways, and only one way works. In fact, the other three ways may ruin the chip.

The key is to find the *marked* corner on both the chip and the socket. One corner has a notch, a dot, an extra hole, or something even harder to spot. Figure 10-2 shows the differences between some chips and sockets.

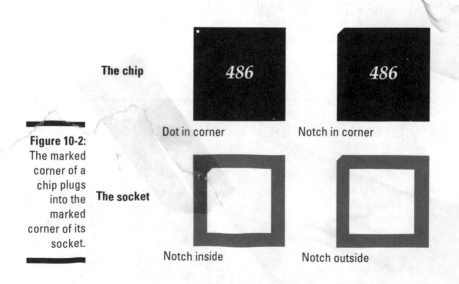

Figure 10-2:
The marked corner of a chip plugs into the marked corner of its socket.

Finally, make sure that your math coprocessor is the same speed — measured in megahertz — as your CPU. The math coprocessor can be faster, but it cannot be slower.

To install a math coprocessor, follow these steps:

1. **Turn off the PC, unplug it, and remove its cover.**

   The Cheat Sheet at the front of this book explains these little chores.

2. **Find the math coprocessor's socket.**

   First, find your CPU. It's almost always the biggest, black, square chip on the motherboard. The numbers 286, 80286, 386, 80386, or 486 are usually printed somewhere along its top.

   The math coprocessor's socket usually lives an inch or two away from the CPU.

3. **Prepare the new math coprocessor chip.**

   Don't touch any chip until you release any pent-up static electricity. Tap on a doorknob, file cabinet, or bare metal part of your desk. *Then* pick up the chip.

   First, make sure that the new chip is the right size to fit in that little socket. Then make sure that all the chip's little pins are lined up straight. The pins need to fit into all those little holes *exactly,* with no legs hanging off the edge.

4. **Press the chip into its socket.**

   The chip's marked corner rests over the socket's marked corner, like in Figure 10-2.

   Finding the chip's marked corner is easy. The socket is a little rougher. Look at the little lines etched onto the motherboard. Sometimes, the little line surrounding the socket has a notched corner, even if the socket itself doesn't. Some sockets have a little dot or extra hole in one corner.

   Lined up the right corners? Make sure that all the little pins are lined up over all the little holes. Then carefully push the chip down into the socket. It should take some pressure, but don't bend your motherboard. If your motherboard bends more than slightly, stop and let the dealer or repair shop finish the job.

   The letters printed on top of the coprocessor usually face the same way as the letters printed on top of your CPU.

   Some sockets have *three* rows of holes, and yet the coprocessor only has *two* rows of pins. If so, line up the pins in the two rows closest to the center.

   Also, the 387SX's socket looks completely different from the 387DX's socket. If something looks wrong, make sure that you bought the right math coprocessor.

5. Plug your computer back in and turn it on.

If the chip came with software, run the software to see whether the chip is working. Didn't come with software? Then run a math-oriented program that knows how to use the chip, and then see whether your computer says *math coprocessor detected* or something just as promising.

If the software can't find the math coprocessor, you probably have to dig out your motherboard's manual. You may need to flip a tiny switch somewhere or tell your computer's CMOS about the new chip. Chapter 18 clears up those pressing details.

If the chip is still not working, check to make sure that the chip is firmly seated in its socket and is facing the right way. Also, check for a wandering pin that didn't go into its hole, like the one in Figure 10-3.

Figure 10-3:
If a single pin misses its hole, the chip won't work.

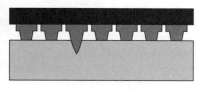

If the math coprocessor is working, put the computer's cover back on and then wipe your hands on your pants. You've earned it.

Can I Put a 486 Chip in My 386 Computer to Make It Go Faster?

Nope. Motherboards and CPUs work together as a team. Think of the motherboard as a city that has roads connecting the houses and the grocery stores. The roads on the 386 motherboard aren't wide enough to carry all the information the 486 chip is capable of trucking around.

However, companies like Cyrix sell special *upgrade* chips. Although technically not a true 486 chip, these 386-to-486 upgrade chips can substantially speed up a 386 computer. You pop out the old chip, slide in the new chip, and your computer thinks it's a 486. Sound too good to be true? Well, it is. Sure, that speedy new chip is thinking speedier thoughts. But it is still talking to the sluggish older parts that haven't been upgraded. And that faster chip is sending the messages over that slow, old 386 motherboard.

There's more bad news. With a faster processor, you'll probably want a bigger, faster hard drive and more memory to go with it.

Plus, that 386's old motherboard probably can't handle any of the fastest local bus or PCI video cards — a slower, accelerated video card is the best you can do. And that leads to the troublesome problem: The cost of a CPU upgrade, more RAM, a bigger hard drive, and an accelerated video card often totals more than a new computer.

But who's got cash falling out their ears? If you find a 386-to-486 chip upgrade at a local swap meet, it may help squeeze a *little* more life out of an aging computer.

How Do I Install an Upgrade Chip to My 386?

IQ level: 100 – 120

Tools you need: Chip puller, screwdriver, and strong fingers

Cost: Varies widely

Things to watch out for:

This one seems deceptively simple — it looks like you just yank out the old chip and push in the new one. But you may encounter several problems.

First, the chip only fits into the socket *one* way. Just as with the math coprocessor chip described earlier in this chapter, the *marked* corner on the upgrade CPU chip needs to match with the marked corner of the socket. The marked corner has either a notch, a dot, an extra hole, or something even harder to spot. Figure 10-2, a few pages back, shows the differences between some chips and sockets.

Second, make sure you buy the right style and speed of upgrade chip for your particular type of 386. For example, the 386DX and 386SX use different types of upgrade chips; so do the different speeds of 386 chips. (For instance, the 20 MHz 386 chip needs a different upgrade chip than a 25 MHz 386 chip.)

Finally, make sure you record your computer's CMOS information before you start poking around inside the case. Specifically, you need to know what type of hard drive your computer uses. (Chapter 18 covers CMOS navigation, and it's easier than it sounds.) Oh, and don't forget to back up all the important stuff on your hard drive — but that's something you should be doing all the time, anyway.

To install a 386-to-486 upgrade chip, follow these steps:

1. **Turn off the PC, unplug it, and remove its cover.**

   The Cheat Sheet at the front of this book explains this.

2. **Find the CPU's socket, and make sure that you bought the right upgrade chip.**

   First, find your CPU. It's almost always the biggest, black, square chip on the motherboard. The number 386 or 80386 is usually printed somewhere along its top. The CPU in IBM's PS/2 line of computers doesn't always say 386, though, so the CPU is harder to find. (PS/2 owners may need to pull out their computer's manual to see which chip is the CPU.)

   Check to make sure the upgrade chip in your hand is the one that is supposed to replace your specific type of CPU. Installing the wrong chip may permanently damage your computer.

3. **Find the CPU's specially marked corner and then remove the old CPU.**

   Don't touch any chip until you release any pent-up static electricity. Tap on a doorknob, file cabinet, or bare metal part of your desk. *Then* it's safe to touch sensitive computer chips.

   One corner of your CPU is marked with a little dot or notch, as seen back in Figure 10-2. Remember which direction that marked corner faces; you need to install the new CPU upgrade chip so it faces the same way.

   The CPU upgrade kit should have come with a special chip removal tool, and instructions on how the tool works. Be careful when prying the chip out of the socket — don't mistakenly try to pry the *socket* off the motherboard. If you're lucky, your chip sits in a ZIF socket: Just lift the lever and the chip comes out.

   The CPU may be buried beneath other parts. Be prepared to remove some cards, a hard drive, or your power supply in order to reach the CPU.

   Some AMD 386DX CPUs are fastened directly to the motherboard, with no socket. Unfortunately, you can't upgrade these chips, so return your upgrade chip to the dealer for a refund. (Or, if you don't like surprises, check the fine print in your computer's manual before trying to upgrade the processor.)

4. **Press the upgrade chip into its socket.**

   The new chip's marked corner rests over the socket in the same direction as the old chip's marked corner, as you noted in Step 3.

   Have you lined up the marked corner of the chip with the marked corner of the socket? Now make sure that all the little pins are lined up over all the little holes. Then carefully push the chip down into the socket. It should take some pressure, but don't bend your motherboard. If your motherboard bends more than slightly, stop and let the dealer or a repair shop finish the job.

Pushing that little chip into the socket can take more pressure than you think. Be very careful not to crack your motherboard while pushing down.

Sometimes slipping a magazine beneath the motherboard can keep it from bending as you push the chip into the socket.

5. **Plug your computer back in and turn it on.**

If the chip came with software, run the software to see whether the chip is working. If the chip isn't working, check to make sure that the chip is firmly seated in its socket and is facing the right way. Also, check for a wandering pin that didn't go into its hole, like the one in Figure 10-3.

6. **Close your computer's case.**

If everything seems to work fine, go ahead and close up your computer's case. You've finished the operation. Whew!

If the computer doesn't recognize your hard drive, check your computer's CMOS setting, as described in Chapter 18. Enter the type of hard drive your computer uses, save the settings, and reboot your computer.

Check the upgrade chip's manual — you may need to stick a *heat sink* on top of the new chip. The heat sink — which looks like a pin cushion — sticks on top of the chip and absorbs heat, keeping the chip from overheating.

What's That OverDrive Stuff?

At the race track, the riders often whip their horses to make 'em run a little bit faster.

Intel does the same thing with its *OverDrive* chips. Many motherboards with Intel's 486 chips contain a special OverDrive socket. When you stick the OverDrive chip in that socket, it whips your CPU and makes it work twice as fast.

✔ Well, not really twice as fast. Technically, your CPU is twice as fast at *thinking* about stuff, not moving information around. Without getting too bogged down in the difference between *thinking* and *moving,* just figure that a 486DX2 OverDrive chip can speed up your computer by about 70 percent. The 486DX4 OverDrive chip isn't *twice* as fast as the 486DX2, but it's noticeably faster than its DX2 cousin.

- Most 486 motherboards can handle those OverDrive chips. (Owners of 386 computers should check out the 386-to-486 upgrade chips discussed earlier in this chapter.) When you see a computer billed as a 66 MHz 486DX2, that means it's really a 33 MHz CPU with one of those OverDrive chips that make it run at 66 MHz.

- Those chips plug in just like math coprocessor chips or 386-to-486 chip upgrades. Some OverDrive chips simply replace the old 486 chips; others fit into an empty OverDrive socket on the motherboard, just like the math coprocessors I described earlier in the chapter. If you're installing an OverDrive chip, head for either of those sections for more details.

- Intel and some third party companies sell chips that upgrade a 486 to Pentium-level performance for around $100. Just pop out the 486 chip and pop in the upgrade.

Before buying a CPU chip upgrade, check into the cost of a new computer. If your computer also needs a new hard drive, more memory, and a faster video card, you can probably save money by buying a new computer instead.

Can I Put a Pentium or 586 Chip in My 486 Computer to Make It Go Faster?

Yep. And to do it, follow the same steps given above for upgrading a 386 chip to a 486 chip. However, remember these two precautions:

- First, make sure you're buying the right chip for the right motherboard. Not all Pentium or 586 upgrades work on all 486 motherboards. You can't simply pop out the old chip and pop in the new one. Your best bet is to call the technical support people at the company selling the chip and see if their wares work on your brand of motherboard. (You may also find the same information on the company's Internet Web site, if they have one.)

- Second, Pentium-level chips usually run at higher temperatures than their predecessors. So, they have it written into their contract that they get a cooling fan. It's a tiny fan — just like the one on the power supply — that clips onto the chip and blows air onto it to keep it comfortable. So, when you install the chip, be sure to plug the fan's power cord into one of your power supply's unused cables.

Can I upgrade my Pentium to make it use MMX?

The latest buzzword in Intel processors is MMX. Intel swears the letters don't stand for anything, but gurus are placing their bets on Multimedia Extensions. That's because the chip speeds up sounds and graphics on specially written MMX programs by more than 200 percent.

So are you stuck if you just bought a new, non-MMX Pentium? Nope. Just replace your CPU with a Pentium OverDrive processor with MMX technology built in. Those new chips not only speed up your computer a little bit, but they let it take advantage of programs optimized to run under MMX technology. They're not cheap; expect to pay several hundred dollars.

Can I Put a New Motherboard into My Old Computer?

Yes, unless you're using an ancient IBM PC or XT. See, motherboards come in two basic sizes: the weird size for the old PC and XT computers, and the size everybody has used since.

Therefore, the newer motherboards just don't fit inside your XT's weird-shaped case. But that's not the biggest problem.

See, even if you could jam a 486 motherboard inside an XT, you would have to buy all new memory. An XT's memory chips don't fit on the new motherboard, so you'd need a new power supply because the old one's not powerful enough. Toss a new keyboard onto the bill, too. Plus, you'd probably want the newer, higher-capacity disk drives.

The plain fact is that a completely new computer costs about the same as all that upgrading. Plus, a new computer has a better warranty. And some dealers toss in a free copy of the latest version of DOS and Windows.

If you use a 286, 386, 486, Pentium or newer computer, you can upgrade your old motherboard. However, be sure to add in the cost of the additional parts that you won't be able to recycle from your old motherboard; as I mentioned before, buying a new computer is usually a better deal.

A few companies went off the deep end when it came to the *standard* motherboard size. Some Compaq computers use weird-sized motherboards, which makes replacement difficult. You'll probably have to go to a Compaq dealer for one of those.

Which motherboard is best?

Shopping for a new motherboard used to be easy. When people wanted a new motherboard, they simply bought a new computer. Today, some cash-conscious computer crafters are picking up a screwdriver to save a few dollars. If you're seriously shopping for a motherboard, here are a few technoid tips:

✔ For years, Intel CPUs were the only players on the block. Today, several companies sell CPUs; in fact, Compaq uses AMD-brand CPUs on some of its machines' motherboards and the moon hasn't exploded. Because the competing chips cost about 20 percent less and seem to be completely compatible with Intel's, don't feel locked into buying a motherboard with an Intel brand name.

✔ Also, look for a motherboard with a ZIF — *Zero Insertion Force* — socket. That means the CPU sits in a socket with a little lever next to it: Pull the lever, and the socket lets go of the chip, letting you drop in newer, fancier chips when they hit the market.

Now, for the numbers: Make sure the new motherboard comes with plenty of room for memory (96MB isn't too much). You also want at least three 16-bit slots for your older ISA cards, and three PCI slots for newer goodies. (Buying a 486 motherboard? Then go with the VESA local bus slots instead of PCI slots.) Also, look for a 256K external cache and a one-year warranty.

Uh, should I really install the motherboard myself?

Don't replace your motherboard unless you're used to fiddling around inside your computer.

Replacing the motherboard is a tedious, laborious chore. You need to remove every wire that plugs into the old motherboard and then plug the wires into your new motherboard. And those wires probably plug into different places!

You have to pull out every card and every bit of memory off your old motherboard. Then you have to stick all that stuff back onto the new one, in exactly the right spots.

Besides, motherboards are fragile things. When bent too far, motherboards break. Oh, you won't see the break because it's just one of those little wires etched along the bottom that breaks.

And the motherboard won't *always* be broken. The motherboard may work fine when you first turn the computer on. But when it heats up in about an hour, the motherboard can expand slightly, which aggravates the break.

That brings on the worst kind of computer problem — a glitch that only happens once in a while, especially when no one's around to believe you.

Don't mess with your motherboard unless you've messed around with all the other parts in your computer first and feel like you've gotten the hang of it.

I just installed a new 486 motherboard, and it's slower than my old 386!

Installing a new motherboard into a computer is like the *Star Trek* episode "Return to Tomorrow" where the crew took that alien's consciousness out of a can and stuck it into Spock. Although Spock still had pointed ears and everything, he was a completely different person.

The same thing happens to your computer. It looks the same, but that new motherboard gives it a completely different consciousness.

In the computer world, that consciousness is called *CMOS*. Your new motherboard has all sorts of new CMOS settings for you to play with. And if the motherboard is moving slowly, you probably need to fiddle with its *cache settings*. In that case, head to Chapter 18 where all those little CMOS setting details hang freely in the wind.

How do I install a new motherboard?

IQ level: 120

Tools you need: Big Phillips screwdriver, little flathead screwdriver, tweezers/needle-nose pliers, two hands, and a *lot* of patience

Cost: Anywhere from $100 – $1,000

Things to watch out for:

Give yourself plenty of time. You need to remove just about everything inside your computer and then put it all back after the new motherboard is inside. Give yourself plenty of room, too. You'll need room to spread out.

If you're dealing with a very old computer, your best bet is to buy a new case along with the new motherboard. That way you can be sure that they match up.

Finally, you are dealing with a lot of your computer's parts here. If you're stuck on the memory step, for example, head for Chapter 11 for memory information. All the cards stuff is in Chapter 15. Just check the book's table of contents to see where your confusing part is discussed.

Good luck. (It's not too late to take this one to the shop, you know. Or just buy a new computer; that might be cheaper.)

To install a new motherboard, follow these steps:

1. **Back up your hard drive and buy the new motherboard.**

   The first step in computer repair is always to back up your hard drive.

   The new motherboard doesn't have to be the same, identical size as your old one. In fact, your new motherboard will probably be smaller. However, the motherboard's little screw holes must be in the same place as the old one, or it may not fit into the case.

2. **Write down your computer's CMOS information.**

   Your new motherboard isn't going to know the same things as your old one. So write down the *type* of hard drive your computer uses. (You can find that information by probing into your computer's CMOS, as I describe in Chapter 18.) Make sure that you know the *density* of your floppy drives, too. (Chances are, they're high-density, 1.44MB drives.)

3. **Turn off your PC, unplug it, and remove its case.**

   All this stuff is described in the Cheat Sheet at the front of this book.

4. **Unplug any wires that connect to the motherboard.**

   Don't touch anything inside your computer until you release your pent-up static electricity. Tap on a doorknob, file cabinet, or bare metal part of your desk.

   Bunches of little wires plug into little pins or sockets on the motherboard. While unplugging each one, write down any numbers, words, or letters that you see next to the spot it was removed from on the motherboard. Those words or letters will help you plug those wires into the right spots on the new motherboard.

   Make sure that you unplug these wires:

   - **Power supply:** The power supply is two, big, multiwired cables that plug into big sockets.

   - **Lights:** Unplug the wires leading to the lights along the front of your computer's case. Most computers have a hard drive light and power light; some fancier computers have more.

   - **Switches:** The wires from your reset button end up on your motherboard somewhere. Usually, the reset button wire goes next to where the lights plug in.

5. Remove all the cards and cables.

The cables from your printer, mouse, monitor, and other goodies all plug into the ends of cards. You need to remove each cable. Then you need to remove all the cards, which are held in place with a single screw at the back of the case. After you remove the screws, each card should pull straight up and out.

Keep track of which card lived in which slot. The cards probably don't need to be reinserted in the same order, but hey, why take chances?

6. Unplug your keyboard.

The keyboard plugs in through a hole in the back of the case. Pull the keyboard plug straight out without turning.

7. Remove all the memory chips.

Chapter 11 covers all of this memory stuff. In that chapter, you find out what type of memory to look for and how to grab it.

You also discover whether or not you can stick that memory on your new motherboard. (The answer is rarely good news.)

Either way, save those chips in Ziploc baggies. Some stores let you trade old chips in for a discount on new chips.

8. Unpack the new board.

Remove the new board from the wrapper and look for anything grossly wrong: shattered plastic, broken wires, gouges, melted ice cream, or anything loose and dangling.

I can't say this enough — don't touch your motherboard until you release any stray static electricity. Touch a doorknob, file cabinet, or bare metal part of your desk. Even then, handle the board by its edges.

Those innocent-looking silver dots on one side of your motherboard are actually savage metal pokers. If they brush across your hand, they leave ugly scratches. If that happens, people just might mistake you for a biker.

Look for any DIP switches; you may need to flick them later. (That DIPPY stuff's all described in Chapter 18.)

9. Put memory chips on the new motherboard.

If you could salvage any memory from your old motherboard, stick it onto your new one. Add as many new memory chips as you can afford, as well. Don't know how? Chapter 11 has detailed instructions for putting memory into its rightful place.

10. Look at how your old board is mounted.

Usually, two or three screws hold the thing in place. Remember where the screws are so you can screw the new ones in the same place.

11. Remove the old motherboard.

Unscrew the screws holding the old motherboard in place. Then gently grasp the board's edge and pull it straight out of the computer. You may need to move the board slightly back and forth until it comes free. You may need to slide yours toward the left before it comes loose.

12. Remove the plastic standoffs.

The screws keep the motherboard from moving around. But little plastic *spacers* keep the motherboard from actually touching the bottom of the case.

You can remove the spacers by pinching their tops and pushing them down into the holes, like in Figure 10-4.

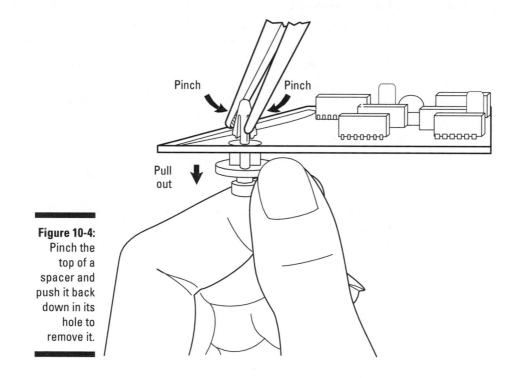

Pinch   Pinch

Pull
out

Figure 10-4:
Pinch the
top of a
spacer and
push it back
down in its
hole to
remove it.

13. Put the little plastic standoffs on the new board.

Then push those little plastic standoffs into the new motherboard. Push them up into the holes from the bottom.

14. Slide in the new board and tighten the screws.

Slide in the new motherboard just like you slid out the old one. Look for the keyboard cable hole — the keyboard plug on the new motherboard needs to go right next to it.

You may have to fiddle with the motherboard for awhile until the little plastic spacers all line up in their little holes. When the board is in firm and all the holes line up, screw it down. Don't screw it in *too* hard because it may crack.

15. Replace the wires.

Is it in? Then hook all those little wires from the lights and switches to their spots on the new motherboard. If you're lucky, the wires are marked. If you're not lucky, you have to flip through the new motherboard's manual.

The red wire always connects to Pin 1. The two black wires always go next to each other on the power supply's two cables.

16. Replace cards and cables.

Put all the cards back in their slots, as described in Chapter 15. Make sure that you don't drop any screws inside the case; if you lose one, curse loudly. Then find the screw before going any further. If a screw lodges itself in the wrong place, it could ruin your motherboard. (Screw extraction tips live in Chapter 2.)

Plug in all your card's cables: the printer, mouse, monitor, and any other odds and ends that need to plug back into the right card.

17. Plug in the keyboard.

The keyboard plugs into its hole in the back of the case.

18. Plug in the PC and turn it on.

This is the big test. Does it turn on? Do you see words on the monitor?

19. Put the cover back on.

If everything works, put the cover back on and breathe a sigh of relief. If the PC is not working, several things could be wrong.

- Make sure that all the cards and memory are sitting firmly in their sockets.

- You may need to adjust the computer's new CMOS settings, as described in Chapter 18.

- Some of your cards may not be compatible with your new motherboard. For example, I had an older VGA graphics card that simply refused to work in a 486 motherboard.

- Through the process of trial and error (and a lot of flipping around from chapter to chapter in this book), you can probably find the culprit. It may be faster to take the whole thing to the computer shop, though. Because you've already installed the motherboard, the shop should charge you a lot less.

What's This BIOS Business?

Sometimes you can stick a new toy in your computer, fire it up, and start playing.

Other times, the computer balks. If, for example, a computer was built in 1983, it's not going to know how to handle the new technology stuff that came out five years later.

For example, you can install a $3^1/2$–inch floppy disk drive into an XT computer. But because that old XT doesn't recognize the drive, it won't be able to use it. That XT computer's *BIOS* — the built-in instructions for handling computer parts — is stuck in the era of $5^1/4$–inch drives and early Madonna singles.

✔ The decrepit BIOS in some computers can't handle Windows, VGA cards, or other new stuff.

   All is not lost, though. BIOS chips are easy to replace. You can pluck the old chips off the motherboard like ticks from a hound dog. Then the new chips plug right into their place.

✔ The problem comes with *finding* those new BIOS chips.

   Try bugging the dealer who sold you your computer. Show the dealer the receipt listing the specific brand of motherboard that you bought many moons ago. The dealer may have some newer BIOS chips in the back room, which are mixed in with the snack foods.

   If you picked up your PC at a garage sale, check the backs of the thickest computer magazines, where the small ads live. Chances are that you can find somebody selling ROM BIOS upgrades.

✔ What BIOS chips do you need? Look for a row of up to four chips, usually with little labels stuck to their tops mentioning the word *BIOS*. For example, my 386 computer has four BIOS chips that say "Mylex, 386 BIOS, ©1986 AMI, 09/25/88." That doesn't mean much to you or me, but it means a lot to the guy on the phone at the mail-order house.

✔ The new BIOS doesn't make your computer run any faster. The BIOS is just a Band-Aid that lets an older computer use some newer parts. New motherboards always come with the newest BIOS chips as part of the package deal.

Some new disk drives come with *device drivers*. After putting the device driver into your CONFIG.SYS file, you can bypass your BIOS. That driver stuff is driven home in Chapter 16.

✔ Your computer probably has several *types* of BIOS chips. For example, a video BIOS chip probably lives on your video card to make sure that the pictures are showing up on the screen. But when you hear the word BIOS dropped in casual conversation, the reference is to the BIOS on your motherboard.

Some of the newest computers have a *flash BIOS*. You can upgrade that kind of BIOS by simply running a software program. Upgrading a flash BIOS is so easy that a lot of nerds are up in arms against it.

How Do I Replace My BIOS?

IQ level: 80

Tools you need: One hand and a chip puller

Cost: Anywhere from $35 – $100

Stuff to watch out for:

Like all other chips, BIOS chips don't like static. Be sure to touch something metal — your computer's case or a filing cabinet — before picking up the chip.

Make sure that the little legs on the chip are aligned in a neat little row. Straighten out any bent legs.

Oh, and make sure that you can take your new BIOS chips back if they don't work. BIOS chips can be finicky in different types of computers, and they may refuse to work.

To replace the BIOS, follow these steps:

1. **Turn off your computer, unplug it, and remove its case.**

   If you're new at this game, head for the Cheat Sheet at the front of this book. And don't forget to touch your computer's case to rid yourself of static before touching any of your computer's sensitive internal organs.

2. **Find your old BIOS chips.**

   They're usually the chips with the word *BIOS* on a stick-on label. You may find anywhere from one to five chips. (You may find a keyboard BIOS chip as well.)

   If you have more than one BIOS chip, look for distinguishing numbers on them: BIOS-1, BIOS-2, BIOS-3, or something similar. Write down which chip goes in which socket and the direction each chip faces. The new BIOS chips must go in exactly the same place.

3. Remove the old BIOS chips.

Some of your cards or other computer paraphernalia may be thoughtlessly hovering in the way. You have to remove that stuff before you can reach the chips.

To make it easy to pry out the old chips, some BIOS retailers toss in a chip puller — a weird, tweezers-looking thing. Don't carry a chip puller around? Try this trick: Using a small screwdriver, gently pry up one end of the chip, and then pry up the other end. By carefully lifting up each side a little bit at a time, you can gently lift the chip out of its socket, like in Figure 10-5.

Figure 10-5:
By gently prying up one side and then the other, you can lift a chip out of its socket.

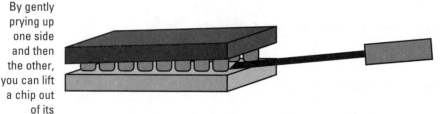

Or look for one of those L-shaped metal things that cover up the slots in the back of your computer. They're called *expansion slot covers,* and they also work to pry out chips, as shown in Figure 10-6.

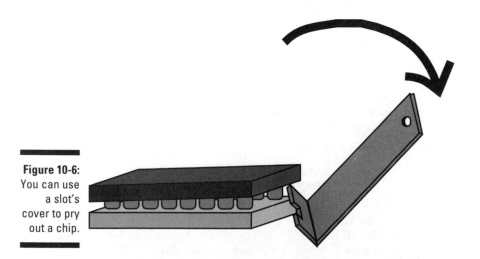

Figure 10-6:
You can use a slot's cover to pry out a chip.

Don't try to pry the chip up from just one side. Doing so can bend or break its tiny little pins. Instead, pry up one side a fraction of an inch and then pry up the other side. By alternating and using gentle pressure, you can remove the chip undamaged.

4. **Insert the new BIOS chips.**

   Find your notes and make sure that you know which chip goes into which socket and the direction the chip should face. Can't find your notes? Then make sure that the *notched* end of each chip faces the *notched* or *marked* end of its socket.

   Next, make sure that the little pins on the chip are straight. A pair of needle-nose pliers can work here. Or you can push them against a flat desktop to make sure that they're all in a straight line.

   Now, follow the steps shown in Figure 10-7.

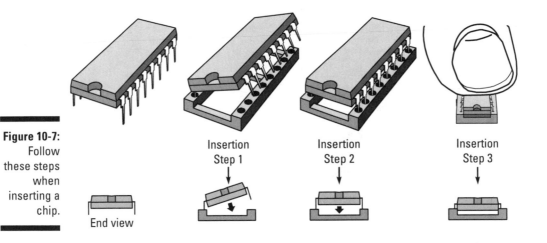

Figure 10-7:
Follow these steps when inserting a chip.

End view   Insertion Step 1   Insertion Step 2   Insertion Step 3

   Put the first row of little pins into their row of holes and make sure that they're lined up perfectly. Next, line up the other row of pins over their holes and push down until the pins are lined up, too. Finally, give the chip a firm push with your thumb until it rests in the socket.

5. **Replace any cards or other items that had blocked your view.**

6. **Replace the computer's cover, plug the computer back in, and turn it on.**

   Your computer should notice its new BIOS chips right away. When you turn on your computer, you can see the chips' new copyright date on the screen's first or second paragraph.

Doesn't work? Then unplug the computer, take off the case, and make sure that you pushed those chips all the way into their sockets. Also, make sure that all those little pins are in their sockets. If one hangs out, like in Figure 10-3, things can get pretty goofy.

Chapter 11

Memory Stuff You Wish You Could Forget

Some parts of your computer are great fun: joysticks, compact disc players, sound cards, and cool games like Disney's age-old Stunt Island, where you can fly a duck around the tops of New York City skyscrapers.

Unfortunately, one part of your computer sends you screaming in the other direction: your computer's memory. Figuring out your computer's memory is the most devastatingly complicated part of IBM-compatible computing.

And besides, memory is awfully boring. In fact, this chapter starts out with awful memory by-products called *parity errors* and closes with migraine-inspired details on pushing memory chips onto your motherboard.

So feel free to ignore this chapter — especially if you're running Windows 95, which does a pretty good job of handling memory details automatically.

If you don't want to be bothered with boring memory details, just let the folks at the computer shop handle your memory problems. Buddha would have taken his abacus to the shop if it used single in-line memory modules (SIMMs). Yech!

My PC Keeps Saying "Parity Error" or Something Equally Weird

That parity stuff means that your computer is not getting along well with its memory, and this isn't good.

If you just installed some new memory, perhaps the computer is just confused. Run your computer's setup program or adjust the CMOS settings, which are described in Chapter 18. Make sure that your computer recognizes your handiwork — its new memory.

If the message persists, though, your best bet is to take your computer to the shop. One of your memory chips is squawking, and the technowizards in the shop can track down the culprit a lot faster than you can. Try a few tricks below before giving up completely, though.

✔ Turn off the computer, remove the cover (see the Cheat Sheet for help), and look for a little graveyard of memory chips lying flat along the motherboard's bottom left-hand corner. See 'em? Give 'em a little extra push with your thumb. Over the years, those chips tend to rise up from their sockets like ghosts.

Before touching any of your chips, touch a plain metal surface to discharge any static electricity. One stray spark can nuke your chips something fierce.

✔ People with newer computers may not have a chip graveyard. Instead, new computer users should turn off their computers and give their memory modules a little push. *Memory modules* are little strips of plastic that have chips hanging off the side. Turn off your computer, take off its case, and give those strips a little push to make sure that they're in there tight.

✔ You can find more of this thumb-pushing stuff at the end of this chapter.

Windows Keeps Saying "Not Enough Memory" or "Insufficient Memory"

Windows uses memory the way baked potatoes use butter: The more you have, the better they taste.

If you don't have enough butter, the potato just sits there and tastes dry. But if you don't have enough memory, Windows reminds you of it constantly, as shown in Figure 11-1.

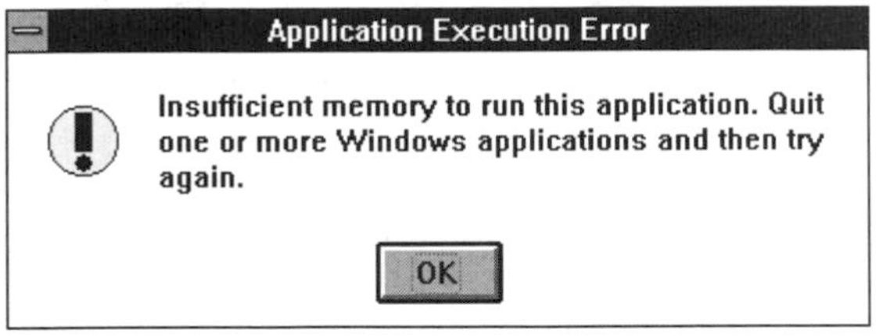

Figure 11-1:
When
Windows
runs out of
memory, it
sends this
uncomfort-
able-
sounding
message.

> **Application Execution Error**
>
> ⊙ Insufficient memory to run this application. Quit
> one or more Windows applications and then try
> again.
>
> OK

You can make Windows stop complaining in two ways. One way is to buy more memory. The other way is to make sure that your computer knows how to use the memory it already has.

✔ Adding memory is usually pretty easy. Just buy more memory chips and stick the chips in the empty sockets inside your computer (after reading the installation instructions at the back of this chapter, that is).

✔ Other computers are maxed out; that is, their motherboards simply can't handle any more memory, even if you won zillions of memory chips from *Reader's Digest.* You simply have to buy a newer, flashier computer with bigger memory bowels. Or, if you're feeling really ambitious, ogle the directions for installing a new motherboard in Chapter 10.

Playing cards by memory

If your XT computer is maxed out, you can buy a memory card to plug into an expansion slot. The computer can transform the memory card into *expanded memory,* and then the computer can dish the memory out to programs that need more memory. Unfortunately, buying an expanded memory card means that you're sinking more money into a dying investment. Think about spending that money on a newer computer instead.

Is your 386 computer stuffed with memory up to its limit? Don't bother with an expanded memory card because it'll be way too slow for those whizbang computers.

Instead, some of those newer computers use special proprietary memory cards, which are available only from the manufacturer. Proprietary memory cards fit in a special 32-bit slot on the motherboard.

Check your motherboard's manual to see whether it has a 32-bit slot before you get too excited about a proprietary memory card. Even if your computer has the slot, those 32-bit proprietary memory cards are expensive.

Confidential to Skip Press in Burbank, California: No, Skip, you can't "hot wire" your 32-bit slot to the $1 slots in Las Vegas. I think your teenage hacker friend has been reading too many adventure novels.

How Much Memory Do I Have?

For the most part, you don't need to know how much memory your computer has. If you don't have enough memory, your computer tells you through a rude message.

If you're curious, though, watch your computer's screen when you first turn it on for the day.

When you flip the on switch, your computer tallies up its memory faster than a grocer can add up double coupons. The computer is testing all the memory it can find so it knows how much room is available for tallying up numbers.

Keep an eye on the screen for the total. That's how much memory your computer has found to play with. (It is possible, through wrong motherboard DIP settings and wrong CMOS settings, for the wrong amount of memory to be shown during bootup. Read on for more information.)

The second easiest way to discover your computer's memory is to look at the receipt to see how much memory you bought. Of course, it's more reassuring to have the *computer* tell you.

Windows 95 users can simply right-click the My Computer icon and choose Properties from the menu that drops down. The Properties window displays the amount of memory, as shown in Figure 11-2.

My computer can't count RAM right!

My computer has 8MB of random-access memory (RAM), and it counts to 7808K each morning. Why doesn't the computer count to 8000K, which is an even 8MB? Well, a megabyte is *really* 1024K, but people tend to round down to 1000K or 1MB.

So 7MB totals 7168K. That's how much *extended memory* my computer has. Then I add the *conventional memory* that DOS can actually use, which is 640K. That brings the total to 7808K, which is the amount my computer displays on-screen.

A 384K chunk of memory is still left over, though. That's the *high* memory, which is where some of your computer's hardware goodies hang their hats.

These weird memory terms all get their due in Table 11-1, which is a little way down the road in this chapter.

How Much Memory Do I Have?

For the most part, you don't need to know how much memory your computer has. If you don't have enough memory, your computer tells you through a rude message.

If you're curious, though, watch your computer's screen when you first turn it on for the day.

When you flip the on switch, your computer tallies up its memory faster than a grocer can add up double coupons. The computer is testing all the memory it can find so it knows how much room is available for tallying up numbers.

Keep an eye on the screen for the total. That's how much memory your computer has found to play with. (It is possible, through wrong motherboard DIP settings and wrong CMOS settings, for the wrong amount of memory to be shown during bootup. Read on for more information.)

The second easiest way to discover your computer's memory is to look at the receipt to see how much memory you bought. Of course, it's more reassuring to have the *computer* tell you.

Windows 95 users can simply right-click the My Computer icon and choose Properties from the menu that drops down. The Properties window displays the amount of memory, as shown in Figure 11-2.

My computer can't count RAM right!

puter has 8MB of random-access
m RAM), and it counts to 7808K each
80(byte doesn't the computer count to
down an even 8MB? Well, a mega-
4K, but people tend to round
So 7M MB.
tended
the conv. That's how much *ex*-
ally use, \ puter has. Then I add
x that DOS can actu-
t brings the total to

7808K, which is the amount my computer displays on-screen.

A 384K chunk of memory is still left over, though. That's the *high* memory, which is where some of your computer's hardware goodies hang their hats.

These weird memory terms all get their due in Table 11-1, which is a little way down the road in this chapter.

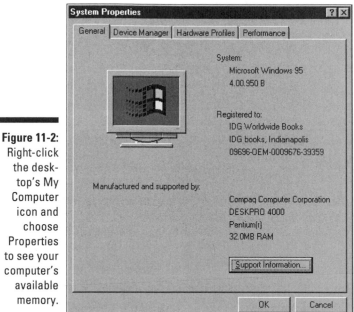

Figure 11-2:
Right-click the desktop's My Computer icon and choose Properties to see your computer's available memory.

Making Windows 3.1 or DOS cough up memory amounts

If you're using Windows 3.1 or DOS 6, look for the helpful little computer nerd program that Microsoft has stashed on your computer. Exit Windows (or just make sure that you're *really* in DOS) and type **MSD** at the `C:\>` thing. The amount of memory your computer thinks that it has appears next to the word `Memory` on the screen. For example, on my computer the MSD program says `640K, 7168 Ext.` So if I divide 7168K by 1024K, I get 7, or 7MB of extended memory. And because I have 1MB of regular memory (that's where the 640K comes from), I have 8MB of RAM in my computer.

Yeah, this memory stuff is pretty complicated. And to make matters worse, sometimes your computer has memory but doesn't know that the memory is there. The memory simply doesn't show up on MSD or any other software program! This calamity is covered in the next section.

And the worst part is the way DOS was designed. When DOS programs complain about needing more memory, they're not saying that you need to buy great gobs of memory chips. They're saying that they need more *conventional memory,* which is that small portion of memory all DOS programs fight over.

I Installed a Bunch of Memory, but My Computer Doesn't Know That It's There!

There are two main reasons for your computer not finding new memory.

First, some PCs aren't smart enough to know that you've spent a lot of time and money to stick little memory chip things inside them. To wise 'em up, you probably need to flip a *DIP* switch on the motherboard. (I'm not making this up, as you find out in Chapter 18's DIP switch section.) Some computers may make you fiddle with their *jumpers,* which Chapter 18 also covers.

To use any more memory than 640K under DOS, you need a special *memory manager* program to dish it around to your programs.

Yep, memory is a horrible, confusing mess. Worse yet, you may need to buy more software.

- ✔ Luckily for thin wallets, Windows and the later versions of DOS come with a free memory manager that can handle some of these complicated memory-dishing chores. When you install the latest version of Windows or DOS, it automatically starts managing your memory.

- ✔ In fact, the memory management system with Windows is so elaborate that it completely takes over all the memory in your computer. When running Windows programs, you don't need to worry about DOS's 640K memory barrier.

- ✔ If you try to run DOS programs under Windows, however, the problems sometimes return. Windows tries to dish out that coveted 640K memory, but sometimes Windows can't scrape up enough memory. That's why some DOS programs don't work right under Windows until they're tweaked just the right way.

    The memory manager in DOS 5 and DOS 6 is called HIMEM.SYS, and it only works if it's mentioned in the first line of your computer's CONFIG.SYS file. When you install Windows, for example, Windows automatically adds the line DEVICE=C:\WINDOWS\HIMEM.SYS to your CONFIG.SYS file. DOS puts that line in there, too.

    Now, back to our regularly scheduled bulleted items.

- ✔ Memory management is an awesome chore, so don't feel bad if you don't get the hang of it right away. In fact, nobody has ever gotten the hang of it.

Why Can't I Move Memory off My Old Motherboard and Stick It onto My New Motherboard?

The packaging has changed on memory chips over the years. The memory chips on your old motherboard are probably a different size from the ones you need for your new motherboard.

The chips just won't fit — like an 8-track tape won't fit in a CD player.

✔ You can usually tell whether or not your memory chips will work by just looking at them. Most memory today comes on long, flat cards called *SIMMs*. Older motherboards used chips called *DIP* or *SIP*. A DIP chip and a SIMM are pictured in Figure 11-3.

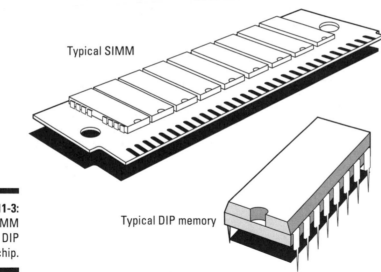

Typical SIMM

Typical DIP memory

Figure 11-3:
A SIMM and a DIP chip.

✔ If you can't reuse your old chips, save 'em anyway. Some computer stores let you trade 'em in for a discount on the type of chips that *will* work.

✔ Other dealers sell converters that let one type of chip plug into another type of socket. This trick only works if your older memory chips can run quickly enough for your fast, new motherboard.

✔ Some men use their obsolete chips to make hip costume jewelry for their wives. Their wives, subsequently, serve their husbands 8-track tapes for dinner.

Only nerds know *all* these memory terms. Memory is merely a chalkboard the computer uses to store information while it's divvying up numbers. Unfortunately, your computer divvies up that big chalkboard into bunches of little sections, and each section has its own name and purpose. Table 11-1 explains what all those words mean, just in case you want to be a memory chip for Halloween.

Table 11-1	Inane Memory Terms
What it's called	*The point of it all*
Memory, alias Random Access Memory (RAM)	Memory comes on "chips" that live on your motherboard. Almost all new computers have at least 8MB – 8,192K — of memory.
	Why 8MB? Because the nerd who created your computer figured that was plenty. Who'd need more?
Conventional memory, alias DOS memory, base memory, or real memory.	Your computer takes the first 1MB of its total memory and tosses 640K (about two-thirds of it) to your DOS programs.
	In fact, all your DOS programs grab for that same 640K memory chunk, no matter how much memory you stuff inside your computer.
	If a program can't find enough conventional memory, it won't run, or may simply stop working; often quite abruptly, and at the worst possible moments.
Upper memory, alias high memory, reserved memory, upper memory blocks.	After a program grabs its 640K of from the 1MB of memory, the computer has 384K left over. The computer uses that for mechanical stuff, like making sure you've *really* put a disk in the floppy drive.
	Your computer's BIOS (Chapter 10) hangs out in that area, as do the brains behind your video card, and other bits of computing viscera.
Expanded memory	As programs grew huffier and puffier, they soon outgrew their little 640K allotment. So, computer nerds stuck extra memory chips onto a "card" and stuck it inside their computers. Then they wrote a complicated memory management program to grab the memory off the card, and slip it over to the DOS program on the sly.

What it's called	The point of it all
	But only DOS programs written specifically for that expanded memory could grab those extra chunks of memory.
	All the other DOS programs were still stuck in their 640K closet.
Extended memory	As the years rolled on, the new 286, 386, and 486 computers hit the stores; they had gobs of memory stuffed right onto their motherboards. Some motherboards came with 4MB; others could hold up to 128MB or more.
	It still didn't liberate DOS programs from their 640K hole, though. But the nerds wrote a special memory manager for that extended memory, just as they'd done for the expanded memory that came on cards. Windows knows how to use extended memory. In fact, it grabs *all* your computer's memory, so it can run bunches of programs, all at the same time.
	But most of your DOS programs are stuck with 640K, no matter how much memory's lying around.
Virtual memory, alias Swap disk	Windows grabs as much extended memory as it can find.
	But when it wants even more memory, it creates its own: Windows grabs part of your hard drive and temporarily stores information there.
	When Windows starts using its newly created virtual memory, everything slows down a little: Your hard drive's much slower than RAM chips. But, hey, it works.

(continued)

Table 11-1 *(continued)*

What it's called	The point of it all
ROM, alias Read Only Memory	Computers normally use memory for calculating numbers. They grab some memory from the pool, work out their problem, and pour the memory back into the pool. But sometimes a computer needs to store something forever. That information's stored on ROM chips. Standing for *Read Only Memory*, ROM chips contain things that never change. Your computer's BIOS is stored on ROM, for example, because it contains instructions for things that never change: the way your computer copies information onto a floppy disk, for example. In fact, that's why you need a new BIOS when a new breed of floppy drive comes out. The old BIOS won't know how to deal with those new drives, and its ROM can't be updated with new information.
Cache, alias Shadow RAM	After your computer's CPU figures out some thing, it copies its answer into a slippery memory receptacle called a *cache*. Then if the computer needs that information again, it just snatches it from the cache. That's quicker than performing the calculation again, or bothering other parts for the answer. A 486 computer comes with an 8K cache built right into the chip. Other computers add CPU caches to the motherboard to further speed things up. Special ultra-fast memory chips are used for caches. They're much faster than the ones used for extended memory. They're also much more expensive.

What it's called	The point of it all
RAM disks	Files normally live on a hard disk or floppy disk. Disk drives are slow, though, because they're mechanical: Little hamsters inside need to run in a treadmill to turn the gears.
	To speed things up, some folks bypass the mechanical stuff. They tell DOS to take some of their memory and turn it into a virtual disk drive.
	Then they copy their most oft-used files to that memory or RAM drive. When the computer needs those files, it sucks them from the RAM. That's a lot quicker than waiting for the tired old hamster.
	It's not as fast as letting Windows 95 use all the memory, however, so RAM disks are obsolete.

Geez, What Memory Should I Buy?

Everybody knows that they need *more* memory to make their computers run better. But what *kind* of memory? Like living rooms, motherboards are all arranged differently. Some motherboards can hold great gobs of memory. Other motherboards can barely squeak by with a sliver.

The only way to know for sure how much memory your motherboard can hold is to dig out the manual and look for the following key words.

Memory type

Some memory chips plug right into the motherboard, like in Figure 11-4. Called a *DIP* (Dual In-line Package) chip, each chip plugs into its own little socket. DIP chips are the oldest type of memory and the hardest to find and install.

Other memory chips, called SIMMs (Single In-line Memory Modules), plug into long slots on the motherboard, like in Figure 11-5. Older SIMMs came with 30 pins; today's models come with 72 pins. Make sure you're buying the right size SIMMs when heading for the store.

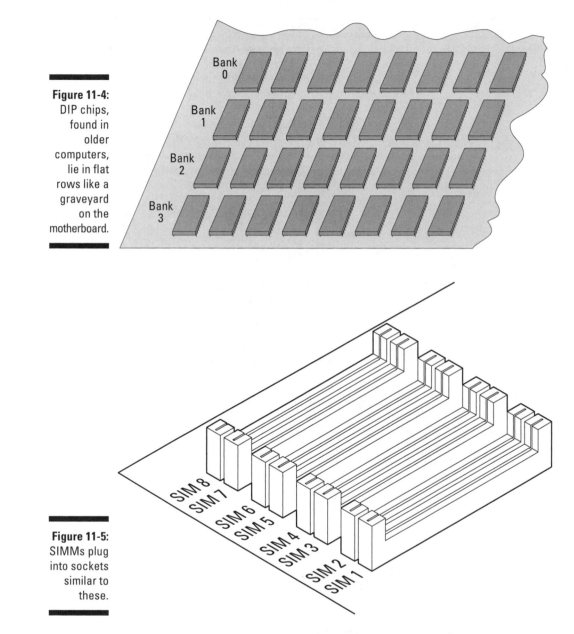

Figure 11-4:
DIP chips,
found in
older
computers,
lie in flat
rows like a
graveyard
on the
motherboard.

Bank 0

Bank 1

Bank 2

Bank 3

Figure 11-5:
SIMMs plug
into sockets
similar to
these.

SIM 8
SIM 7
SIM 6
SIM 5
SIM 4
SIM 3
SIM 2
SIM 1

Another older type of memory, called a SIP (Single In-line Package), plugs into little rows pretty much like the ones in Figure 11-5. The sockets have little holes rather than a slot to accommodate the little feet on the chips.

Although most new computers these days use SIMMs because they're the easiest to install, the push for increasing amounts of RAM has brought a new type of memory: the DIMM (Dual In-line Memory Module). Pushed onto a 168-pin circuit, these memory modules work best on Pentiums, which take advantage of the better technology.

Parity or non-parity

A SIMM usually comes with nine DIPs. But of those nine DIPs, the computer only uses eight for storing information. The last chip is used for *parity checking* — a computerized way of making sure the other chips aren't messing up.

But some manufacturers say DIP chips don't screw up very often — if at all. So they pull the ninth chip off the SIMM to save some cash in construction costs.

Other manufacturers say there's no sense in building a computer that you can't rely on, so they keep the parity chip enabled. In fact, they design their motherboards so the memory has to have its parity enabled.

✔ Parity chips cost more to manufacture because they have an extra chip. Some manufacturers get sneaky by pricing the two types of chip the same, but here's the catch: They're usually selling slower parity chips at the same price as faster non-parity chips. (Memory speed comes up in the next section.)

✔ Make your own decision about parity. The price difference is usually less than 10 percent.

Memory speed

Buy chips that are the same speed or faster than your current memory chips. Buying faster chips won't make your computer run faster. Motherboards run at their own, internal limit.

Also, don't buy chips that are slower than your current crop of chips, even though they *are* cheaper.

Chip speed is measured in *nanoseconds*. Smaller numbers mean faster chips: A 70 nanosecond chip is faster than a 100 nanosecond chip.

Dunno how fast your current chips can scoot? Look at the string of numbers written across the roof of the chips. The numbers usually end with a hyphen and are followed by another number or two. Table 11-2 shows what that magic number after the hyphen means.

Table 11-2	The Numbers after the Hyphen Display Your Chip's Speed	
The Number on the Chip	*The Speed of the chip*	*Computers That Like the Chip*
-6 or -60	60 nanoseconds	Most Pentium and Pentium Pro
-7 or -70	70 nanoseconds	Most 386, 486, Pentium, and newer
-8 or -80	80 nanoseconds	Most 386, 486, and newer
-10	100 nanoseconds	Most ATs or 286s
-12	120 nanoseconds	Most ATs or 286s
-15	150 nanoseconds	XTs and PCs
-20	200 nanoseconds	Very old PCs

Memory capacity

Here's where things get even weirder. For example, suppose that your motherboard says it can handle 64MB of memory. Your computer only has 16MB, and you're rubbing your hands in anticipation of an easy, plug-in-the-chip upgrade.

But when you open your computer, you see that all your SIMM sockets are full of chips, just like in Figure 11-6. How can you fit more memory in there? Where's the crowbar?

- ✔ The problem is the capacity of the SIMMs that are sitting in those sockets. Those little strips can hold memory in the amounts of 1MB, 2MB, 4MB, 8MB, 16MB, or more.

- ✔ In this case, those eight SIMMs must each be holding 2MB of memory. Eight sockets of 2MB SIMMs total up to 16MB of RAM.

- ✔ So to upgrade that computer to 64MB of memory, you need to yank out all those 2MB SIMMs and put the higher capacity 8MB SIMMs in their place.

- ✔ Yes, that means those old 2MB SIMMs are useless to you. Some dealers let you trade old chips in for a discount on your new chips. Other dealers make you store your old chips in the garage until you forget about them.

- ✔ Actually, there's finally a better way, and it's called a SIMM expander. These little circuit boards plug into a SIMM socket and protrude above the other SIMMs. The expanders then let you plug two additional SIMMs into their own SIMM sockets (see Figure 11-7).

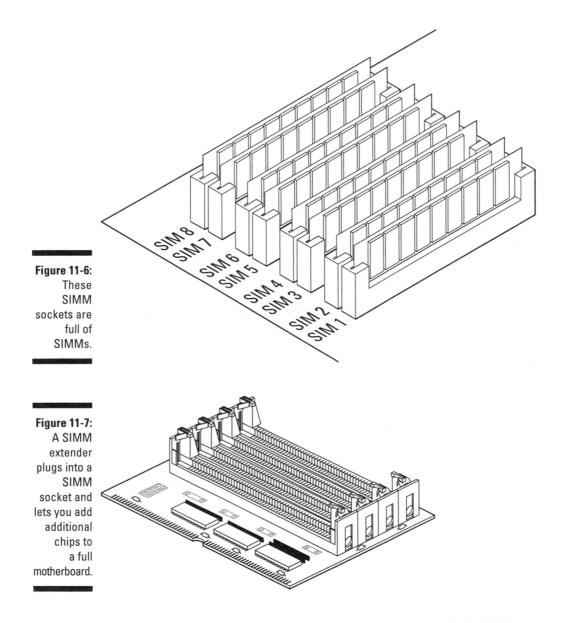

Figure 11-6:
These
SIMM
sockets are
full of
SIMMs.

Figure 11-7:
A SIMM
extender
plugs into a
SIMM
socket and
lets you add
additional
chips to
a full
motherboard.

✔ So, in the case above, you would only have to pull two 2MB SIMMs, plug
in a SIMM expander, and plug both of the 2MB SIMMs into the SIMM
expander's socket. That leaves you with an empty SIMM socket to
insert more RAM — and you don't have to waste any of your existing
memory.

How Do I Install More Memory?

IQ level: 100

Tools you need: Your motherboard's manual, screwdriver, chip puller (optional), and screwdriver

Cost: Anywhere from $30 – $80 per megabyte

Stuff to watch out for:

Memory has more rules than Mrs. Jackson during her shift on lunch duty:

- First, be sure to buy memory that fits in your motherboard's sockets. Several different sizes exist.
- Second, buy memory that's the right speed so your computer can use it without tripping.
- Third, buy memory that's the right capacity. Different motherboards have different limits on how much RAM they can handle.

These three details are covered more fully in the "Geez, What Memory Should I Buy" section. And be sure that you pull out your motherboard's manual to see what rules to follow.

Actually, installing the memory is the easy part. The hard part is figuring out which chips to buy and where to put them.

If this stuff sounds confusing, feel free to pass this job over to the computer shop, especially if you don't have a manual for your motherboard. The folks in the back room can upgrade memory chips in just a few minutes.

Finally, some companies (IBM included) used some oddball chip sizes. If any of these instructions start sounding weird or something is the wrong size, take the whole thing to the shop.

To install new memory chips, perform the following steps:

1. **Turn off the computer, unplug it, and remove the case.**

   These steps get the full treatment in the Cheat Sheet at the front of this book.

2. **Figure out what memory your computer uses.**

   Dig out your motherboard's manual to see what sort of memory it's craving. Check for the memory's *type* (motherboards use DIPs, SIMMs, DIMMs, or SIPs), *speed* (measured in nanoseconds, or ns), and *capacity* (the memory size, listed in kilobytes [K] or megabytes [MB]).

The most amiable motherboards can handle several different capacities and chip speeds.

3. **Figure out whether there's room for more memory.**

Ogle your motherboard to see whether it has any empty chip sockets. DIP chips are usually arranged in rows of nine sockets lying flat on your motherboard, as in Figure 11-3. Are any of them empty?

Sockets for SIMMs or SIPs are in little rows, usually in a corner of your motherboard. Spot any empty ones, as in Figure 11-8? If so, then you're in luck!

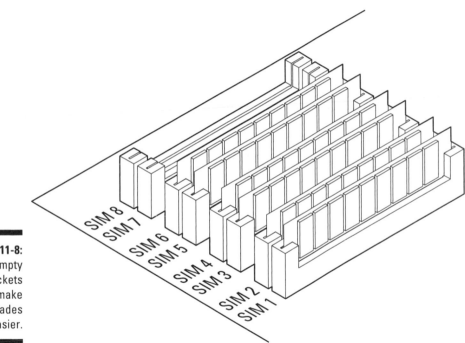

Figure 11-8:
Empty
sockets
make
upgrades
easier.

You can add as much memory as you want, under two conditions. First, don't add more memory than your motherboard can handle. (You can find its limit listed in the manual.) Second, your computer organizes those little sockets into *banks*. Some motherboards say that two sockets make a bank. Other motherboards say that four sockets make a bank. Still others say that one socket is a bank.

Regardless, motherboards either make you fill up a bank completely or leave the bank empty. You can't leave a bank half full, or the motherboard will belch.

Also, you can't mix amounts of memory in a bank. For example, you can't put a 1MB SIMM and a 2MB SIMM in a single bank. You either have to use all 1MB SIMMs or all 2MB SIMMs.

If you don't see any empty sockets, your memory upgrade gets a little more complicated. Check your motherboard's manual to see whether it's maxed out. Your motherboard may already be stuffed to the brim and simply can't handle any more RAM.

If the manual says that the motherboard *can* handle more memory but the sockets are all full, you have to yank out some of the old chips and replace them with higher-capacity chips. If you must remove existing SIMMs, be careful not to break the plastic clips that are on some SIMM sockets.

If your sockets are full but your computer can handle more RAM, buy a SIMM extender described in the "Memory capacity" section. It shows how to add more memory to a maxed-out motherboard.

4. Buy the right type of new memory chips.

By now, you should know whether you need to buy DIPs, SIMMs, DIMMs or SIPs. And your pocketbook (and the motherboard's limit) decides what capacity of chips you buy.

But make sure that you buy the right *speed* of chips, as well. There's really only one rule: Don't buy chips that are *slower* than your current ones.

Don't know the speed of your current chips? Head for the "Geez, What Memory Should I Buy?" section of this chapter for pointers.

5. Install the new memory chips.

Make sure that you ground yourself by touching something metallic before picking up any of the chips, or you could destroy them with static electricity.

If you're working in a dry area with lots of static around, take off your shoes. Working barefoot can help prevent static buildup. If you have your own office, feel free to take off all your clothes. Compute naked!

Check your motherboard's manual to make sure that you're filling up the correct sockets and rows.

SIMMs or DIMMs: Look for the notched end of the SIMM or DIMM. That notch lets the chip fit into its socket only one way. Position the SIMM or DIMM over the socket and push it down into place. When the chip is in as far as it goes, tilt it slowly until the little metal tabs snap into place. The whole procedure should look like the three steps in Figure 11-9.

Some SIMMs, like the ones in Figure 11-6, just push straight down and lock in place. Other SIMMs, like the ones in Figure 11-9, need to be tilted while they're being inserted. Some SIMMs need to be tilted *after* being inserted. If you're careful, you'll figure out which way the chips fit.

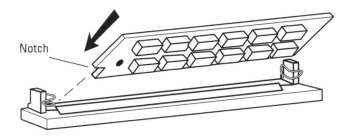

Notch

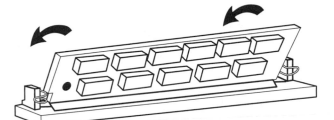

Figure 11-9:
Some
SIMMs are
pushed in at
an angle
and then
straightened
out, like this;
other
SIMMs are
pushed
straight in
and then
pushed
down at
an angle.

Be sure that you fill up the bank where you're adding SIMMs. Also, many Pentium machines have a 64-bit memory bus and must be upgraded in matched pairs.

DIPs: Make sure that the little pins on the chips are straight. A pair of needle-nose pliers can help flatten the pins. Or you can push the chips against a flat desktop to make sure that the pins are in a straight line.

Make sure that the notched end of the chip is over the notched or marked edge of the socket. Then put the first row of little pins into their row of holes, making sure that the pins line up perfectly.

Next, line up the other row of pins over their holes. Then push down until the pins line up, too.

Finally, give the chip a slow, firm push with your thumb until it rests in the socket. Repeat the process until you've filled up the row.

The process is shown in Figure 11-10.

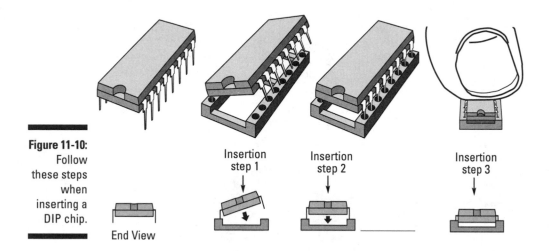

Figure 11-10:
Follow these steps when inserting a DIP chip.

End View

Insertion step 1

Insertion step 2

Insertion step 3

SIPs: Make sure that the *notched* or *marked* end of the SIP is aligned with the *marked* side of the socket. Then carefully push the SIP's little legs into the holes until it's firmly in place.

As with the other SIPs, make sure that you fill up the sockets *one bank at a time*.

6. Double-check your work.

Make sure that all the DIP chips face the right way and make sure that all the legs are in the holes. Also, check the legs to be sure that none are bent underneath or are hanging over the sides.

Check your motherboard's manual to make sure that you filled up the banks in the right order.

7. Flip appropriate DIP switches or jumpers on the motherboard.

Some computers don't automatically recognize the chips you agonizingly inserted. The computer requires you to flip a DIP switch or move a jumper to tell it how much memory you've added.

Which do you do? Check your motherboard's manual. The manual is the only place you can find these secrets.

Unsure about how a jumper or DIP switch works? Jump to Chapter 18.

8. Replace the case, plug in the computer, and turn it on.

Your computer should greet you with an error message about memory mismatch or something weird. The message sounds scary, but it's good news! Your computer found the memory chips you stuck inside it.

Your computer is grateful, but it's also a little wary. Your computer wants to show you the amount of memory it found and ask you to confirm that yes, indeed, you did put that much memory inside it.

All this stuff happens in your computer's CMOS area or setup screen. And all that stuff's tucked away in Chapter 18. (It's not nearly as hard as it sounds, either.)

XTs don't have a setup program or CMOS area, so XTs just take your word on how much new memory you've installed, based on the DIP switches and jumpers you moved around.

If your computer still doesn't recognize your new memory chips, turn it off and push those chips into their sockets a little more firmly. That may do the trick.

9. **Put the case back on.**

Whew. You did it. Boot up your computer and see how much faster it runs!

Chapter 12
Floppy Drives

• •

In This Chapter

▶ Tracking down disk errors

▶ Formatting floppy disks

▶ Installing a new floppy drive

• •

*I*nstead of redecorating their living rooms every year, the technical types who work at the world's computer hardware and software factories redesign floppy disks. They either figure out a way to store more information on a disk, or they make the disk smaller. Most likely, they do both.

Then everybody needs to rush out and buy the latest disk drives, or they can't read the new disks. It's a never-ending cycle, like an old dishwasher that's stuck on rinse.

Several years ago, people needed to upgrade to a $3^1/_2$-inch disk drive just to be able to install software. Today, you're not in vogue unless you can listen to Garth Brooks on a CD-ROM drive while formatting your floppy disks.

Luckily, most new computers already come with CD-ROM drives and $3^1/_2$-inch disk drives, so you won't have to bother with this chapter unless your floppy drive is giving you grief. If your floppy drive is acting suspiciously, this chapter explains how to track down the problems and fix it, or simply install a new floppy drive.

My Computer Barfs on My Friend's Disks!

A floppy disk may work fine in your friend's computer but not in your computer. Instead of reading the disk, your computer barfs a weird error message onto the screen.

For example, my friend Wally could store stuff on his disks with no problem. Unfortunately, no other computers in the office could read his disks.

That's because Wally's disk drives were slightly out of alignment with the computers in the rest of the world. A few PC repair shops can tune up a disk drive if its disks don't work in other machines, but the alignment almost always costs more than a brand new drive. Wally didn't buy a new drive, so everybody just avoided his computer. (We still ate lunch with Wally, though.)

Alignment problems aren't the only causes of disk weirdness, however. Some other causes for disk barfs include the following:

✔ If you have the older, *low-density* drives (the ones that only read 360K or 720K floppies) your computer will barf on a friend's newer, *high-density* floppies (the ones that hold 1.2MB or 1.44MB of data). The older drives simply can't decipher that newer, fancier format.

✔ Also, IBM-compatible computers and Macintosh computers don't like each other. (Neither do their owners, but that's a different story.) PCs and older Macs can't read disks used by the other because each sticks stuff on a floppy disk using a different *format*.

✔ The newer Macintosh computers are much friendlier. They can automatically tell when an IBM disk has been stuck in their mouths, and they can read the information off the disk without causing a fuss. (With some particularly slow and expensive software called SoftWindows, some Macs can run an IBM PC's Windows programs, too.)

When I Put In a New Disk, It Says "Invalid" Something or Other

A couple of gremlins could cause this `Invalid` stuff. The number one culprit is an *unformatted disk*.

Your computer can't always use floppy disks right out of the box. Unless the box specifically says "formatted," your computer needs to format the floppies first. A new floppy disk is like an empty wall. When a computer formats the disk, it sticks little electronic shelves on the wall so it can store data on them.

Windows 95 users can right-click the My Computer icon and choose Format from the pop up menu.

DOS users can format a disk in drive A by typing the following command:

```
C:\> FORMAT A:
```

In other words, type **FORMAT,** a space, and then **A:** (for drive A). The computer responds by telling you to insert a disk in drive A and press the Enter key. Did you put the disk in there? Then press Enter. When the computer asks whether you want to format another disk, press N. Your newly formatted disk is now ready to roll.

Regardless of your operating system — Windows or DOS — the computer lets you choose a *volume label*. That's a fancy computer word that translates roughly to *name*. So, type in **Tina** or **Lars** or **Ulrich** or whatever name you prefer and then press Enter. (Or just press Enter to forget about the volume label. Instead, write a name on the disk's sticker where you can see it.)

Don't ever format drive C (or D, E, F, or G). Any drive with a letter higher than B isn't a floppy disk. It's probably a hard disk, and formatting wipes a hard disk clean. You need to format a hard disk only once, after it's first installed. Then you never format it again.

If your disk is properly formatted, you may get an Invalid message for several other reasons:

✔ You get an Invalid message if you try to use a high-density disk in a low-density drive.

✔ Sometimes a floppy disk simply goes bad. If this happens to all your disks, your floppy drive may be acting up. If it just happens on an occasional floppy, just toss that floppy and use another.

✔ If you see the Invalid message when using your hard drive, you're in for some serious disk trouble. Make a backup copy of your hard drive *immediately.*

✔ If your computer has trouble reading its own disks, it may have forgotten what kind of disk drive it owns. To remind it, head for its CMOS area or setup screen to make sure that it lists the right type of drive. (Better head for Chapter 18 for more information on this one.)

✔ Finally, your drive's *controller card* may be on vacation. Turn off your computer, take off the case, and look for a card with a flat ribbon cable snaking out of it. Push that card down into its socket to make sure that it's snug. Make sure that all those cables are snugly fastened, too. What are controller cards? They're explained near the "How Do I Install a New Floppy Drive?" section later in this chapter.

Who cares why a 1.2MB disk holds more than a 360K disk?

Computers measure stuff by the metric system, which works out great for everybody except Americans, who've been using yardsticks and rulers since kindergarten.

Mainly, computers measure the amount of data they can store either in *kilobytes (K)* or *megabytes (MB)*. One megabyte is a lot more than one kilobyte. It's *1,000* times as much. Actually, it's exactly 1,024 times as much, but everybody rounds it down to 1,000 during general everyday breakfast conversation.

So, a 1.44MB disk can hold *twice* as much as a 720K disk. And a 1.2MB disk can hold *four* times as much as a 360K disk.

The disks that can hold 1.44MB or 1.2MB of data are called *high-density* disks. The others, the 360K and 720K disks, are called *low-density* disks, although some manufacturers call them *double-density* to confuse the issue.

Finally, the newest disks can hold 2.88MB, and they're called *extended-capacity* disks. You find out more about these in the sidebar entitled "What's an extended capacity disk?".

My Computer Says That My Sector Isn't Found or My FAT Is Bad!

This is particularly discouraging news.

If you see a message to this effect while using a floppy disk, try your best to copy the floppy's contents to another floppy or to your hard drive. If you're lucky, you may be able to salvage some of its contents.

If you're not lucky and you *really* need that data back, head to the software store's utilities aisle and buy a *disk rescue program.* For example, both Norton Utilities and CyberMedia's First Aid 95 can rescue some data off a disk that's gone bad. Without one of these special programs, however, there's not much you can do.

If the error message pops up while you're trying to read something off your hard drive, try saving your current work and then push your computer's reset button. Sometimes that fixes it.

If the message keeps popping up, though, you'd better start saving money for a new hard drive. First, though, give one of the rescue programs a shot at it. They're a lot cheaper than a new hard drive, and they can often grab information from a disk you thought was a goner.

What's an extended-capacity disk?

The newest breed of floppy disk, dubbed *extended capacity,* can hold 2.88MB of data. That's twice as much as the former storage champs, the high-density disks. (If you're curious about high-density disks, check out the sidebar entitled "Who cares why a 1.2MB disk holds more than a 360K disk?"

✔ These new disks are still 3¹/₂-inches wide, just like the older guys, but they have the letters *ED* stamped on a corner.

✔ Extended-capacity disks are rare; hardly anybody uses them. I've never seen one, but everybody says that they're out there somewhere.

✔ If you want to use the extended-capacity disks, you need to buy a special, more expensive disk drive. (I've never seen one of those either, although high-end IBM PCs come with this drive as standard.)

✔ The special, more expensive disk drives can still read the other two varieties of 3¹/₂-inch disks: 720K disks and 1.44MB disks.

✔ These new disks and drives have been slow to catch on. But, hey, Hollywood snobs booed *Citizen Kane* during the Academy Awards in 1941.

✔ Computers toss information onto disks in little areas called *sectors.* When a sector goes bad, it's like a shelf collapsing in the garage: Everything spills onto the floor and gets mixed up.

✔ In the old days, almost all hard drives came with a few bad sectors. However, DOS put warning signs next to those sectors so it wouldn't store any information on them. Because the hard drive's hundreds of other sectors still worked, nobody complained.

✔ Your *file allocation table,* dubbed *FAT,* is your computer's index to what stuff it has stuffed in what sectors. When your FAT goes bad, your computer suddenly forgets where it put everything. A bad FAT is even grosser than it sounds.

✔ If you don't have a rescue program and don't feel like buying one, try running the disk tools that come with Windows 95. Described in Chapter 18, these freebies can often fix a misbehaving disk, which means you won't have to buy utility software.

✔ Still using DOS or Windows 3.1? Try running CHKDSK or SCANDISK, the funny-sounding programs that I describe in Chapter 13. They come with MS-DOS, so there's nothing else to buy.

How Do I Install a New Floppy Drive?

IQ level: 80

Tools you need: One hand and a screwdriver

Cost: Anywhere from $50 – $120 for combo drives

Stuff to watch out for:

If you're adding a second floppy drive, better check under your computer's hood to see whether there's room to slide one inside. That magic spot is called a *bay;* see the upcoming Figure 12-3 for a picture of one. Sometimes a second hard disk or tape backup drive can hog all the available bays.

Make sure that your PC doesn't require its own peculiar brand of floppy drive, like IBM's PS/2 or some Compaq computers.

 Don't have a drive bay for another drive? Buy a Combo Drive from Teac. It squeezes both a 3¹/₂-inch floppy drive and a 5¹/₄-inch floppy drive into one small unit that fits in a single drive bay. That immediately frees up enough room for more exciting toys like internal CD-ROM drives or tape backup units.

 If you're adding one of those high-density 3¹/₂-inch floppy drives, make sure that you're using DOS 3.3 or later. That's the first version of DOS that can handle those drives. If you're using an ancient PC, you may need to update its BIOS chips before you add a new floppy drive. (That's described in Chapter 10.) Or just swear loudly and buy a new computer.

 Don't want to buy new BIOS chips for your ancient computer? Buy a new controller card along with your new high-density floppy drive. Some controller cards come with a Band-Aid BIOS that lets an older computer work with a newer drive.

 Your new floppy drive may need rails or mounting brackets before it can fit inside your PC. Some drives come with that stuff right in the box; others don't. If you're *replacing* a drive, you can swipe its old rails. If you're adding a second drive and need rails or brackets, they cost a couple bucks at the computer store.

 Forced to use an ancient 5¹/₄-inch floppy drive for drive B? Then look for its *terminating resistor* jumper or switch, as shown in Figure 12-1. Sometimes it's marked *TR*. Remove that jumper to use the new drive as drive B; leave it in place if you want the drive to be drive A.

See, your computer needs a "plug" on the end of its ribbon cable. Because drive A is at the cable's end, it needs the plug to keep the signals from flowing out the end. If drive B has the terminating resistor, or plug, the signals have to work too hard to reach drive A on the cable's end. If jumpers leave you stumped, check the drive's manual and Chapter 18.

To add or replace a floppy drive, follow these steps:

1. **Turn off the computer, unplug it, and remove the case.**

   These chores are covered in the Cheat Sheet at the front of this book.

2. **Remove the cables from the old drive.**

   Found the old drive? Floppy drives have two cables plugged into them:

   Ribbon cable: The flat ribbon cable connects the drive either to a controller card (on older computers) or to a special socket built right onto the motherboard of newer computers. Look to see which kind you have so you can replace it if it falls off.

   If you're replacing the drive, grab its ribbon cable by the plug and pull it straight off the drive. It should slide off pretty easily. You can see a picture of the cable and connector coming up in Figure 12-6.

   Power cable: The other cable is made of four wires that head to the power supply. Like the ribbon cable, the power cable pulls straight off the drive's connector, but it usually takes a _lot_ more pulling. Don't pull on the wires themselves; pull on the cable's plastic connector. Sometimes a gentle back-and-forth jiggle can loosen it.

   Drives can use one of two power supply plugs, pictured with their sockets in Figure 12-2.

Figure 12-2:
Power
supply
cables
come in two
sizes. Each
size plugs
into its own
socket.

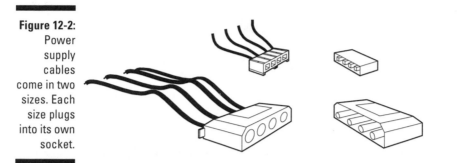

Adding a second floppy drive? Then look at the flat ribbon cable connected to drive A. Do you see a second, vacant connector on it, as shown in the upcoming Figure 12-5? (Most cables come with two connectors.) If not, head back to the store for a new ribbon cable with two connectors. Got the new cable? Then jump to Step 5.

3. **Remove the mounting screws holding the drive in place.**

   Drives fit inside your computer in two main ways:

   Rails: Some drives let you screw little rails onto their sides. The rails hold the drive in place as it slides into the computer. Finally, two screws along the front keep the drive from sliding back out. To remove the drive, just unscrew the screws, as shown in Figure 12-3.

   Choose short screws to attach rails to the drive. If you use long ones, they may damage the drive.

   No rails: Some drives also slide in but without rails to hold them in place. Instead, they're secured by screws along their sides, as shown in Figure 12-4. The screws along one side may be hidden from view by a particularly long card or even another drive mounted on its side. You have to pull out the card to get at the screws, cursing all the while. Note that using long screws may damage the drive.

4. **Slide the drive out of the front of the computer.**

   After you remove the drive's screws and cables, grab the drive from the front and slide it straight toward you.

5. **Slide the new drive in where the old one came out.**

   Slide your new drive into the spot where the old drive lived. You may need to remove the rails from the old drive and screw them onto the new drive.

   Adding a second drive? Find an available bay either above or below the other drive and slide the second drive on in.

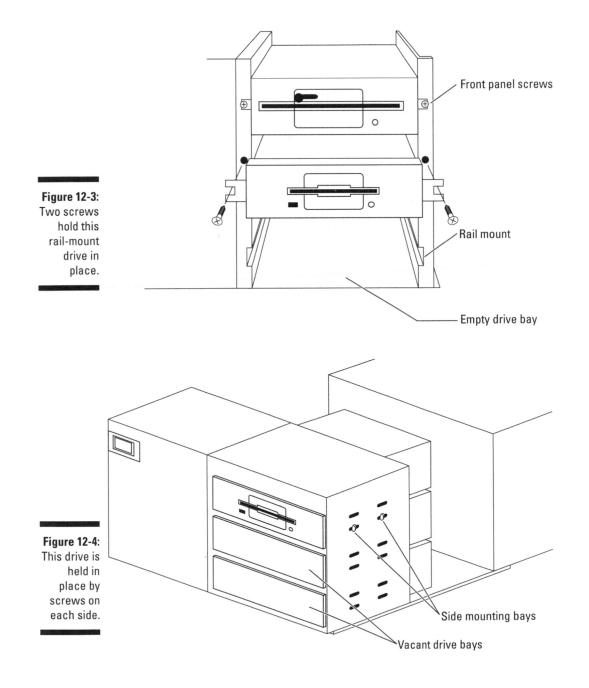

Figure 12-3:
Two screws
hold this
rail-mount
drive in
place.

Front panel screws

Rail mount

Empty drive bay

Figure 12-4:
This drive is
held in
place by
screws on
each side.

Side mounting bays

Vacant drive bays

6. Attach the two cables to the drive.

Sometimes it's easier to attach the cables if you slide the drive back out a little bit first.

Ribbon cable: The plug on the *end* of the ribbon cable attaches to drive A; the plug in the ribbon cable's *middle* goes to drive B, as in Figure 12-5. A little barrier inside the ribbon cable usually makes sure that it can only plug in one way: the right way.

Sometimes the ribbon cable can fit either way. Horrors! Look closely for little numbers printed near the connecting tab on the drive. One edge of the tab has low numbers; the other side has larger numbers in the 30s. The colored edge of the ribbon connector always faces toward the low numbers. It should look like the one shown in Figure 12-6.

The connector on some 3$^{1}/_{2}$-inch drives doesn't look like the one in Figure 12-6. Instead, it has a bunch of little pins, like the one shown in Figure 12-7. You may have to head back to the computer store for an adapter if one wasn't included in the drive's box.

Power supply: The power supply cable only fits into the drive's socket one way. Even so, check carefully to make sure that you're not forcing the two together the wrong way.

If you're adding a second drive, look at all the cables coming out of the power supply and grab one that's not being used. All used up? Then head back to the store and ask for a *Y adapter* for your power supply's drive cable.

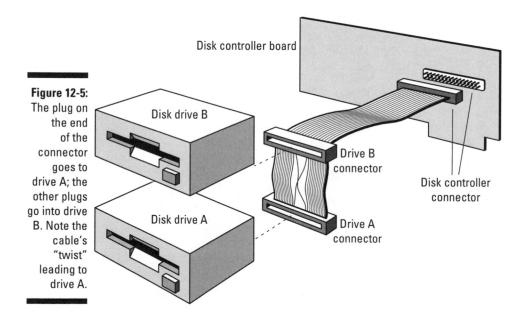

Figure 12-5: The plug on the end of the connector goes to drive A; the other plugs go into drive B. Note the cable's "twist" leading to drive A.

Disk controller board

Disk drive B

Disk drive A

Drive B connector

Drive A connector

Disk controller connector

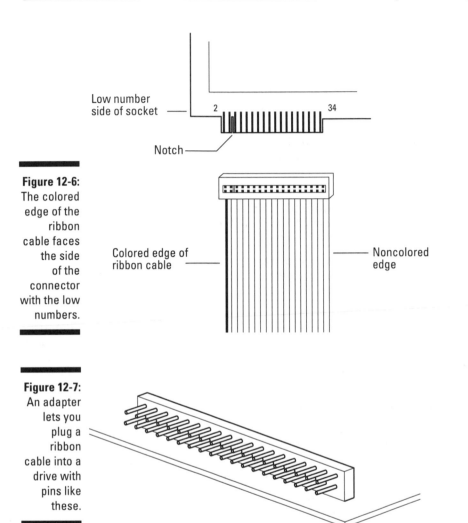

Low number side of socket

2   34

Notch

Figure 12-6: The colored edge of the ribbon cable faces the side of the connector with the low numbers.

Colored edge of ribbon cable

Noncolored edge

Figure 12-7: An adapter lets you plug a ribbon cable into a drive with pins like these.

7. Screw the new drive in place.

If the drive's inserted right, its holes line up with the holes in the computer's case. Got it? Then put the screws back in the right holes. You may need to slide the drive a little farther in or out until the holes line up.

Make sure that you use a screw of the right length to keep from damaging the disk drive.

8. Test the drive.

Plug in your computer, turn it on, put a disk in the drive, and see whether the drive works. Okay? Then turn if off, unplug it, and replace the cover. You're done!

However, if the drive doesn't work, turn off the computer, unplug it, and try a couple of things before pounding the walls. First, are the cables lined up right? Plugged in firmly?

Check the connection where the ribbon cable plugs into the controller card or the motherboard. Sometimes all that jiggling around can pull it loose.

If you did anything more than simply replacing a dead drive, you probably need to tell your computer about your accomplishment. Computers aren't smart enough to figure out what kind of drive you installed. Here's what you do:

XT: If you added a drive to an ancient PC or XT, you'd better pull out your computer's manual. You probably need to flip a switch or change a jumper on the motherboard. (That's covered in Chapter 18.)

AT, 286, 386, 486, and Pentiums: For these computers, you probably need to change your computer's CMOS or setup screen. (That's covered in Chapter 18, too.)

If you're installing one of those new combo drives (the ones with a 5$^{1}/_{4}$-inch drive and a 3$^{1}/_{2}$-inch drive in one little unit), you need to fiddle with the drive's jumpers. That's how the computer knows which one will be drive A and which will be drive B. The drive's manual should explain which way to jump.

Twisted cable tales

Some floppies don't get along with their ribbon cables. It boils down to whether or not the ribbon cable has a little twist near its end. Some do and some don't. You need to set the drive's *DS switches* accordingly.

Where are those DS switches? They're little switches or jumpers on the side of the floppy drive, as illustrated in the accompanying figure. The drive's manual can tell you what to start flipping.

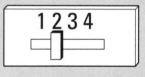

✔ If your ribbon cable has a *twist* in its middle, like the one in Figure 12-5, set both your drives' switches to *DS2*. (Most likely, they already came set that way.)

✔ If there's *no* twist in the ribbon cable, set drive A to DS1 and drive B to DS2. (If your switches start at DS0, then set drive A to DS0 and drive B to DS1. Hey, I didn't design this stuff....)

✔ If your drives already work fine, ignore all this stuff. Finally, for the lowdown on jumper flippin', head for Chapter 18.

Chapter 13

Hard Drives, CD-ROM Drives, Zip Drives, and Tape Backup Drives

● ●

In This Chapter

▶ Defragmenting a hard drive

▶ Fixing disk errors

▶ Understanding types of hard drives

▶ Installing a new hard drive

▶ Installing a CD-ROM drive

▶ Exploring backup drives

▶ Installing a tape backup drive

▶ Installing a Zip drive

● ●

*N*early every computer on the market comes with a hard drive buried deep in its bowels. In fact, you can't run Windows without one. If your computer doesn't have a hard drive, you may find some Paleozoic termites buried in its internal fossil resins — it's that old.

Even if your computer has a hard drive, however, it probably still has a problem: Hard drives are rarely big enough. Luckily, you easily can replace your hard drive with a larger model, provided your wallet's large enough to cope.

This chapter shows how to install a hard drive or fix your old one before it gives up the ghost completely. Plus, it shows how to make backup copies of your old hard drive, either by installing tape backup units or the trendy new Iomega Zip drive.

Finally, this chapter shows you how to install or replace your CD-ROM drive. (Even if your new computer came with a CD-ROM drive, it's probably a real crawler compared to the snappy models on the market today.)

Does My Hard Drive Need to be Defragmented?

When your computer first copies a bunch of files onto the hard drive, it pours them onto the disk in one long strip. When you delete some of those files, the computer runs over and clears off the spots where those files lived.

That leaves holes in what used to be a long strip. When you start adding new files, the computer starts filling up the holes. If a file's too big to fit in one hole, the computer breaks the file up, sticking bits and pieces wherever it can find room.

After a while, a single file can have its parts spread out all over your hard drive. Your computer still can find everything, but it takes more time because the hard drive has to move around a lot more to grab all the parts.

To stop this *fragmentation*, a concerned computer nerd released a defragmentation program. The program picks up all the information on your hard drive and pours it all back down in one long strip, putting all the file's parts next to each other.

Windows 95 users can defragment a disk drive — either a hard drive or a floppy drive — by following these steps:

1. **Right-click your slow drive and choose Properties, as shown in Figure 13-1.**

   Right-click the drive from either My Computer or Windows Explorer.

2. **Choose Tools from the menu.**

   Windows 95 tells you how much space you have left on your drive. If your hard drive still runs slowly even after you defragment it, the drive may be too full. Better consider buying a larger hard disk.

3. **Click the Defragment Now button.**

   Windows 95 peeks at your drive and lets you know whether your disk is defragmented. Follow the program's on-screen advice; unless you use your computer constantly, you probably won't have to defragment your drive very often.

   Some people tell their computers to defragment their drives during the evening or lunch hour when they're not working on them. Windows 95 can defragment a drive in the background while you're working, but it often slows things down.

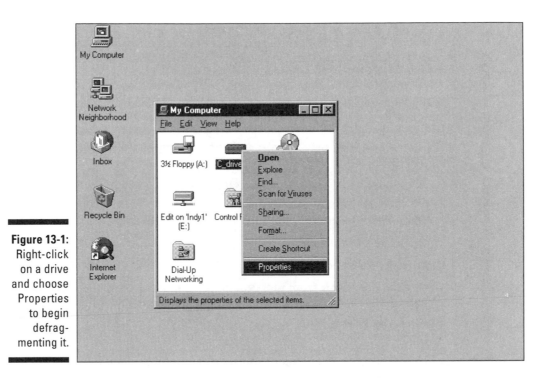

Figure 13-1:
Right-click
on a drive
and choose
Properties
to begin
defrag-
menting it.

Still using an earlier version of Windows or DOS? DOS 6 comes with a
built-in defragmentation program. From DOS, type **DEFRAG** at the
command line, and the program recommends how your disk should be
optimized. Press Enter, and the program starts raking your fragmented
data back into one big pile again. Users of older versions of DOS have to
pick up a defragmentation program at the software store.

Compact discs don't have a defragmentation problem because computers only *read* information from them. Because they're not constantly
erasing and adding new information to the discs, the information on the
discs is never broken into pieces.

Defragmenting a drive can take several minutes, especially if you
haven't done it for a while. In fact, on some slow drives, the process
may take up to an hour. The more often you defragment a drive,
however, the less time it takes.

How Can I Check for Disk Errors?

Ever lost your train of thought after somebody snuck up and tapped you on
the shoulder? The same thing can happen to your computer.

If the power goes out or a program crashes while a computer's working, the computer loses its train of thought. Your computer forgets to write down where it put stuff on the hard drive. (That's why you should always close your programs before turning off your computer.)

These lost trains of thought result in "disk errors," and Windows 95 fixes them pretty easily when you follow these instructions.

1. **Right-click your drive's icon and choose Properties, as shown earlier in Figure 13-1.**

   Right-click the drive's icon from either My Computer or Windows Explorer.

2. **Choose the Tools from the top of the Properties page.**

3. **Click the Check Now button.**

   A new window pops up, full of options.

4. **Choose Thorough from the Type of test box, and click the Automatically fix errors box to put a check mark inside it.**

5. **Click the Start button.**

   Windows 95 examines your disk drive, looking for suspicious areas and fixing the ones it can. A large hard drive can take a long time; floppy drives don't take nearly as long.

   When Windows 95 finishes the process, the proud little program leaves a window on the screen summing up the number of errors it found and fixed.

If you're using an older version of Windows or DOS, exit Windows and type the following command at DOS:

```
C:\> CHKDSK /F
```

That is, type **CHKDSK**, a space, a forward slash, and then press F. Your computer responds with some computer words too bizarre to mention here. But if the program asks you, Convert lost chains to files (Y/N)?, press Y.

Depending on the way your drive's error-patching program is set up, your computer gathers any unused file scraps and stores them in files like FILE000.CHK, FILE001.CHK, FILE002.CHK — you get the point. Feel free to delete those files. They contain nothing worthwhile, as you quickly discover if you try to open them with your word processor.

What's a Controller Card?

A *controller card* plugs into one of the slots inside your computer. Long flat cables run from the controller card over to your disk drives, as illustrated in Figure 13-2.

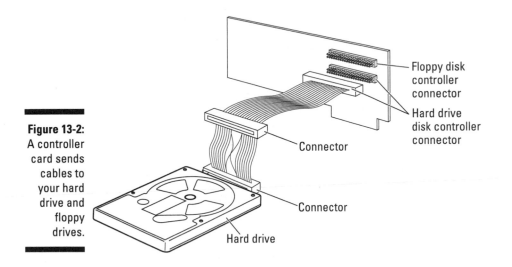

Floppy disk controller connector

Hard drive disk controller connector

Connector

Connector

Hard drive

Figure 13-2: A controller card sends cables to your hard drive and floppy drives.

When your computer wants some information, it tells the controller card. The controller card grabs the right information from the drive through the cable and shoots it back to the computer.

WELL-WORN

- In the big, bulky days of yesteryear computing, controller cards were big, bulky things with lots of circuitry and expensive little chip things. Then engineers began creating IDE drives: speedier drives with most of the circuitry hot-wired right into the disk drives themselves. IDE drives skip the controller card, and their cables plug right into special sockets on the motherboard.

- Most of the hard drives sold today are *EIDE drives.* Short for *Enhanced Integrated Drive Electronics,* they're just like IDE drives, but they can handle more than 1GB of information.

- If your current hard drive plugs straight into your motherboard, your floppy drives probably do the same thing. They usually plug in near the power supply — in the back right corner of your computer. (That's the same location where the tuba players sit in an orchestra pit.)

✔ If your older motherboard *doesn't* have those special IDE or EIDE sockets, buy an IDE or EIDE controller card. They're cheap little things that plug into a slot and gives you a place to plug in the drive's cables. (EIDE controller cards cost about $10 more than IDE controller cards.)

Should I Buy an ST506, a SCSI, an ESDI, an IDE, or an EIDE Drive?

Today, everybody wants to upgrade from their old-technology drives. Not only are the older drives dying fast, but they have ugly, old-technology names like *ST506* and *ESDI*. (In an attempt to spice things up, the nerds sometimes refer to the ST506 drives as *MFM* and *RLL* drives, so don't be confused.)

Some rich folks prefer *SCSI* drives because those drives are quick and can hold gobs of data. But if you're installing a new drive today, the choice is pretty clear: Most of the drives on the shelves are the new EIDE drives.

These Enhanced IDE drives are a step up from last year's IDE drives; they don't need fancy controller cards, described in the preceding section. They can also hold a lot more information than an IDE drive. They're the easiest drives to install, too. Good news!

If you're replacing your old-technology hard drive with a big new EIDE drive, you need to replace your old controller card also. Luckily, a controller card for an EIDE drive only costs around $30.

IDE and EIDE drives turn up their noses at older-technology drives. If you want to add an IDE or EIDE drive as a second hard drive, your *first* hard drive must be the same type. If you've been using an older-style ST506 drive, you have to ditch it.

✔ If you're using older-style drives, don't feel too bad about ditching them for IDE or EIDE drives. IDE and EIDE drives are faster and more reliable than the older ones. Plus, most newer computers come with special sockets designed specifically for EIDE or IDE drives.

✔ If you're adding a second EIDE drive to a new computer, you probably won't need to buy a new controller card at all.

✔ Some folks are excited about SCSI-style hard drives. Theoretically, you can plug a SCSI card into your computer and "chain" up to seven other computer toys, including hard drives, CD-ROM drives, scanners, and tape backup drives. Unfortunately, SCSI drives are harder to set up, more expensive, and prone to conflicting standards. Want more technical information? Visit the more technical sidebar box called *"The raging SCSI versus EIDE debate."*

    ✔ Dunno what all those other hard drive words mean? Check out Table
      13-1.

Table 13-1	What Do All Those Hard Drive Words Mean?	
This Word	*Means This*	*So Look for This*
Capacity	The amount of data it can store.	The more megabytes (MB), the better. If you use Windows 95, you want at least 500MB. Buy the biggest drive you can afford. In fact, nobody will laugh if you get a 1GB drive — it can hold twice as much information as a 500MB drive.
Access or Seek time	How long it takes your drive to locate stored files, measured in milliseconds (ms).	The smaller the number, the better. You want speed, and 15 ms is considered pretty speedy. CD-ROM drives are considerably slower. The slow ones are called *2X*, while the fastest ones are *8X* or even *12X*.
Data transfer rate	How fast your computer can grab information from from files after it finds them.	The higher the number, the better. Don't place *too* much stock in it, though; it has become a meaningless statistic bandied about by vendors.
MTBF	Mean Time Between Failures	The higher, the better. This is the number of hours the drive should last. For example, an MTBF of 30,000 means the drive will last about 3½ years of continuous spinning. (That's about 10 years of 8-hour days.)
Cache	The ability to remember frequently accessed information.	The bigger, the better. Because memory chips are faster than hard drives, these chips remember frequently acquired pieces of information. If the computer needs the information again, it can grab it from the cache, saving some time.

My CD-ROM Drive Doesn't Work When I Leave Windows 95!

Because its an evolutionary era, where the old world of DOS is transforming
into the new world of Windows, some things remain in transition.

What's DVD?

Short for *Digital Video Disc,* DVD is a new type of CD technology that holds seven times as much data as a normal CD. Unfortunately, DVD has been slow to catch on: Few companies are making DVD CDs or the special drives that can run them.

Some companies have jumped onto the bandwagon, piling nationwide phone number directories onto the discs; others are making huge multimedia programs and elaborate games. But for the most part, industry players are eyeing each other to see whether this expensive new technology will take off before it's replaced with something even newer and more exciting.

See, Windows 95 can automatically recognize most CD-ROM drives on sight. DOS, by contrast, needs a special piece of software called a *driver* that tells it the drive's there and translates all the talking back and forth.

To avoid using up precious memory, Windows 95 doesn't bother loading the driver. After all, it doesn't need it. But that means that when you move to DOS — either by using the Restart the Computer in MS-DOS mode command or by running a DOS program — the driver won't always be there to tell the computer about the CD-ROM.

The solution? You need to locate the CD-ROM's driver and put it in your computer's AUTOEXEC.BAT and CONFIG.SYS file. Usually a CD-ROM drive's installation program can do this automatically. But if it's giving you problems, head for Chapter 16.

How Do I Get the Drive Lights to Turn On and Off?

If your hard drive's light comes on when you use the drive but never turns off, check out Step 6 of the installation section, coming up in the "How Do I Install or Replace an EIDE or IDE Hard Drive?" section. Somebody may have fastened the flat ribbon cable connector upside down when pushing it onto the disk drive.

Also, some disk drives mount inside your computer where they're never seen. That means you can't see the light regardless of whether it's on or off.

The raging SCSI versus EIDE debate

The two most popular types of hard drives today are SCSI and EIDE, and the price difference between the two is narrowing. The drives use different controllers — the electronics that control how the data flows. So, which is better, SCSI or EIDE? Like anything else, the answer depends on how you want to use your computer.

EIDE drives are easier to set up than SCSI drives, and their EIDE controllers are cheaper than SCSI controllers — in fact, most new computers let you plug an EIDE drive directly into the motherboard. You won't even have to buy a controller.

SCSI controllers, however, let you "chain" a group of devices together. First, you plug a SCSI controller card into a slot on your computer. Then you can link several SCSI devices to the card using a chain of cables. For example, one controller card can handle a hard drive, a tape backup drive, and a CD-ROM drive. You only need one slot to control all those devices. And, because the SCSI standard handles all the internal mechanics, those devices won't use up as many IRQs and DMAs (covered in Chapter 18) as they would have had they been plugged into their own individual slots.

Like external modems, you can usually move SCSI devices around to different computers without a problem: A SCSI hard drive or CD-ROM drive works on either a Macintosh or a PC.

If you have the money and want to expand your PC with several new peripherals, look into the current SCSI standard, known as SCSI2. Some of the best sound cards come with SCSI controllers built in so you can connect a CD-ROM drive; check to see if the sound card's SCSI controller can handle other SCSI devices, as well. It may be just what you need to slip in that tape backup unit that you've been thinking about.

But if you're thinking of just adding a single component — a larger or additional hard drive, for example — then SCSI may be an unnecessary expense.

If the hard drive light on the front of your computer never comes on, you need to push the light's little wires onto a *jumper* that lives on your hard drive or controller card. (I discuss jumper pushing in Chapter 18.)

Some hard drives even have a little jumper that lets you choose one of two options: You can keep the little light on all the time, or you can have it turn on when the hard drive's actually fetching data. (Traditionalists stick with the fetching data option.)

How Do I Backup My Hard Drive?

Nothing lasts forever, not even that trusty old hard drive. That's why it's important to keep a copy — a backup version — of your hard drive for safekeeping. Table 13-2 shows some of the most popular ways and their pros and cons.

Table 13-2	Ways to Backup a Hard Drive	
Method	*Pros*	*Cons*
Backup Program and Floppy Disks	Cheap	If you have a small hard drive, you can get away with a backup program and bunch of floppy disks. The program copies the disk onto floppies for safekeeping. The size of today's large hard drives makes this impractical, though.
Backup Program and Tape Drive	Relatively in-expensive, slow	Although easy to install, these are slow and losing popularity.
Removable-cartridge disk drive, like Iomega's Zip drive	Relatively in-expensive, fast, and portable	The current winner. These work just like floppy disks that hold a lot of information.
Read/Write CD-ROM drives	Expensive	These CD-ROM drives let you write information to discs. They're too expensive for most needs, however, although the price is dropping quickly.
Optical drives	Expensive	These write information to special discs, like Read/Write CD-ROM drives. They're too expensive for consumers, however, and are usually used in business settings.

How Do I Install or Replace an EIDE or IDE Hard Drive?

IQ level: 100

Tools you need: One hand, a screwdriver, and a system disk

Cost: Roughly $200 – $400; high-capacity ones can cost $1,000 or more

Stuff to watch out for:

If you're replacing your current hard drive, make sure that you have a system disk on hand. Don't have one nearby? Race back to Chapter 2 for instructions. You need some of the programs on that disk.

EIDE drives don't work with the older-style ST506 (MFM or RLL) drives. If you have one of those, pull it out and try to sell it. That old drive was probably going to die soon, anyway.

If your computer used an older-style ST506 (MFM or RLL) drive, you need to buy a new controller card to go with your new EIDE or IDE drive. (Those two drives use different types of controllers, too.)

If you're adding a *second* IDE or EIDE drive to accompany your first IDE or EIDE drive, you have to tell your computer which drive you want to be drive C. (Drive C is the one the computer looks at first and boots from.) That drive's the *master,* and the second is the *slave.* You need to move a little jumper on the second drive to make that drive work as the slave (see Figure 13-3).

Figure 13-3:
This hard drive has a power supply connector, a ribbon cable connector, and a master/ slave jumper.

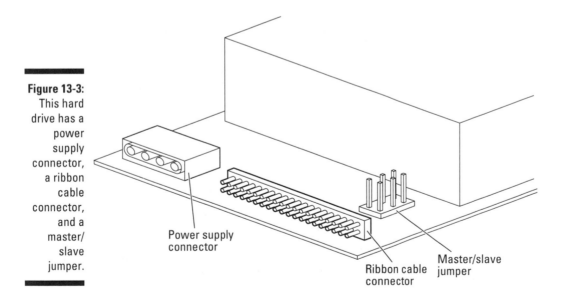

Power supply connector

Ribbon cable connector

Master/slave jumper

Some hard drives also ask you to move a jumper depending on whether you're using one hard drive or two. Others automatically set themselves up for one hard drive if they're set up as the master. You may have to check the drive's manual on this one.

XT computers can't handle two IDE drives. The newer computers can't handle more than two IDE drives, or things start getting *really* complicated; you may find yourself in a mess involving IRQ14 monitoring, or other scary, high-tech terms.

You may need rails to mount your hard drive inside your computer. Some drives come with mounting rails; others don't. If you're replacing an old drive, you can often unscrew its old rails and swipe them. Otherwise, you may need to head back to the store buy some. (They're usually pretty cheap.)

If you're adding a hard drive to a PC that's never had one — or adding a second hard drive to a PC — you may need a new power supply. Your PC's going to draw a little more power now. Chapter 14 puts power supplies into perspective.

The following steps show you how to install an EIDE or IDE hard drive.

1. **Back up your hard drive, turn off the computer, unplug it, and remove the case.**

   Be sure to backup your hard drive before playing with it. You don't want to lose any of your data. You can find instructions for removing the computer's cover in the Cheat Sheet at the front of this book.

2. **Remove cables from the old drive.**

   Hard drives have two or three cables plugged into them.

   Ribbon cable: The ribbon cable leads from the hard drive to its controller card. Older-style drives have *two* ribbon cables going to the controller card. Either way, ribbon cables pull straight off the drive pretty easily.

   Power cable: The other cable is made of four wires that head for the power supply. Power cables come in two sizes, as shown in Figure 13-4. Like the ribbon cable, the power cable pulls straight off the drive's socket; it usually takes a *lot* more pulling, though. Don't pull on the wires themselves; pull on the cable's plastic connector. Sometimes a gentle back-and-forth jiggle can loosen it.

   Adding a second IDE drive: If you're adding a second IDE drive, check out the flat ribbon cable connected to the first drive. Do you see a second, vacant plug on it, like the one shown in Figure 13-2? If not, head back to the store for a new ribbon cable. It needs to have *two* connectors. (Most already do, luckily.) You second-drive installers can jump ahead to Step 5.

3. **Remove the mounting screws holding the drive in place.**

   Some drives are held in place by two screws in front. Other drives are held in place by screws in their sides. The screws on one side may be hidden from view by a particularly long card, or even another drive,

Figure 13-4:
Your hard
drive uses
one of
these two
sizes for the
power
cable.

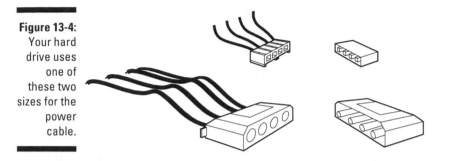

mounted on its side. That means you have to pull out the card or remove the obstructing drive just to get at the screws!

4. Slide the old drive out the computer's front.

After you remove the old drive's cables and screws, you can slide the old drive out of the front of the computer. Give it a gentle tug.

Drives that mount on their sides slide out toward the computer's center; be sure not to gouge your motherboard while pulling out the drive.

Replacing a controller card: Are you pulling out your old-style drive to replace it with an EIDE or IDE drive? Then pull out your old controller card as well. You can see a picture of one in Figure 13-2. Look for the card where all the ribbon cables end up. Found it? Pull all the ribbon cables off, including the ones heading for your floppy drives.

See that tiny screw holding the controller card in place? Remove the screw and pull the card straight up out of its slot. (For more card details, head for Chapter 15.)

5. Slide the new drive in where the old one came out.

Your new EIDE or IDE drive should slide in place right where the old one came out. Doesn't fit? If the new drive's smaller than the old one, you need to add rails or mounting brackets to make it fit.

When handling drives, be careful not to damage their exposed circuitry by bumping it into other parts of your computer. Also, be sure to touch your computer's metal case to get rid of any static electricity before picking up your drive.

Adding a second IDE drive? Slide it into a vacant bay, which usually is next to the first drive. Check your computer's manual; you may be able to mount the drive on its side in a special spot inside your computer.

6. Add the new controller card if necessary.

Are you replacing an older-style drive with an EIDE or IDE drive? Then you need a new controller card to go with it.

Handling the card by its edges, push it down into the slot where the old controller card sat. Then fasten it down with the screw. (You can find more card installation tips in Chapter 15.) Check the controller's manual; you need to push ribbon cables onto the controller's connectors for your floppy disks and hard disk.

7. **Attach two cables to the hard drive.**

   Try sliding the drive out a little bit to connect the two cables more easily.

   Ribbon cable: The plug on the ribbon cable should push onto little pins on the end of the drive. The other end of the cable goes either to the controller card or to a socket on the motherboard.

   If you're installing a second hard drive, the ribbon cable should have a spare connector on it. (If not, head back to the store.) It doesn't matter which connector goes onto which drive; the computer looks at the drives' master/slave jumpers to figure out which one's drive C.

   Power supply: The power supply cable only fits into the drive's socket one way. Even so, check the ends to make sure that you're not forcing it in the wrong way. Check out Figure 13-4 to make sure that you've found the right power cable socket.

   Power supply cables come with both large and small connectors. The connectors are supposed to fit only one way, but the small ones often fit either way. The trick? Look for the number 1 somewhere near the drive's little socket. The power supply connector's red wire fastens onto the number 1 prong.

   Adding a second IDE drive: If this is your second drive, look for its master/slave jumper. Make this second drive the slave drive. You can see the jumpers in Figure 13-3. The drive's manual tells you where to put the jumper. (Chapter 18 tells you how to set those jumpers.)

   Note that some hard drives also ask you to move a jumper depending on whether you're using one hard drive or two. Others automatically set themselves up for one hard drive if they're set up as the master. You may have to check the drive's manual on this one.

   IDE and EIDE drives usually come configured as master drives. If you're installing just a single IDE or EIDE drive in your computer, you usually don't need to mess with any of the jumpers.

8. **Replace the screws.**

   Cables attached? Master/slave jumper set? Then fasten the drive in place with those little screws. Make sure that they are short screws to prevent damage to the inside of the hard drive.

9. **Replace the cover, plug in the computer, and turn it on.**

   Chances are, your hard drive won't work right off the bat. Hard drives must be prepared before they start to work, unfortunately. Take a deep breath before heading for the next step. Exhale. Now move on.

10. Configure CMOS for the new drive.

Here's where things get the most complicated. Your computer needs to know some arcane details about the drive you've just installed.

Your absolute best bet is to buy a hard drive setup program like EZ-Drive from MicroHouse (to order, call 303-443-3388). This program introduces your new hard drive to your computer and has the drive shaking hands with DOS in less than 60 seconds. (In fact, EZ-Drive comes bundled with some new hard drives, making them easy to install.)

If you bought a used hard drive from a friend, it may boot right up, in which case you won't have to fiddle with this stuff. If you have a new hard drive, though, holler for a computer guru friend, hand your guru the following section, and tell him or her to break in your new hard drive. No guru around? Then you may have to brave it yourself. You won't break anything; the drive just won't work until it's set up right.

Breaking in a New Hard Drive

Here are the last few hoops you need to jump through before your computer starts speaking to its new hard drive:

1. Set the CMOS.

Your CMOS, which I describe in Chapter 18, is where your computer keeps track of the equipment connected to it. It needs to know what kind of hard drive you installed before you can use it. EIDE and IDE drives deal with the CMOS in three possible ways:

- Some drives check the CMOS to see what hard drive your computer expects to find and then automatically mimic that drive. Blissfully simple! Move on to Step 2.

- Other EIDE and IDE drives let you pick *any* hard drive that's listed in your computer's CMOS table. So just choose any drive that's the same capacity (in megabytes) as your EIDE or IDE drive, and all will be fine. A bit bothersome, but still workable. Head for Step 2.

- The pickiest IDE and EIDE drives make you look for information buried in their manuals. Specifically, you need to look for the drive's recommended *cylinders, heads,* and *sectors.* Then you need to plug those numbers into your CMOS' *user-defined* area. Yeah, it's a little complicated. But if you're lucky, the first two options work. If you're unlucky, head for Chapter 18.

Some older computers need to have a BIOS upgrade before they can work with the large EIDE drives. You can plug these new BIOS chips into your motherboard (Chapter 10) or upgrade them by simply running a program.

2. Partition the drive.

Partitioning a drive completely wipes out any information stored on it.

When you're through setting the CMOS, you need to *partition* your new drive. Windows 95 users get lucky: Many new EIDE drives come with a Disc Wizard that easily handles all chores of setting up and partitioning your new hard drive.

Not using Windows 95? Then the simplest method is to make one big DOS partition. Type **FDISK** at the DOS prompt; that brings the partition program to the screen.

If you replaced your old drive, tell FDISK to make a *Primary DOS Partition.* To do that, press Enter twice and then press Y.

If you added a second drive to be a slave to your first, you see a new option, `Change Current Fixed Disk Drive`. Pick that option to switch to your second drive; then create a *Logical DOS Partition* to make that drive your drive D.

When you exit FDISK, it reboots your computer. If you just installed a single hard drive, better put a system disk in drive A so your computer will start up.

3. Format the drive.

The Disc Wizard or EZ-Drive installation programs bundled with most new EIDE drives automatically handles this as part of the installation process.

Formatting a disk completely wipes out any information stored on it.

Never try to low-level format an IDE drive, no matter what anyone tells you.

DOS users need to *format* the new drive after it is partitioned. If your computer only has one hard disk, insert your system disk and press the computer's reset button. Then type the following at the A:\> prompt of your system disk:

```
A:\> FORMAT C: /S
```

If you installed a second drive and partitioned it to be drive D, format it by entering this command:

```
A:\> FORMAT D:
```

Done? Then remove the system disk from drive A and reboot your computer, and everything should work fine.

If it doesn't work, start by double-checking all your cables. On tight? Upside down? In the right place? Is the drive partitioned right? Formatted correctly? If you installed a second disk drive, twice as many things could have gone wrong.

If your two IDE drives just won't work right, try switching the master/slave relationship. Sometimes IDE drives from different manufacturers just don't like to work with each other, no matter who's in charge. You may have to exchange one IDE drive for one that's the same brand as the other.

If you have to turn your computer on several times in the morning before the hard drive starts working, you may need a new power supply. The power supply may not provide enough power to bring the drive up to speed quickly enough. You can find power supplies dissected in Chapter 14. (Or, if your drive is old, it may simply be worn out.)

How Do I Install a CD-ROM Drive?

IQ level: 90

Tools you need: One hand and a screwdriver

Cost: Anywhere from $50 – $500

Stuff to watch out for:

Compact disc players (CD-ROM drives) come in two types, *internal* and *external.* The external ones are little boxes that take up room on your desk. The internal ones slide into the front of your computer like a floppy disk. They may also be IDE or SCSI.

Both kinds come with a card that plugs into one of your computer's slots, although some new IDE CD-ROM drives plug straight into the motherboard. Better pop the cover and make sure that you have an empty slot before doing anything else.

A new breed of CD-ROM drive lets you write information to a disc as well as read information from its drive. They currently cost about three times as much as a regular CD-ROM drive, but the price is constantly dropping. They're installed in the same way as a normal CD-ROM drive.

Installing an external CD-ROM drive

1. **Turn off your computer, unplug it, and remove its case.**

   You can find complete instructions in the Cheat Sheet at the front of this book.

2. **Plug the CD-ROM drive's card into one of your available slots and screw it down.**

   Chapter 15 describes cards and how to stick them in the right place.

3. **Replace your computer's cover and plug in your PC.**

4. **Plug the CD-ROM drive's cable into the card.**

   You can find a thick cord in the box with the CD-ROM drive. One side of the cord plugs into the connector now peeking from the back of your PC; the other end fits into the back of the CD-ROM drive.

5. **Plug in the CD-ROM drive and turn it on.**

   External CD-ROM drives have a power cord that needs to be plugged into the wall.

   Don't have enough power outlets? Head back to the computer store and buy a power strip. These gadgets let you plug in six or more accessories into one outlet.

6. **Turn on your computer.**

   When Windows 95 boots up, it may recognize the new CD-ROM drive off the bat and automatically install it for you. If not — or if you aren't using Windows 95 — move to Step 7.

7. **Install the CD-ROM's software.**

   If you're not using Windows 95, put the CD-ROM's installation disk in drive A and type **INSTALL** or **SETUP**, depending on what your manual says.

   Chances are, the program sticks a *device driver* into your computer's CONFIG.SYS file and then reboots your computer. That driver stuff's hammered down in Chapter 16.

   For a few extra tips and tricks, head to the end of the "Installing an internal CD-ROM drive" section.

Installing an internal CD-ROM drive

1. **Turn off your computer, unplug it, and remove its case.**

   You can find complete instructions in the Cheat Sheet at the front of this book.

2. **Plug the CD-ROM drive's card into one of your available slots and screw it down.**

   Cards — and how to install them — are described in Chapter 15.

3. **Slide the CD-ROM drive into the front of your computer.**

   You need a vacant drive bay, which is an opening where your disk drives normally live. The drive should slide in the front. For tips, check out Chapter 12. The CD-ROM drive slides in the same way as a floppy drive.

Don't have an empty drive bay for your CD-ROM drive? Buy a Combo Drive from Teac. It squeezes both a 3¹/₂-inch floppy drive and a 5¹/₄-inch floppy drive into one small unit that fits in a single drive bay. That immediately frees up enough room for an internal CD-ROM drive.

4. Connect the cables.

First, connect the cable between the CD-ROM drive and the card you installed in Step 2. It should only fit one way.

Next, rummage around the tentacles of wires leading from your power supply until you find a spare power connector. That plugs into your CD-ROM drive. Those drives usually use the small-sized connector shown back in Figure 13-4.

5. Screw the drive in place.

Although some drives screw in from the sides, most fasten with two screws along the front.

6. Replace your computer's cover, plug the computer in, and turn it on.

When Windows 95 boots up, it may recognize the new CD-ROM drive and automatically install it for you. If not — or if you aren't using Windows 95, move to Step 7.

7. Run the CD-ROM drive software.

The software should take over the rest of the installation chores. If it tosses bits of weirdness, like *interrupts* or *drivers,* page on ahead to Chapters 16 and 18.

CD-ROM drives almost always use SCSI ports and cards. If you already have a SCSI card in your computer, things can get either better or worse. Here's why:

The Good News: SCSI ports can chain a handful of other SCSI devices. That means that you can hook your CD-ROM drive into your chain. For example, if your sound card comes with a SCSI port, you don't need the CD-ROM drive's card. Just plug the CD-ROM drive's cable into the sound card's SCSI port, saving time and, more importantly, a slot.

The Bad News: Different brands of SCSI ports aren't always compatible with each other. Sometimes they work; sometimes they don't. Before investing in SCSI devices, call the manufacturers to be sure the devices can all get along.

How Do I Install a Tape Backup Unit?

IQ level: 90

Tools you need: One hand and a screwdriver

Cost: Anywhere from $200 – $800

Stuff to watch out for:

The easiest tape backup units live in little boxes. You just plug a cable between the box and your parallel port. That's it! Just pop its installation floppy in your disk drive and you're through.

An internal backup unit is a little rougher to install, but not much. Just follow these steps:

1. **Turn off your computer, unplug it, and remove its cover.**

   The Cheat Sheet at the front of this book covers this step.

2. **Push the unit into a drive bay.**

   You need a free drive bay — one of those spots into which you can slide floppy disk drives. If you don't have one, you can remove drive B to make room. Be sure to tell your computer's CMOS that it doesn't have a drive B anymore, however. I explain the cautious task of informing your CMOS in Chapter 18.

3. **Fasten the unit down.**

   If the unit has rails on the sides, fasten it in place with two screws along the front. If it doesn't use rails, put two screws in each of its sides.

4. **Attach the cables.**

   Power cable: Find a spare power cable hanging out of your power supply. Don't have one? Head to the store for a Y adapter.

   Ribbon cable: The drive comes with its own ribbon cable. Unplug your floppy drive's old ribbon cable from your controller card and plug in the new backup unit's cable.

   See the extra connector on the backup unit's ribbon cable, about an inch away from where it's plugged into the card? Plug your floppy drive's cable into that new little connector. Then plug the end of the backup unit's new ribbon cable into the backup drive.

   The cables fit only one way, but look at the ribbon's colored edge: That's the side that plugs into Pin 1.

5. **Replace the computer's cover, plug in the computer, and turn it on.**

   That should do the trick. Now you have to run the tape backup unit's installation software.

Whew. No more feeding 40 backup disks to the computer every week. Don't you wish you bought this a year ago when you first bought your computer?

If any of these steps leave you scratching your head, flip to Chapter 12. You install tape backup drives almost exactly like floppy drives.

So What's a Zip Drive Anyway?

Iomega and Epson both make *Zip drives* that work like floppy disks — but hold up to 100MB of information. The large memory capacity makes Zips handy for backing up hard drives, storing enormous multimedia files, or keeping clandestine data away from prying eyes. You can also use Zip disks to transport files from work to home and back to work again.

Zip drives are external drives that plug into a parallel port or SCSI drive (see the next section for all the installation information), but some new computers now come with Zip drives already installed. Iomega is also developing a smaller model for use with laptops.

Iomega also makes Jaz drives, which look similar to Zips, but can hold up to 1GB of stuff, and Ditto drives, which can hold up to 2GB.

How Do I Install a Zip drive?

IQ level: 90

Tools you need: One hand and a screwdriver

Cost: Around $150 – $200

Stuff to watch out for:

Although Windows 95 took its time getting used to these little cartridges, Iomega Zip and Windows 95 seems to have patched up their differences.

Zip drives come in two types: One type simply plugs into your parallel port, and the other requires a SCSI drive. The parallel port model is slower and may be a little cheaper; the SCSI drive model costs more and works faster.

To install a Zip drive from either Iomega or Epson, follow these steps:

1. **Shut down your PC, unplug your printer cable, and identify the connectors on the back of your Zip drive. SCSI-model users move to Step 3.**

   Zip drives come with two connectors. Parallel drives have one 25-pin male connector for the cable that connects to your PC and one 25-pin female connector for your printer's cable to plug into.

   SCSI drives have two identical-looking 25-pin female connectors.

2. **Connect the Zip drive's cable between your computer's printer port and the parallel drive's connector. Go to Step 5.**

3. **Don't already have a SCSI card? Then plug the card in as described in Chapter 15 and connect the drive to the card.**

4. **Already have a card? Connect the cable from the Zip drive to your PC's external SCSI connector. Set the drive's SCSI ID number by flipping its little rotary switch (usually with a small screwdriver.)**

   You may need to tell your SCSI adapter to recognize the new device.

5. **Plug the Zip drive's AC power connector into a wall socket and plug it into the Zip drive.**

6. **Double-check all your connections and turn your computer back on.**

   Some Zip drives have a power switch; most remain on all the time.

7. **Install the Zip drive's installation software.**

   Run the drive's setup software from within Windows 95 or DOS and place a Tools disk in the drive to complete the process.

Chapter 14
Power Supplies

*Y*ou can't see it, but you can sure hear it: Your computer's power supply sits inside one corner of your computer and whirs away.

This chapter covers that restless little beast that sucks up electricity all day long. When the power supply stops grabbing power, this chapter tells you how to grab the power supply and replace it with a new one.

My Computer Makes a Whining Noise

Some power supplies wail like a Volkswagen from the early '60s. Other power supplies purr quietly like a BMW.

The noise comes from the fan inside the power supply that blows air across the power supply's innards. The fan cools off the inside of your computer at the same time.

As for the racket? Well, many power supplies are just noisy little beasts. There's just no getting around the racket.

✔ If your power supply is absolutely *too* noisy, consider replacing it. Today's power supplies are often a little quieter than the rumblers released five or more years ago.

✔ If your power supply doesn't make any noise at all, you're in even *worse* trouble. Hold your hand against the fan hole in the back. If you don't feel any air blowing out, the fan has died. Buy a new power supply —

right away. Your computer can overheat like a car in the desert, and suddenly die without warning.

Don't try taking apart your power supply and quieting down the fan. Power supplies soak up electricity and can zap you, even when they're unplugged. Don't mess around inside a power supply.

Nothing Happens When I Turn On My PC

Nothing? No little lights go on along the front? No purr from the fan whirring merrily? If you're sure that your computer is plugged in, then your power supply probably died during the night.

My Computer Forgets the Date, Even After I Changed the Batteries!

Drinking fountains never work the same way. Some fountains make you bend down really low and press your cheek against the gross, crusty metal part to get any driblets of water. Other fountains squirt up and hit you in the forehead.

Power supplies, however, are specifically designed to provide a steady stream of electricity at just the right voltage. If the power level strays from the norm, even by just a few volts, it can interfere with your computer's lifestyle.

If your power supply is not dependable, replace it. Uh, how can you tell whether your power supply is dependable? The following list should help.

- ✔ If your computer constantly forgets the date and the hard drive type, even after you change the battery, the power supply is a likely suspect. Sometimes, the power supply won't deliver enough power to keep your computer's settings in place. Try a second replacement battery, though — they're cheaper.

- ✔ After you change the power supply (or battery), head for Chapter 18 to restore your computer's settings to the right place. Luckily, XT computers don't have these setting problems. Unfortunately, XTs have enough other problems to keep their owners busy.

Is it your hard drive, or is it your power supply?

Sometimes it's hard to differentiate between a noisy power supply fan and a noisy hard drive. Both have a constantly running motor, so both are susceptible to the burned-out bearing syndrome.

To tell whether the noise is from your power supply or your hard drive, turn off your computer, unplug it, and open the case. Then pull the power supply's cable out from the back of your hard drive. Plug your computer back in and turn it on. Because the hard drive won't be getting power, it won't turn on with the rest of your computer. If you hear a noise, it's your power supply.

If you don't hear a noise, it's your hard drive. Unfortunately, hard drives cost a lot more to replace, as I discuss in Chapter 13.

✔ First, plug a lamp in your power outlet to make sure that the outlet *really* works. You may have a blown circuit breaker. That's a lot cheaper.

✔ A lightning bolt that barrels down your electric line can kill your power supply. The power supply has been designed to sacrifice itself for the good of the whole computer. Chances are that you can replace the power supply, and then everything will return to the pre-lightning state.

✔ Power supplies are pretty easy to replace. Just grab a screwdriver and page ahead to the section "How Do I Install a New Power Supply?"

✔ Your computer's power supply and its battery are two different things. The power supply gives your computer electricity when it's turned *on* so it can accomplish computer-like things. The computer's battery provides electricity when your computer is turned *off* so it can remember what computer-like things have been installed.

✔ Have you had to replace any of your computer's disk drives lately? The power supply may be at fault, producing too much power. Being off just a few volts can burn up your computer's disk drives or make them work erratically.

✔ If you recently added a second hard drive or extra cards to a computer with an older power supply, consider upgrading your power supply. The old one may not be putting out enough watts to support all the extra gadgets. See the "What Kind of Power Supply Should I Buy?" section later in this chapter.

What's a UPS or Backup Power Supply?

When your computer loses its power, *you* lose your work. Everything that you haven't actually saved to a disk just sort of dribbles away.

If the power suddenly fails and the lights go out, your computer will go out, too. To protect against such scariness, some people buy an *uninterrupted power supply,* which is often called a *UPS.*

The UPS is a big box that connects your computer and its power outlet. The big box constantly sucks up power and stores it, like a huge car battery. Then if the power dies, the big box instantly turns itself on and provides uninterrupted power to your computer.

Then the big box provides you with a rewarding feeling of accomplishment for having bought and installed a UPS before the power died.

- The more money you spend on your UPS, the more time you'll be able to work in the dark. Common times range from ten minutes to a half hour.

- For the most part, the UPS isn't designed to keep your computer running all day in the dark. The UPS just keeps your computer going when the power dies, which gives you a few extra minutes to save your work, turn off your computer, and drink a Pepsi until the lights go back on.

- Some uninterrupted power supplies also work as a *line conditioner,* which filters out any nasty voltage spikes or surges that may come through the power lines. A line conditioner can make your computer last longer.

- A UPS isn't cheap; one costs anywhere from $120 to $400. Still, a UPS can be an important investment if you live in an area prone to power outage problems.

What Power Supply Should I Buy?

If you expand your living room by knocking down a wall, you'll need more than a single 100-watt bulb to light everything up. Computers work in a similar way.

Like a light bulb, a computer's power supply is rated in watts. The more gizmos you've plugged into your computer, the more watts you need to feed them.

An XT can survive with a 135-watt power supply, while an AT computer is more reliable with a 200-watt power supply.

If you're using a 386, 486, Pentium or faster computer, make sure that your power supply is rated at 250 watts or more. A sticker on the power supply displays the wattage rating.

✔ Don't think that more is *always* better. For example, there's no reason to stick a 235-watt power supply in an XT. Your electricity bill might rise, but your computer's performance won't.

✔ If you've been upgrading a lot of computer parts lately — a new motherboard, a second hard drive, extra cards, or a tape backup drive — your next purchase should be a more powerful power supply.

How Do I Install a New Power Supply?

IQ level: 90

Tools you need: One hand and a screwdriver

Cost: Approximately $50

Stuff to watch out for:

Power supplies can't be repaired; they're simply replaced. Throw the old power supply away.

Don't ever open your power supply or try to fix it yourself. The power supply stores powerful jolts of electricity, even when the computer is turned off and unplugged. Power supplies are safe but only when they are not open.

Also, the shelves in the back room of the computer store are filled with different kinds of power supplies. To find the right replacement, bring in your old power supply and say, "I need another one of these." Or check with the place that sold you the computer. If you're upgrading your power supply to a higher wattage, tell the dealer "I need a power supply like this but rated at a higher wattage."

To install a new power supply, perform the following steps:

1. **Turn off your PC, unplug it, and remove its cover.**

   If you've never gone fishing inside your computer before, the Cheat Sheet at the front of this book covers how to remove your computer's cover.

2. **Unplug the power supply cables from the motherboard, the drives, and the power switch.**

   Your power supply is that big, boxy, silver thing in your computer's top right-hand corner. Bunches of cables run out of a hole in the power supply's side.

Each cable has one of several types of plugs on its end. The plugs are all shaped differently to keep them from plugging into the wrong place. Even so, put a strip of masking tape on the end of each plug and write down its destination. You and your computer will feel better that way.

Here's a rundown of the plugs, their shapes, and their destinations:

Motherboard: The two biggest plugs attach to connectors on the motherboard, as in Figure 14-1.

Figure 14-1: These rectangular-shaped plugs pull straight up and off sockets on your motherboard.

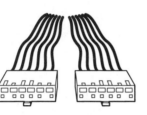

Drives: Disk drives, tape backup units, and other internal goodies get their power from two different sizes of plugs, as shown in Figure 14-2.

Switch: Some older power supplies have an on/off switch built right into their chests. Other power supplies have a wire that connects to an on/off switch along the computer's front or side. Those power supplies have little connectors like the one in Figure 14-3.

The plugs only fit into their sockets one way. The power switch tabs can be rough, though, so draw a picture of which colored wire connects to which tab.

Unless your computer is packed to the brim with goodies, you probably have a few stray cables left over. Those cables are thoughtfully supplied to power any future additions.

3. **Remove the screws holding the power supply to the back of the computer's case.**

Look on the back of your computer near the fan hole and you see several screws. Some of these screws hold your power supply in place. But other screws hold your fan inside your power supply.

With the case off, you can usually tell which screws hold the power supply in place. Try loosening the screws slightly; that sometimes makes it easier to tell which screws are which.

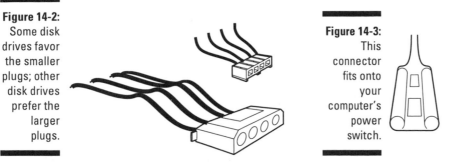

The screws that hold the power supply in place are generally closer to the outside edge of the computer's rear. The screws that hold the fan are generally closer to the fan's edge. Don't loosen the fan's screws if you can help it.

4. Lift out the power supply.

Does the power supply come out easily? If the power supply is cramped, you may need to loosen the floppy drives and pull them forward a bit. (I describe how to loosen floppy drives Chapter 12 if you're not sure how the floppy drives are mounted.)

If the power supply still won't come out, make sure that you've removed all the screws. Some power supplies have extra screws around their base to hold them down.

Some XT power supplies are held in place by little metal tabs; if so, slide the power supply toward the front of the case, and it should come loose.

Power supplies are pretty hardy beasts, so don't be afraid to pull hard.

5. Take the power supply to the store and get a new one.

That's the best way to make sure that you get the right-sized replacement. If you're planning on adding some other computer toys — such as compact disc players or sound cards — or filling up your slots with more gadgets, consider buying a power supply with a higher wattage.

6. Put the new power supply where the old one sat.

Sometimes it's easier to reconnect the cables before sliding the power supply in place.

7. Reconnect all the cables to the motherboard, the drives, and the power switch.

Grab any little pictures you drew and look at any masking tape labels you put on the old power supply's cables. (Forgot to label them? Well, it doesn't really matter which disk drive gets which plug.)

On the motherboard, the *black* wires on the two plugs almost always face each other. But make sure that you hook up the power switch connectors according to your notes. There aren't any hard and fast rules.

8. **Replace the screws holding the power supply to the back of the computer's case.**

   Do you have the cables back on? If so, screw the power supply back into place. Be sure that you tighten down any disk drives you may have loosened.

   Also, check to make sure that you haven't knocked any other cables loose while moving around inside your computer.

9. **Make sure that the voltage is set correctly.**

   Look on the back of the power supply, which is near the fan. A switch usually lets you toggle the power to either 120 volts or 220 volts. If you're in the U.S., make sure that the switch is set to 120 volts. Otherwise, flip the switch to the 220-volt setting.

   If you're working on a computer in a country other than the U.S., be sure that you toggle the voltage setting switch appropriately. Also make sure that you have the proper cord for 220 — look on the cord's little yellow tag for this rating.

10. **Reconnect the power cord.**

    Plug your computer back in; its power cord should push into the socket near the fan.

11. **Turn on the power and see whether it works.**

    Do you hear the fan whirring? Does the computer leap to life? If so, then all is well. If the fan is not spinning, though, something is wrong with the new power supply or your power outlet.

    Try plugging a lamp into the outlet to make *sure* that the outlet works. If the outlet works, take the power supply back. The computer store sold you a bad power supply.

12. **Turn off the computer and put the case back on.**

    Is everything working right? If it is, turn off the computer, put its case back on, and put a cool glass of iced tea in your hands. Congratulations!

Chapter 15

Stuff on Cards

• •

In This Chapter

▶ Making cards fit in slots

▶ Repairing cards that aren't working

▶ Understanding card varieties

▶ Installing new cards

• •

Most computer upgrades are a shoehorn process: trying to force an old computer to do something it wasn't really designed to do.

Adding expansion cards, however, is a different story. Cards provide the 100 percent approved way of upgrading your system. That means that this is going to be easy. So, relax. Smile! You're playing with cards, remember?

My Card Doesn't Fit!

Unlike other computer organs, expansion cards have remained remarkably uncomplicated over the years. In fact, most people need to worry about only one thing: card size.

For years, cards came in two main sizes — big and small. The small ones are called *8-bit cards* and look like the one shown in Figure 15-1.

The bigger versions are called *16-bit cards*. They're a newer breed, so the gray-haired XT computers don't have any of them. Figure 15-2 shows a 16-bit card.

You can plug an 8-bit card into a slot of any size. No problem there. But you can't plug a 16-bit card into an 8-bit slot. Well, you can, but the card usually won't work.

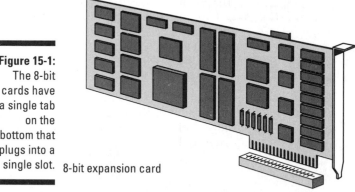

Figure 15-1:
The 8-bit cards have a single tab on the bottom that plugs into a single slot.

8-bit expansion card

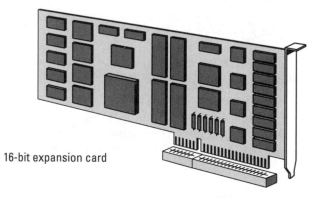

Figure 15-2:
The 16-bit cards have two tabs that plug into a longer slot inside your PC.

16-bit expansion card

✔ Because the old XT computers don't have 16-bit slots, they can't handle the latest, fanciest sound cards, video cards, and other goodies. Also, some really picky old XT computers don't like just *any* card in the slot closest to the power supply. Save that slot for last.

✔ Sometimes a card is too long. If you push the card into the slot, the end bumps into some memory chips or something near the front of your computer. These troublesome long cards are called *full-length cards*. Luckily, they're a dying breed.

✔ Some cards are too fat. They fit into the slot but bump up against the cards in the slots next to them. This problem pops up most often on really old cards.

✔ How do you handle cards that are too fat or too long? Well, you can break off the troublesome parts that don't fit. But then the card doesn't work. Your best bet is to move the cards around to different slots, trying different positions until they all fit. It's kind of like packing bags in the car trunk on the way home from the grocery store. You have to try different combinations before the trunk lid will close.

✔ Finally, some fancy computers support fancier types of cards. If the terms Local Bus, PCI, or EISA don't sound familiar, then check out Chapter 3. You can find descriptions and pictures of what those cards look like and what they're supposed to do.

My Card Doesn't Work!

Not much can go wrong when you install a card. The biggest problem is remembering to turn off the power to your computer first.

Always turn off the power to your computer and unplug it before inserting or removing a card. If you forget, you may see sparks and a dead card (or worse).

Chances are, your nonfunctioning card *does* work; the computer just doesn't know it's attached. The card lies unnoticed, like a dribble of spaghetti sauce on the corner of a mouth.

Which bus are you on?

Computer nerds call a computer's row of expansion slots a *bus.* Although there are several types of buses, you probably have a *PCI* or *ISA bus.* The majority of cards on the store shelves are PCI or ISA cards, so they work in your computer without any problems.

If your computer has an *EISA bus,* you spent a lot more money for it. An EISA bus can still use the same old ISA cards filling the shelves. It also can use the more expensive EISA cards, if you can find one.

The people who need to watch out are those who have an *MCA bus.* Short for *Micro Channel*

Architecture, IBM designed the MCA for its PS/2 series of computers. If you have an MCA bus, you can't use the ISA or EISA cards everybody else is buying. You must ask for MCA cards *specifically,* or the cards won't work on your computer.

There's more. Most people have a combination of ISA cards and a couple of the fancier cards, either *PCI* or *VESA Local Bus.* Those two fancy cards speed up a computer's ability to sling graphics onto the screen. You can find lots more information about cards and slots in Chapter 3.

✔ Windows 95 comes with "Plug and Play" technology that recognizes most newly inserted cards and puts them right to work. Check out Chapter 17 for more information on Windows and Plug and Play.

✔ Many cards also come with an installation program. The program tells the computer to make contact with the card and report its progress. It usually takes three steps.

    • The installation program may put a *driver* program onto your computer's hard disk.

    • The program may tell you to change a *jumper* on the card.

    • The program may ask you to flip a *DIP switch* on the card.

✔ All this stuff's covered in Chapter 18. (Windows users can find more information in Chapter 17.)

If one of your older cards stops working, turn off your computer, unplug it, remove the cover, and remove the card. Then take a plain old pencil eraser and rub it over the contacts on the part of the card that fits into the slot. This can remove any corrosion or buildup of crud. Also try pushing the card more firmly into its slot. Sometimes the cards creep up and out with age.

Older cards sometimes stop working if their driver is disturbed. You need to check your AUTOEXEC.BAT or CONFIG.SYS file, as I describe in Chapter 16.

What Kinds of Cards Can I Buy?

Hundreds of cards fill the store shelves. But here's a look at the most popular. You probably have at least two of these cards inside your computer right now.

Video cards: These give your monitor a place to plug into. Every computer has a video card, except for the ones from the early '90s that came with the video circuitry built right into the motherboard. (In fact, you may need to disable that motherboard circuitry if you ever put a video card in a slot. Better check the motherboard's manual.)

Computers expect only one video card. Don't confuse your computer by leaving your old video card in place after adding a new one.

An *accelerated* video card can display images faster than the boring old cards. They cost a little more, but they can really speed up Windows and other graphics-hungry programs on older computers. Pentium and Pentium Pro computers usually use PCI video cards and slots to speed up graphics. Local bus — VL-Bus — video cards speed things up even more, if your computer has VL-Bus slots: three slots that line up with a VL-Bus card's three tabs. (You can find pictures of these cards in Chapter 3. PCI slots resemble MicroChannel slots — don't confuse them.)

I/O cards: You know where your printer plugs into the back of your computer? It's probably plugging into the back of your I/O card. Chances are, there's a serial port above your printer port, too. (A mouse or modem usually plugs into that port.) I/O cards are a vanishing breed, however, because more computers include those ports directly on the motherboard.

Controller cards: All sorts of flat ribbon cables sprout from these cards. The cables connect to your floppy drives and hard drives. Some newer computers recently got rid of their controller cards. The ribbon cables just plug straight into the motherboard on these machines.

Put your controller card in a slot close to the power supply; that way, the ribbon cables don't have to reach as far to connect to your drives.

Sound cards: Bought a sound card? Fun! Unless you're using Windows 95, the hard part is configuring them to a special *IRQ address.* I cover that technical stuff in Chapter 18.

You won't hear anything from a sound card unless you also bought speakers. Another alternative is to buy a *long* phono cord and run it from the sound card to your stereo's tape or auxiliary jack. The hard part then becomes trying not to trip over the cord.

Modems: Modem cards cause two main problems. First, you need to configure the modem cards for a COM port so your computer has an electronic doorway to yell in and out of. (COM ports are covered in Chapter 17.)

Second, modem cards come with *two* phone jacks on them. Your phone line plugs into one, and you plug your telephone into the other. But those phone jacks are rarely marked. Which one goes where? Grab that manual or just try connecting the wires one way; if it doesn't work, try the opposite plug.

Memory cards: Some people, hungry for more memory, stick memory chips on a card and then stick the cards into their computers. It's a last-resort operation, though, reserved for when your computer's motherboard is already filled up with memory chips. Memory on a card always works more slowly.

Some older 386 computers come with a *proprietary* memory slot. You can buy a memory card for that slot from the computer's maker, but no other card will work. The card looks different from the other cards, so you don't have to worry about getting your memory cards mixed up. It's just as fast as any other memory, but it costs a lot more.

Interface cards: You plug in one of these guys to put a new connector on the back of your computer. For example, you can plug in a CD-ROM drive, a mouse, or a PC Card reader for those little credit-card-sized laptop cards. Some Roland music synthesizers use an interface card, as do the latest robotic arm controllers.

Video capture cards: Hook up the camcorder to a video capture card and record movies directly onto your PC. Make digital Christmas cards by the open fire and mail them on floppy disks to your friends! (Oh, and television tuner cards can turn your $2,500 PC into a $79 television.)

- All types of cards plug in the same way. No special tricks.

- Not all cards start working right away, though. You may have to flip some switches on them or move some jumpers around. That's covered in Chapter 18.

- After you buy the right card for your particular computer, the biggest problem you'll probably have with cards is finding room for them. Most computers come with six or eight slots. After you plug in your video card, controller card, and I/O card, you'll realize how quickly those slots get used up.

When fastening a cable to the back of a card, look for little screws or clips on the cord's end. Some have big thumbscrews designed especially for clumsy people. (Thank goodness.) Others have tiny screws that frustrate the myopic. Either way, fasten the cord tightly onto the back of your computer. That keeps it from falling off whenever you adjust your computer's position on your desk.

How Do I Install a New Card?

IQ level: 90

Tools you need: One hand and a screwdriver

Cost: Anywhere from $70 – $300 and more

Stuff to watch out for:

Cards are particularly susceptible to static electricity. Tap your computer's case to ground yourself before touching the card.

Be careful not to bend the cards while installing them. That can damage their circuitry.

Cards are pretty easy to install. They're self-contained little units. For example, they suck electricity right out of that little slot they plug into. You don't need to plug special power cables into them.

Cards are delicate. Handle them only by their edges. The oil from your fingers can damage their circuitry.

Also, those little silver dots on one side of the card are actually sharp metal pokers that can leave scratches across the back of your hand. In fact, the scratches on one computer nerd's hand resembled a tattoo so closely that chummy hoodlums dragged him into a biker bar. (He ended up recalibrating the Quiz Whiz arcade unit.)

Different-sized cards need different-sized slots. You may need to rearrange some of your cards to accommodate different lengths and thicknesses.

To install a card, follow these steps:

1. **Turn off your computer, unplug it, and remove the cover.**

   Don't know how that cover comes off? Flip to the Cheat Sheet at the front of this book for the answers.

2. **Find the right size slot for your card.**

   See the row of slots along the back wall of your computer, as shown in Figure 15-3? Your new card will plug into one of those slots. Don't confuse your computer's expansion slots — the ones where the cards plug in — with its memory slots, where the memory-chip-laden SIMMs plug in.

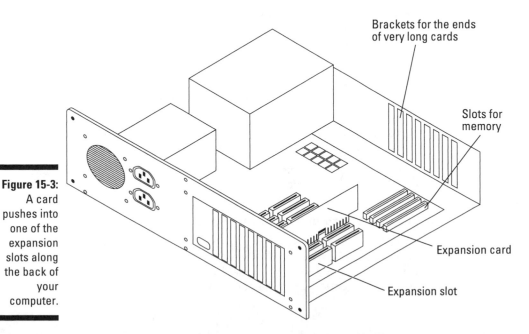

Brackets for the ends of very long cards

Slots for memory

Figure 15-3: A card pushes into one of the expansion slots along the back of your computer.

Expansion card

Expansion slot

Check out the pictures in Figures 15-1 and 15-2 so you know whether you have an 8-bit or 16-bit card. Or just look at its bottom: Two tabs make it a 16-bit card; just one tab makes it an 8-bit card.

Three tabs on the card? Then you're probably dealing with a VESA Local Bus card, which needs a VESA Local Bus slot. (You can find pictures of cards and their appropriate slots in Chapter 3.)

You can stick an 8-bit card in a 16-bit slot, but rarely vice versa.

You may have to shuffle your cards around until there's room for the new card.

If you have a lot of room, keep your cards spaced as far apart as possible. That keeps them cooler.

3. Remove the slot's cover.

Unused slots have a little cover next to them to keep dust from flying in through the back of your computer. With a small screwdriver, remove the screw that holds the cover in place. Don't lose the screw! You need it to secure the card in place.

Dropped the screw in there "somewhere?" Head for Chapter 2 for tips on getting it back out. (You can't just leave it in there, or your computer will choke on it and possibly electrocute itself.)

Got the screw out? Keep it handy, and keep the little cover bracket, too. You can use it as a makeshift chip puller, as seen in Figure 10-6 in Chapter 10.

4. Push the card into its slot.

To spare yourself some possible aggravation, first check your card's manual to see if you need to flip any of the card's switches or move any of its jumpers. Then you won't have to take the card back out if it's not working right.

Holding the card by its edges, position it over the slot. The edge with the shiny metal bracket should face toward the *back* of your computer. Got it?

Push the card slowly into the slot. You may need to rock it back and forth gently. When it pops in, you can feel it come to rest. Don't force it!

Don't let any card come into contact with any other card. That can cause electrical problems, and neither the card nor the computer will work.

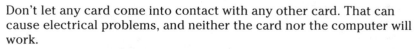

5. Secure the card in the slot with the screw.

Yep, all those expensive cards are held in place by a single screw. Make sure that you *use* a screw, however; don't just leave the card sitting there. Cards need to be grounded to the computer's case. Without a secure connection, they may not work.

6. **Plug the computer back in, turn it on, and see if Windows 95's Plug and Play feature recognizes and installs the card.**

   Windows 95 usually recognizes newly installed cards and sets them up to work correctly. If something goes wrong, head for Chapter 17 for quick-fix tips.

7. **If it works, carefully put the cover back on. You're done!**

If the card still doesn't work — or you're not using Windows — you probably have to run the card's installation software. Still doesn't work? Then try the following:

- ✔ Check the manual to make sure that the card's switches and jumpers are set right.

- ✔ Sometimes you have to run the card's software and then reboot your computer before it will work. That's because the card puts a driver in one of your computer's special files. Your computer only reads that file when it's first turned on or when it's rebooted.

- ✔ Make sure that the card is seated securely in its slot and screwed in reasonably tight.

- ✔ Make sure that the card's in the right slot: 8-bit or 16-bit.

- ✔ VL-Bus (local bus) video cards work correctly only if they're plugged into local bus slots, which have three little slots to line up with the card's three little tabs. (Feel free to plug a 16- or 8-bit card into a local bus slot, however.)

- ✔ It can take some fiddling to get a card working right.

- ✔ Nine times out of ten, the problem lies with the software. The card's sitting in the slot just right; the software is conflicting with some other software or not talking with the card correctly.

- ✔ If the card still doesn't work, root around in its box for the manual. Most manuals list a technical support phone number you can call for help. Be sure to read the tail end of Chapter 4 before calling; it can save you a lot of time.

Part IV
Telling Your Computer What You've Done

The 5th Wave — By Rich Tennant

"I'M WAITING FOR MY AUTOEXEC FILE TO RUN, SO I'M GONNA GRAB A CUP OF COFFEE, MAYBE MAKE A SANDWICH, CHECK THE SPORTS PAGE, REGRIND THE BRAKEDRUMS ON MY TRUCK, BALANCE MY CHECKBOOK FOR THE PAST 12 YEARS, LEARN SWAHILI, ..."

In this part . . .

Upgrading a computer is kind of like recording something on a VCR. The easy part is stuffing the videotape inside. The hard part is making the VCR automatically record the late show while you're snoozing so you can watch the show the next day and fast-forward through all the commercials.

Computers present a similar situation. The easy part of upgrading your computer often turns out to be sticking in the new part. The hard part is making the computer recognize that new part and start putting it to work.

That's where this part of the book comes in. It helps avert that sinking sensation — that feeling you get when you've finally tightened the last screw, but the ungrateful computer *still* doesn't recognize your handiwork.

Hold on; you're almost there.

Chapter 16

That AUTOEXEC.BAT and CONFIG.SYS File Stuff

In This Chapter

▶ Understanding your CONFIG.SYS file

▶ Understanding your AUTOEXEC.BAT file

▶ Taking a look at paths

▶ Creating a PATH statement

▶ Adding a driver to a CONFIG.SYS file

▶ Changing your AUTOEXEC.BAT file

▶ Understanding what really happens when you turn on your computer

*G*reat news: Windows 95 users don't need to bother with this chapter because Windows 95 doesn't really bother with these files. You see, Windows 95 has outgrown them.

This chapter's still here for the Windows 95 holdouts, however; those 100 million or so people who still use DOS or an earlier version of Windows. If you're one of them, computing life goes like this:

When your computer wakes up in the morning, it reaches for its cup of coffee. However, a computer thinks *everything* is either a file or piece of electronic circuitry, so its cup of coffee certainly isn't made by Folgers.

No, the coffee for a newly awakened computer consists of two small files: AUTOEXEC.BAT and CONFIG.SYS.

You've probably seen those weird names either in a directory on your hard drive or in a manual somewhere. Normally, you don't have to mess with these files, thank goodness. But when a program or manual tells you to *modify your AUTOEXEC.BAT/CONFIG.SYS files,* follow the numbered steps in this chapter.

What's a CONFIG.SYS File?

A CONFIG.SYS file is simply a file filled with text. However, it's designed for your *computer* to look at, not you. That's why its contents look like the fine print on a bottle of multivitamins. For example, look at the nerdy verbiage in the CONFIG.SYS file shown in Figure 16-1.

```
DEVICE=C:\WINDOWS\HIMEM.SYS
DEVICE=C:\WINDOWS\EMM386.EXE NOEMS
DOS=HIGH,UMB

DEVICEHIGH=C:\UTIL\DEV\MDSCD FD.SYS /D:MSCD000 /N:1
DEVICEHIGH=D:\COMM\FAX\SATISFAX.SYS IOADDR=0310
DEVICEHIGH=D:\SOUND\PROAUDIO\MVSOUND.SYS D:3 Q:7

STACKS=9,256
FILES=80
BUFFERS=40
LASTDRIVE=Z
```

Figure 16-1:
A typical
CONFIG.SYS
file; yours
may differ
from this
one.

What is all that stuff? Well, a CONFIG.SYS file contains mostly the names of *drivers* — pieces of software that help your computer talk to mice, sound cards, extra chunks of memory, and other gadgets. The CONFIG.SYS file lists where all those drivers live on your hard drive; it's sort of like a phone book for computer parts.

Whenever you turn on or reboot your computer, it flips open its CONFIG.SYS file to see all the drivers listed in there. As it reads each driver's name, it finds that driver's software on the hard drive. It then reads the driver to learn how to carry on a conversation with whatever component the driver represents.

The computer immediately forgets about the drivers as soon as you turn it off. But when you turn it back on again, it heads straight back to the CONFIG.SYS file and calls those drivers back into action. Sure, it's repetitious. But computers never get bored.

- ✔ If your computer can't find a part's driver, it probably won't be able to find the part, either. In fact, it won't even know it's supposed to *look* for the part. And if it stumbles across the part accidentally, it won't know how to talk to the part, leading to arguments and general discomfort.

- ✔ When everything's working correctly, your computer reads its CONFIG.SYS file so quickly and automatically that you don't have to mess with the file at all — except when you need to toss a new driver's name in there.

✔ Some computer parts come with installation programs that automatically place the names of their drivers into the CONFIG.SYS file. Other computer parts are lazy and make you list the drivers yourself.

✔ Your computer looks at the CONFIG.SYS file only when it's rebooted or turned on. That's why so many installation programs want to reboot your computer when they're through — it's how they force your computer to notice their changes.

✔ Not *all* computer parts force you to fiddle with a CONFIG.SYS file or a driver. Some make you fiddle with an AUTOEXEC.BAT file instead. (That's the file I describe next.) Some make you fiddle with both. Others don't make you fiddle with *anything:* The computer handles all the fiddling chores itself. The boxes that the parts come in rarely give much of a clue as to what you should expect, unfortunately.

✔ The lines listed in a CONFIG.SYS file aren't commands you can type at the DOS prompt. Your computer will probably spit out an error message if you try. Your computer can only understand those lines when they're packaged in the CONFIG.SYS file.

✔ Your computer's picky about the location of its CONFIG.SYS file. It only looks for CONFIG.SYS in your *root* directory — that C:\> directory. If you move the file to a directory like C:\DOS> or C:\WINDOWS> or any other directory with words in the name, your computer won't be able to find it.

✔ When you flip on the power switch, your computer always reads the CONFIG.SYS and AUTOEXEC.BAT files — even if you use Windows or Windows 95. (Windows 95 needs to know what a DOS program might want to see, in case you decided to run one from within its domain.)

What's an AUTOEXEC.BAT File?

Imagine that it's your first day on the job. You walk into a new, unfamiliar office and don't know where to start. Then you see a "to-do" list the boss tacked to the desk.

An AUTOEXEC.BAT file is a "to-do" list for your computer. It's simply a text file filled with commands you'd normally type at the C:\> prompt. You can see a sample of an AUTOEXEC.BAT file in Figure 16-2.

Whenever you turn on or reboot your computer, it looks for a file called AUTOEXEC.BAT. If it finds one, it reads the file line by line and carries out all the instructions in the file. It AUTOmatically EXECutes all those commands when you first turn it on. (Get it?)

Figure 16-2:
A typical
AUTOEXEC-
.BAT file.
Yours may
differ from
this one.

```
PATH C:\DOS;:\WINDOWS
SET TEMP=C:\DOS
C:\WINDOWS\SMARTDRV.EXE
C:\WINDOWS\MOUSE.COM
PROMPT $p$g
```

An AUTOEXEC.BAT file is a sneaky way to make computers do some of their start-up work automatically so you don't have to boss them around for every little thing.

✔ An AUTOEXEC.BAT file contains a list of commands for the computer to run whenever it's turned on or rebooted. In fact, those are the only times the computer ever bothers reading the AUTOEXEC.BAT file.

✔ If the AUTOEXEC.BAT file ever changes, the computer won't notice until the next time it's rebooted. That's why the installation programs for most new computer parts insist on rebooting your computer. Rebooting forces your computer to notice their changes.

✔ Like the CONFIG.SYS file, the AUTOEXEC.BAT file lives in your root directory, the one you see when you type **DIR** at the C:\> prompt. Sure, you can put those two files anywhere on your hard drive you want. However, your computer can't find them unless they're in the root directory.

✔ Some computer parts want to stick some lines into your CONFIG.SYS file. Others prefer adding to the AUTOEXEC.BAT file. Some want to put a line in *both* files. Other, more easygoing parts don't use *any* drivers or programs, sparing you from bothering with this entire chapter.

✔ There's no surefire way to tell whether a certain computer part prefers to stake its mark in the CONFIG.SYS file or the AUTOEXEC.BAT file. It depends on the manufacturer and whoever invented the part. Only the manual knows for sure.

Keep a backup copy of your AUTOEXEC.BAT and CONFIG.SYS files on a floppy disk. If something goes wrong, you can copy them back over to your root directory. Feel free to keep a printout of them on hand, too. Just be sure to update your printout or floppy disk whenever the files change.

What's a Path?

Computers aren't terribly clever beasts. When you copy a file or program to your computer's hard drive, your computer doesn't always pay attention. Your computer can't automatically find the file or program later.

That's why a *path* comes in so handy. A path is a computer's road map — it shows where a particular file is located.

For example, perhaps your file COUGH.EXE is in your C:\SYMPTOMS subdirectory. After the C:\> prompt, you type **COUGH** and press Enter, like this:

```
C:\> COUGH
```

But your computer doesn't run COUGH. Instead, it gives off the following confused shout: Bad command or file name.

That's because the computer couldn't find COUGH. What your computer did was look in the directory that it was in at the time — the C:\> directory — and couldn't find COUGH, so it gave up.

However, if you add COUGH's *path,* the computer knows where to look for the file. So to make the computer run COUGH, you type the subdirectory as well as the filename, like this:

```
C:\> C:\SYMPTOMS\COUGH
```

The point? If all the programs and drivers in your CONFIG.SYS and AUTOEXEC.BAT files include paths, your computer will always be able to find them.

- ✔ If you see the words Bad command or file name while your computer is booting up, it's a sure sign that the computer couldn't find a file listed in your AUTOEXEC.BAT file.

- ✔ The problem probably occurred because the file's name or path is spelled wrong, no matter how subtly. Or it may be that you moved the file to a different place on your hard drive. If you did, your computer can't find it anymore — you have to update the file's path in your AUTOEXEC.BAT file to reflect its new location.

- ✔ When your computer can't find something in your CONFIG.SYS file, it's a little more specific about the problem: Your computer not only lists the name of the driver it can't find, but also the line number in your CONFIG.SYS file that's causing the problem.

PATH=C:\WHO\CARES>

This path stuff is a bother. Why can't the computer just look *everywhere* on the hard drive and find files automatically? Well, because that can take a long time. If you have an old computer and an older hard drive, it can take a *very* long time.

DOS offers a compromise. It lets you put your most popular directories on a special list. When you type the name of a program at the C:\> prompt, the computer searches for the file in the current directory, just as it normally does. But if it doesn't find the program there, it *also* searches the directories you placed on the special list.

This special list is called the PATH statement, and it lives in the AUTOEXEC.BAT file. In the AUTOEXEC.BAT file in Figure 16-2, for example, the PATH looks like this:

PATH C:\DOS;C:\WINDOWS

See those subdirectories listed after the word PATH? Those are the directories your computer staggers through when searching for files. In Figure 16-2, for example, the computer automatically searches through the C:\DOS and C:\WINDOWS directories for your programs.

Listing a program's directory on the PATH can make things easier. You can type a program's name from anywhere on your hard drive, and if its directory is on the path, your computer finds and runs the program.

In fact, that's part of the problem. Because it's so easy to find and run a program that's on the PATH, almost *every* installation program wants to put its directory on the PATH.

DOS bylaws decree that a PATH statement can be no longer than 127 characters. The solution? When your PATH gets too long, open up your AUTOEXEC.BAT file and give it a trim. You need to keep Windows and DOS in there, that's for sure. But you may be able to cut out some other, less frequently used directories. The PATH may list some directories that you deleted years ago in a fit of hard-drive housekeeping.

How to Edit a CONFIG.SYS or AUTOEXEC.BAT File

Sooner or later, some new program or gadget will send you a blast of rudeness. From out of the blue, its manual tells you to modify your CONFIG.SYS file or edit your AUTOEXEC.BAT file. If you spot a floppy disk in the box with your new computer part, chances are that the program on that disk wants to fiddle with your CONFIG.SYS or AUTOEXEC.BAT file.

Some installation programs make all the changes automatically; others make *you* wear the file-changing hat. When you're forced to change your CONFIG.SYS or AUTOEXEC.BAT file, carefully follow these steps.

Before starting, make sure that you're at the *real* DOS prompt and not at the counterfeit DOS prompt that Windows sometimes hands you. Not sure which is which? Then type **EXIT** at the C:\> prompt and press Enter. If Windows doesn't pop back up on your screen, you're safe: Windows wasn't lurking in the background after all.

1. **Find the file.**

   Your CONFIG.SYS and AUTOEXEC.BAT files live in a place called the root directory. That's the place that gives you a simple-looking C:\> prompt. To get there, type the following command:

   ```
   C:\> C:
   ```

   In other words, press C, a colon, and the Enter key. That takes you to drive C even if you're currently visiting drive D, a CD-ROM drive, or something even more expensive.

   Next, type this command:

   ```
   C:\> CD \
   ```

   That is, type CD, a space, and the backslash character (*not* the slash that shares the ? key), and then press Enter.

   These two steps always bring you to your root directory, home of your CONFIG.SYS and AUTOEXEC.BAT files.

2. **Make a backup copy.**

   Before fiddling with these important files, make a backup copy so you have a place to turn if the weather starts getting rough. Type the following two commands at the C:\> prompt, pressing Enter after each line:

   ```
   C:\> COPY CONFIG.SYS CONFIG.GOD
   C:\> COPY AUTOEXEC.BAT AUTOEXEC.GOD
   ```

   By entering these commands, you make a backup copy of each file. The names of the backup files end in GOD — that stands for "Good" file. (Of course, a little divine intervention doesn't hurt either.)

   Feel free to put a copy of the files on a floppy disk, too. Type the following at the C:\> prompt, pressing Enter at the end of each line:

   ```
   C:\> COPY CONFIG.SYS A:
   C:\> COPY AUTOEXEC.BAT A:
   ```

   Make sure that you have a floppy disk in drive A. You can never have too many backup copies.

3. **Open the file.**

Now you're ready to start changing the file. If the manual says to add a line to your CONFIG.SYS file, type the command below:

```
C:\> EDIT CONFIG.SYS
```

That is, type **EDIT**, a space, and **CONFIG.SYS**. Then press Enter.

Or if you're supposed to add a line to your AUTOEXEC.BAT file, type **EDIT**, a space, and **AUTOEXEC.BAT**, and press Enter:

```
C:\> EDIT AUTOEXEC.BAT
```

The Edit program pops up on the screen, letting you see your weird-looking CONFIG.SYS file.

Not using DOS 5 or greater? Then you don't have the convenient Edit program, and you just see an error message. You have to use a word processor to do your editing. And here's another catch: You need to save the file in a special format called *ASCII* or *Plain Text* or *DOS text*. Windows' Notepad will do the trick. If something goes horribly wrong, however, you can head back to steady seas with your backup files — that's described at the end of this section.

4. **Add the new line.**

Do you see the contents of your file inside the Edit program? If you edit your CONFIG.SYS file, for example, your screen looks something like the one shown in Figure 16-3.

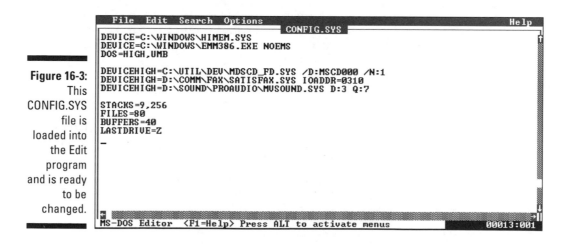

Figure 16-3: This CONFIG.SYS file is loaded into the Edit program and is ready to be changed.

Whether you're adding the new line to the CONFIG.SYS or AUTOEXEC.BAT file, put it at the very bottom of the file. Unless the manual says otherwise, that's probably the safest spot.

Hold down the Ctrl key, press the End key, and release them both. That moves you to the last line of the file. Press Enter.

Now type in the line you're supposed to add. You can find that line listed in the new part's manual or whatever else is forcing you to do all this nonsensical stuff.

Be sure to include the file's path so the computer can find the file. (Paths have their own section earlier in this chapter.) Check for typos, too. If you don't spell everything 100 percent correctly, your computer will grow a hair bun and give you cross looks.

Done typing in the line? Then press Enter.

5. Save the file.

Did you double-check your work? Then it's time to save the file. Press and release Alt and then press F. A little menu drops down from the top of the screen.

Press S to Save the file.

6. Exit the program.

The computer saved your work, so press and release the Alt key and press F. Again, the little menu appears. This time, however, press X for Exit. The Edit program disappears into nothingness, leaving you at your C:\> prompt.

7. Reset the computer.

Your computer only reads its AUTOEXEC.BAT and CONFIG.SYS files when it's rebooted. So push your computer's reset button or turn it off, wait 30 seconds, and turn it on again. The screen clears, your computer gathers itself together, and you're ready for the big moment: It reads those AUTOEXEC.BAT and CONFIG.SYS files.

- After you change these files, watch your computer closely when it reboots. If the screen says something like Bad or missing file name or Error in CONFIG.SYS line 13, something's wrong. Jump back to Step 3 and check to see that you spelled everything right and the program's path is correct.

- If you did everything correctly, your computer won't toss anything strange onto the screen, not even a thank-you message. Try using your new part or program; chances are, your computer will finally recognize it.

- If you mess something up terribly and your computer freaks out, here's how to restore sanity. Simply copy your backup copies over the messed-up ones. Type the following commands at the C:\> prompt:

```
C:\> COPY CONFIG.GOD CONFIG.SYS
```

```
C:\> COPY AUTOEXEC.GOD AUTOEXEC.BAT
```

Then reboot your computer, and it should come back to normal. You still need to find a computer guru to make those changes for you, however. Tell 'em you made an honest effort at doing it yourself. That and a fresh box of Count Chocula cereal often get a guru's attention.

Sometimes you need to *change* a line, not add a new one. To be safe, find the line you need to change and type the word **REM** in front of it. For example, a program may want you to change an AUTOEXEC.BAT file line that looks like this:

```
PROMPT $p$g
```

To change the line, type the word **REM** in front of it and type the new, changed line directly beneath it, like this:

```
REM PROMPT $p$g
PROMPT $D$_$T$_$P$G
```

The REM stands for *remark*. Because remarks are designed for humans, DOS ignores any line starting with REM.

If something goes wrong with your change, delete the line that messed things up and remove the REM from the original line — the one that worked. Doing that brings things back to normal. Well, as normal as computers can be, anyway.

One last note: If you try this tactic in a version of DOS earlier than 3.3, DOS says `Unrecognized command in CONFIG.SYS` when the computer boots up. Just tell the computer to hush up; everything's fine.

Do you want your computer to start Windows 3.1 or Windows 3.11 automatically when you turn it on? Then add this word to its own line at the very end of your AUTOEXEC.BAT file:

```
WIN
```

Your computer reads that line when it reboots and loads Windows automatically.

What Are Those Weird Sounds and Words When I Turn On My Computer?

A computer jumps through the same hoops whenever you press its Reset button or flip its on switch. Here's a rundown of its same ol' runaround:

1. You turn the switch on, and electricity starts flowing.

When you first turn on your computer, you hear the power supply's fan start to spin and your hard drive begin to whir. All the circuits inside your PC get a waking burst of electricity.

2. The BIOS begins.

After the computer's CPU wakes up, it heads straight for its *BIOS* — basic, gut-level instructions stored inside special *BIOS* chips on the motherboard. (More BIOS babble bubbles in Chapter 10.) By reading its BIOS, the computer knows how to talk to its floppy drives and other basic parts.

3. The computer tests itself (POST).

After the computer figures out how to talk to its parts, it begins testing them with the *POST,* or *power-on self test.* I describe the POST is more fully in Chapter 4.

XT: On these oldsters, the POST looks at the DIP switches on the motherboard. The switches tell the POST what parts are inside your computer, and then the POST goes looking to make sure that the parts are *really* there.

Other: If you're using a 286, 386, or newer computer, the POST looks for the equipment list stored in your computer's CMOS. The CMOS, which I cover in Chapter 18, contains a battery backed-up list of the parts inside your computer. The POST grabs the list and starts looking for everything that's listed.

As the POST goes around kicking tires, it lets you know what's going on. For example, you see an on-screen tally as the POST counts your memory chips. You hear your floppy drives gnash their teeth as the POST gives 'em a quick spin. Your hard drive's little red light flashes as the POST peeks inside.

If the POST finds something askew, it flings out a coded series of beeps (which Chapter 24 decodes) or flashes a cryptic error message (decryptified in Chapter 23). Or both.

If everything's fine and dandy (most of the time), the computer gives one affirmative, head-nodding beep and moves to Step 4.

4. The computer looks for an operating system.

The computer first looks for an operating system on drive A. That's because *everybody* used to keep their system disk in drive A. (Hard drives weren't invented yet.)

The computer is searching for the *boot sector.* If the computer finds a disk in drive A but there's no boot sector to be found, it stops dead, leaving this epitaph:

```
Non-system disk or disk error
Replace and strike any key when ready
```

Odds are, you accidentally left a normal, everyday disk in drive A. The computer couldn't find its life-giving boot sector, so it gave up. Remove the disk, tap the spacebar, and the computer will continue.

When it can't find a disk in drive A, the computer moves on to the hard drive, looking there for the boot sector.

5. The computer looks for the CONFIG.SYS file.

Next, the computer looks for a CONFIG.SYS file. Described earlier in this chapter, this file contains mostly drivers: bits of software that help a computer deal with things like compact disc players, memory managers, mice, video cards, and other gadgets attached to it.

6. The computer runs the COMMAND.COM program.

You may have noticed this file sitting on your hard drive or a floppy disk. It contains more basic DOS stuff — form-letter reactions to commands you type at a C:\> prompt, for example.

7. The computer runs AUTOEXEC.BAT.

The computer's had its fun; now it gives the user a chance to jump in. It reads each line in the AUTOEXEC.BAT file, covered earlier in this chapter. The computer treats each line as if the user typed in the command at the DOS prompt.

For example, if you end your AUTOEXEC.BAT file with the line WIN, your computer ends its reboot flurries by loading Windows. Quick and convenient. Unless, of course, you were just turning on your computer to grab a quick phone number from your files, and now you have to wait for Windows to finish loading before you can call out for the pizza.

Boring boot sector balderdash

What's the computer looking for in the boot sector? Two files with important operating system information. Normally, the two files are invisible, so you don't have to bother with them, thank goodness.

One file, called IBMBIO.COM or IO.SYS depending on your version of DOS, helps DOS communicate with your computer's hardware. The other file, called either IBMDOS.COM or MSDOS.SYS, holds computer-language answers to bare-bones DOS questions: What are files, what is memory, and other questions answered in *DOS For Dummies,* 2nd Edition, by Dan Gookin (IDG Books Worldwide, Inc.).

While you work in some programs, you may see these two files sitting on your hard drive. Don't delete them, or your computer won't be able to get out of bed.

Chapter 17

Fixing Squeaky Windows

● ●

In This Chapter

▶ Upgrading your computer for Windows 95

▶ Telling Windows 95 about new hardware

▶ Adding a different keyboard

▶ Adding a new monitor or video card

▶ Adding a new mouse

▶ Adding a new sound card, CD-ROM drive, or other gadget

▶ Adding a new printer

▶ Changing video modes

▶ Finding new drivers

▶ Optimizing Windows 95's performance

● ●

*I*t's an old joke by now. One of Windows 95's greatest features, dubbed as "Plug and Play," claimed that it could instantly recognize any new device you plugged into your computer. The pitch was that with Plug and Play, Windows 95 could set up computer parts so they wouldn't squabble with previously installed gadgets, and the world would be a glorious place.

Unfortunately, "Plug and Play" can turn into "Plug and Pray" when something goes wrong. In that case, you probably have to doff your hat and *personally* introduce Windows 95 to your new part, or the two will never get along. Of course, if you're using Windows 3.1, you have to do that anyway.

Windows 95 can automatically recognize a lot more computer parts than Windows 3.1 can, even if they're *not* built to the official Plug and Play standards. You don't have to stick with exclusive Plug and Play parts. Windows 95 still can run your old Windows software, too. However, older versions of Windows can't run Windows 95 versions of software.

This chapter explains how to upgrade to Windows 95, if you're considering it. It also helps you tell Windows 95 and Windows 3.1 about new hardware that you've added to your computer, as well as how to make adjustments to the goodies already installed.

Finally, this chapter tells you how to lift the hood and make a few adjustments so that Windows 95 can run at its greatest power.

Upgrading Your Computer to Run Windows or Windows 95

Just as an old Model T Ford can't pull a 46-foot sailboat, some old computers can't run Windows or the newly polished Windows 95. Those oldsters just don't have enough oomph. But how much oomph is enough? Oomph Table 17-1 has the answers.

Oomph Table 17-1	Computers Need This Much Oomph to Run Windows	
Computer Requirements Politely Recommended by Microsoft	*What Your Computer Really Needs to Run Windows or Windows 95*	*Why?*
4MB of memory (RAM)	At least 8MB of memory	Windows 95 crawls across the screen with only 4MB and moves much more comfortably with 8MB. If you plan to run several large programs, however, bump that to 16MB or more. Power users may want to consider even 32MB. When buying a computer, make sure that you can upgrade its RAM inexpensively (check out Chapter 11 for all info on RAM).
45MB of hard disk space	More than 500MB	That 45MB can hold Windows 95 but little else. Where do your programs go? Where do your files go? Some Windows programs want 20MB to 80MB of space just for themselves. Don't be afraid to buy a hard disk that's 500MB or larger.
A 386DX microprocessor	A Pentium	While at the store, compare Windows 95 running on different speeds of computers. The faster the computer, the less time you spend waiting for Windows 95 to do something exciting.

Computer Requirements Politely Recommended by Microsoft	What Your Computer Really Needs to Run Windows or Windows 95	Why?
A 3¹/₂-inch floppy drive	At least one high-density 3¹/₂-inch floppy drive	Many Windows programs come packaged on high-density, 3¹/₂-inch disks.
Color VGA card	Accelerated color Super-VGA card, VL-Bus card, or PCI bus card	Because Windows 95 tosses so many little boxes on-screen, you need to get an accelerated high-resolution SuperVGA card.
MS-DOS version 3.31 or later; Windows 3.0 or later	MS-DOS version 3.31 or later; Windows 3.0 or later	Microsoft is selling Windows 95 as an upgrade to its older products. Not upgrading from an older version of Windows? Then you have to buy the more-expensive version of Windows 95 at the software store.
Miscellaneous	A 15-inch monitor	The bigger your monitor, the bigger your desktop: Your windows won't overlap so much. Unfortunately, super-large monitors are super-expensive.
Miscellaneous	CD-ROM drive for Windows 95	Yep, Windows 95 says it's time you joined the multimedia explosion.
Miscellaneous	Modem	You don't need a modem, but without one you can't dial up the online services that come packaged with Windows 95, and you can't water ski across the Internet using Microsoft's freebie Internet Explorer. (And isn't it time you joined the Internet revolution, anyway?)

Telling Windows 95 about New Hardware

When you wolf down a sandwich for lunch, you know what you ate. After all, you picked it out at the deli counter, chewed it, swallowed it, and wiped the bread crumbs away from the corner of your mouth.

But when you add a new part to your computer, it's turned off — Windows 95 is asleep. And when you turn the computer back on and Windows 95 returns to life, it may not notice the new part.

Here's the good news, however: If you simply tell Windows 95 to *look* for the new part, it can probably find it. In fact, Windows 95 not only spots the new part, but it introduces itself, and starts a warm and friendly working relationship using the right settings. Ah, the beauty of modern Plug and Play convenience.

Here's how to tell Windows 95 to examine what you stuffed into its belly and make it put those new parts to work:

1. **Click the Windows 95 Start button found in the screen's bottom left corner, choose <u>S</u>ettings from the pop-up menu and choose <u>C</u>ontrol Panel.**

   The Control Panel's Add New Hardware icon, shown in Figure 17-1, handles the process of introducing Windows 95 to anything you recently attached to your computer.

Figure 17-1:
The Control Panel contains the Add New Hardware program, which introduces Windows 95 to new computer parts.

2. **Double-click the Control Panel's Add New Hardware icon.**

   The Windows 95 Add New Hardware Wizard, shown in Figure 17-2, pops out of a hat, ready to introduce Windows 95 to whatever part you've stuffed inside your computer.

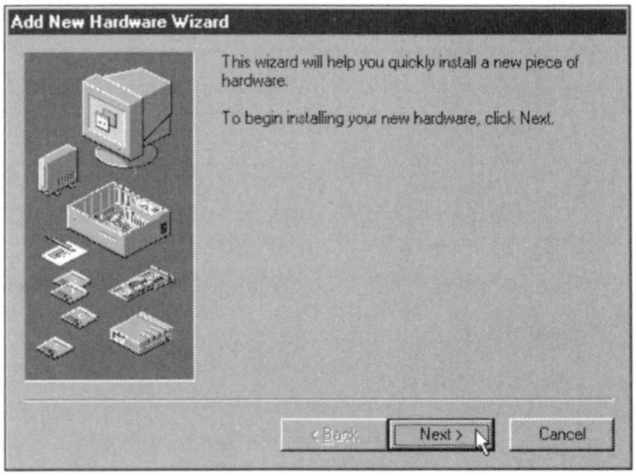

Figure 17-2:
The
Windows 95
Add New
Hardware
Wizard
automatically
installs
most
computer
parts.

3. **If you've already installed your new part, make sure you close all your currently running programs, and then click the Next button, shown in Figure 17-3.**

Figure 17-3:
Windows 95
can
recognize a
wide range
of computer
parts.

Windows 95 peers into the inner workings of your computer, spots the new device, and automatically sets everything up to work right. You're done!

If Windows 95 *doesn't* find your new part, however — or you don't trust Windows to find your new gadget automatically — click the No button and then click the Next button to move to Step 6, which presents a list of parts and brand names.

4. **From the list, click the name of the computer part you installed, and then click the Next button.**

Usually, you have an inkling as to what you installed: a new video card (Windows 95 calls them display adapters), a new modem, or perhaps a sound card or CD-ROM drive. If so, click the gadget's name from the box, and Windows 95 shows you a list of manufacturers.

Click the manufacturer that made your particular part, and Windows 95 shows you a list of models made by that manufacturer. See yours listed? Then click the Finish button and follow the instructions. If Windows 95 can't find your new device or can't make it work right, you need to contact the manufacturer of your new part and ask for a *Windows 95 driver*.

Or, if a driver came in the box, put the disk the manufacturer provided in your A drive and click the Have Disk button. Windows 95 grabs the driver from the disk, copies it to the hard drive, and, hopefully, talks to your computer's new part.

As Windows 95 grows in popularity, so will the number of manufacturers offering Windows 95 drivers.

✔ Adding a new modem? Then Windows 95 wants to know your current country and area code, as well as whether you dial a special number (like a "9") to reach an outside line (or *70, to turn off call-waiting). If you want to change this stuff later, double-click the Control Panel's Modem icon — that brings you to the same page that the Add New Hardware icon does.

✔ Windows 95 is pretty good about identifying various gadgets that people have stuffed inside the computer, especially if your computer is Plug and Play compatible — and you're installing a Plug and Play part.

✔ If you're not sure what type of part you've installed but you know the company that made it, then choose "Other devices" from the Add New Hardware Wizard's "Hardware types" box. Then when Windows 95 lists a bunch of companies, click the company that made your part. Windows 95 lists all of that company's parts it can recognize.

✔ Found an updated driver for a computer part? Head for the "Fine-tuning Windows 95 System Properties" section at the end of this chapter for the lowdown.

✔ In Windows 3.1, you had to know where you were going in order to get something done. Windows 95 is much more forgiving, and lots of the icons' functions are overlapping. If you install a new modem, for example, you can use the Add New Hardware icon or the Modem icon to introduce it to Windows 95. Added a new printer? Use either the Add New Hardware icon or the Printer icon; both take you to the same place — the spot where you tell Windows 95 about your new printer.

Telling Windows 3.1 about New Hardware

You need to beat Windows 3.1 about the head and shoulders a little more before it understands that you've added new hardware to your computer. The next few sections explain where to strike.

Introducing Windows 3.1 to a new mouse, keyboard, video card, or monitor

Sometimes Windows 3.1 works like the easy-to-use wunderkind that's advertised on TV: It recognizes your new part automatically, and everything works, with no button-pushing or mouse-sliding on your part.

For example, if you merely replace your mouse, keyboard, video card, or monitor with another one of the same kind, you needn't do anything special. Just plug it in, and Windows treats it just like the old part.

When you buy a part that uses a different *mode,* however, you have to make some changes. Here's a rundown of the modes that various computer gadgets use:

Mouse: Most mice operate in two modes: *Microsoft mode* and some other funky, third-party mode, like *Logitech* or *Genius.* If your new mouse runs in the same mode as your old one, you don't need to fiddle with Windows. If it runs in a different mode, however, you need to follow the steps later in this section. (More mouse information lives in Chapter 6.)

Your best bet is to set your new mouse to Microsoft mode and choose that mode when installing the mouse. Microsoft mode seems to cause the fewest problems.

Keyboard: Most new keyboards today are Enhanced Keyboards, which have 101 keys. If you're just replacing your old Enhanced Keyboard, you don't have to mess with Windows. If you're upgrading from an 84-key keyboard or adding some offbeat third-party brand of keyboard, however, follow the steps later in this section. (Chapter 5 is packed with keyboard stuff.)

Video card: Video cards can work in many different modes. The different modes let you choose the number of colors your monitor can display and the monitor *resolution* — the amount of information that can fit on the screen.

If you upgrade to a fancier video card, Windows still boots up on your screen, but it looks like it did with your old video card. To make Windows take advantage of your new card, follow this section's instructions on installing your new card's Windows driver. Then head for the section on switching between video modes, also in this chapter. You can try your new card's different video modes until you find one you like.

Monitor: Bought a new monitor? You need to tweak Windows under only one condition: if you finally bought a monitor that can take advantage of your video card's fancier video modes. To try out those new modes, you need to change the Windows Display options, which I describe later in this chapter.

To introduce Windows 3.1 to your new brand of mouse, keyboard, or video card, follow these steps:

1. Double-click the Windows Setup icon in the Program Manager's Main window.

The Windows Setup icon lets you tweak the major Windows hardware settings.

2. In the Windows Setup window's menu, choose <u>O</u>ptions, and then <u>C</u>hange System Settings.

The Change System Settings dialog box pops up, as shown in Figure 17-4. Here's where you can change your display, keyboard, mouse, or network. If you're at the office, though, you'll probably get yelled at for fiddling around with the network. Don't click that one.

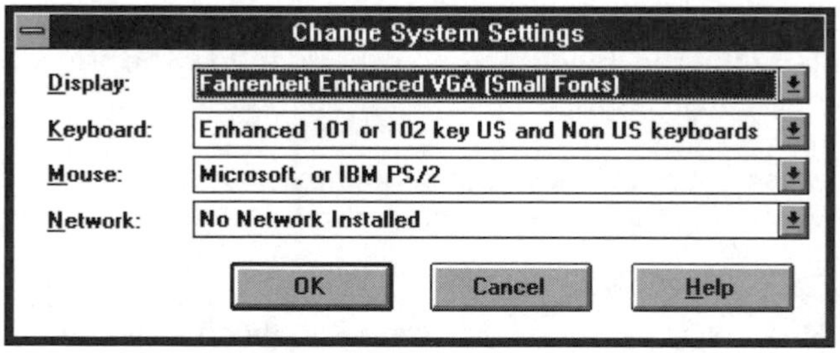

Figure 17-4:
This dialog box lets you change your display, keyboard, mouse, or heaven forbid, your network.

3. Click the box next to the kind of toy you want to add.

For example, to change to a different brand of mouse, click inside the box next to the word <u>M</u>ouse. A menu drops down, as shown in Figure 17-5.

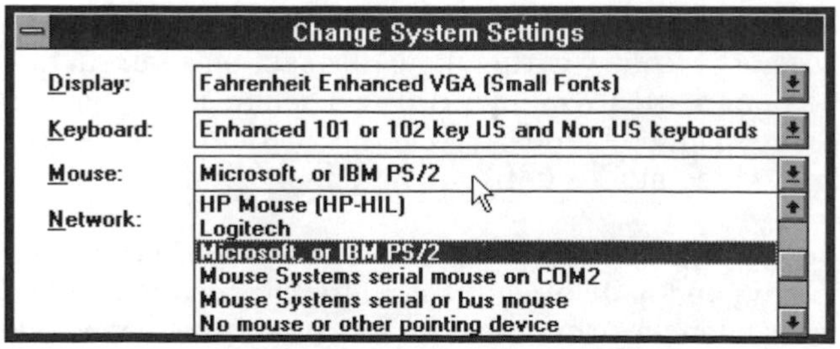

Figure 17-5:
Choose your new brand of mouse from the list that drops down.

Press your up arrow or down arrow to see all the listed brands. If you're lucky, Windows 3.1 lists your toy's particular brand by name.

If you're *not* lucky, click Other (Requires disk from OEM) and jump to Step 6. That "Other" business means Windows 3.1 doesn't have a driver for your mouse; you need to use the driver on the disk that came with the mouse.

4. Click the name of the gadget you installed.

When you click one of the listed gadgets, the menu snaps back into position and looks just like it does in Figure 17-4. This time, however, the box lists the gadget you just selected from the list.

5. Click the OK button.

The Windows Setup dialog box appears, as shown in Figure 17-6. If Windows 3.1 asks you to put one of your Windows 3.1 disks in drive A, rummage around in your Windows 3.1 box until you find the correctly numbered disk. Then stick it in drive A and press Enter.

Figure 17-6:
Insert the
correct disk
into drive A
and press
Enter.

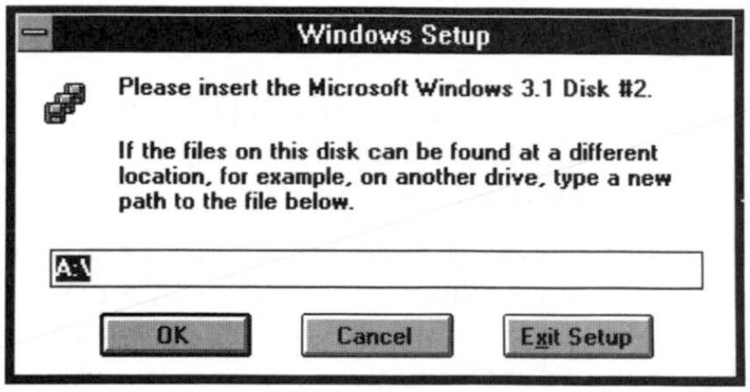

Windows Setup

Please insert the Microsoft Windows 3.1 Disk #2.

If the files on this disk can be found at a different location, for example, on another drive, type a new path to the file below.

`A:\`

| OK | Cancel | E**x**it Setup |

Or if you clicked the Other (Requires disk from OEM) option in Step 4, rummage around in the new gadget's box for a floppy disk. Then stick *that* disk in drive A and press Enter.

If your disk only fits in drive B, feel free to stick it in there. Then change the A:\ in the Windows 3.1 Setup dialog box to B:\ and press Enter.

Either way, Windows 3.1 copies the files it needs onto your hard drive so it can use your new toy. Next, Windows 3.1 almost always asks permission to reboot your computer.

6. Click the R̲estart Windows button when you see the Exit Windows Setup dialog box, as shown in Figure 17-7.

Windows 3.1 disappears and then reappears. This time, however, it's ready to use your new part.

About time, eh?

Figure 17-7:
Don't
reboot your
computer
manually
when you
see this
dialog box;
instead,
click
<u>R</u>estart
Windows
to let
Windows
3.1 handle
the reboot
chores by
itself.

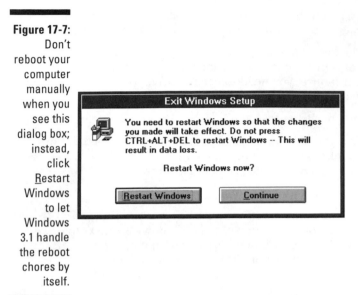

Exit Windows Setup

You need to restart Windows so that the changes
you made will take effect. Do not press
CTRL+ALT+DEL to restart Windows -- This will
result in data loss.

Restart Windows now?

[<u>R</u>estart Windows]   [<u>C</u>ontinue]

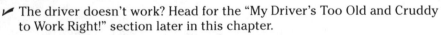

✔ Sometimes Windows 3.1 doesn't ask you to insert a floppy disk. Instead, it automatically knows how to talk to your new gadget, saving you the bother of rummaging around for the right disk.

✔ Other times, Windows 3.1 says it *already* has a driver for the new gadget on board. Go ahead and install the driver that came in the gadget's box anyway, though. Those drivers that came with Windows 3.1 are getting pretty old by now. The one that came with your gadget probably is more up to date.

✔ The driver doesn't work? Head for the "My Driver's Too Old and Cruddy to Work Right!" section later in this chapter.

✔ If you install a new video card, Windows 3.1 may be so disturbed that it doesn't even show up on the screen. If you can't get Windows 3.1 off the ground, head for the "I changed video modes, and now Windows 3.1 is broken!" sidebar later in this chapter.

✔ If your new mouse doesn't work in Windows 3.1, making it impossible for you to switch to the mouse's new driver, head for the sidebar "I changed video modes, and now Windows 3.1 is broken!" It shows you how to use the DOS version of Setup so that you can avoid the Windows 3.1 Setup program.

✔ The Windows 3.1 Setup program works well for switching to a new mouse, keyboard, video card, or monitor. But that's *all* it can set up. If you added a sound card, compact disc drive, satellite dish controller, or something even more fun, head for the "Introducing Windows 3.1 to a sound card . . ." section, coming up next.

✔ Some parts, usually video cards, don't make you use the Windows 3.1 Setup program. Instead, these cards come with their own installation software. If your card says it has its own setup or installation program, use it — that software will probably work better than the Windows 3.1 Setup program.

Introducing Windows 3.1 to a sound card (or CD-ROM drive or other gadget)

Windows tends to segregate its toys. For example, you install the keyboard, mouse, and video card through the Setup program, which I describe earlier in this chapter.

Everything else (including the *really* fun stuff) gets introduced through a second program: the Windows Control Panel. The following steps explain how to tell Windows about your new sound cards, CD-ROM drive, or anything else that's not a keyboard, mouse, or video card:

1. **Double-click the Control Panel icon in the Program Manager's Main window.**

   The Control Panel dialog box appears, letting you add drivers for new computer gadgets.

2. **From the Control Panel dialog box, shown in Figure 17-8, double-click the Drivers icon, which looks like a little recording studio.**

   The Drivers dialog box appears, listing the drivers that Windows is currently using, as shown in Figure 17-9.

Figure 17-8: Double-click the Drivers icon.

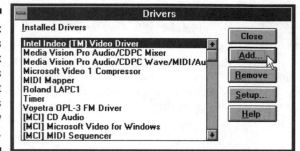

Figure 17-9:
The Drivers
dialog box
lists drivers
that
Windows is
currently
using.

3. Click the Add button.

The Add dialog box, like the one shown in Figure 17-10, pops up. The box contains a list of brand names.

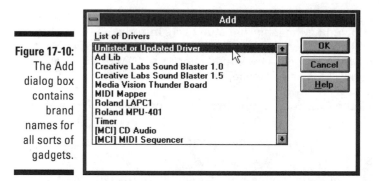

Figure 17-10:
The Add
dialog box
contains
brand
names for
all sorts of
gadgets.

4. When you see your gadget's brand name, click it.

Do you see the name of your particular gadget? Press PgUp or PgDn on your keyboard to scroll through the list. When you see your gadget, double-click its name. If your gadget's *not* listed, double-click the Unlisted or Updated Driver option.

The Install Driver dialog box, like the one in Figure 17-11, appears. This dialog box asks you to insert one of your Windows disks, or if you chose the Unlisted or Updated Driver option, to insert the disk that came with your new gadget. Either way, insert the disk in drive A and press Enter. (If you're inserting your disk in drive B, change the A:\ to B:\ first. Otherwise, you hear that terrible gnashing sound as your disk drive tries to read a floppy that's not there.)

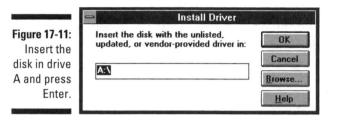

Figure 17-11:
Insert the
disk in drive
A and press
Enter.

5. Let Windows restart your computer.

After Windows copies the drivers off the disk, it asks politely whether it may restart your computer, as shown in Figure 17-12. Click the Restart Now button. The screen clears, and Windows reappears. This time, however, Windows 3.1 recognizes your new gadget.

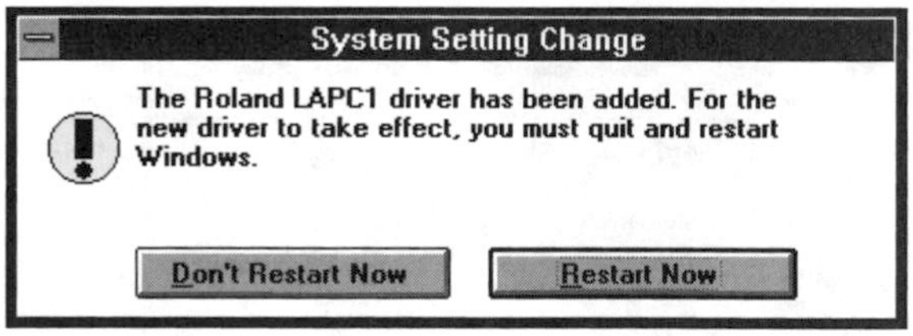

Figure 17-12:
Don't
reboot your
computer
manually
when you
see this box;
instead,
click Restart
Now to let
Windows
handle the
reboot
chores by
itself.

> ✔ If Windows doesn't recognize your new gadget when it reboots, try turning your new gadget back on. If Windows 3.1 still doesn't recognize it, you may need to change some of its settings.
>
> ✔ Before Windows can recognize some gadgets such as compact disc drives, you need to install drivers in DOS. Make sure that you run any installation programs that come with your new toy. *Then* try to install it in Windows 3.1.
>
> ✔ Windows 3.1 is getting old. Some of the drivers that came with it — the ones for the SoundBlaster sound card, for example — don't work well anymore. Instead, use the driver that comes in the box with your new gadget.

✓ If the driver that came with your new gadget doesn't work, it may be old, too. Head for the section entitled "My Driver's Too Old and Cruddy to Work Right!" for tips on finding the most up-to-date driver available.

Adding a New Printer

Congratulations! Don't you love that "new printer" smell? If you're installing a new printer in Windows 95, head back to the "Telling Windows 95 about New Hardware" section earlier in this chapter. Windows 95 treats printers like any other piece of hardware.

If you're using Windows 3.1, however, you need to introduce your new printer through the Windows Control Panel, as described next:

1. Double-click the Control Panel icon.

The Control Panel icon lives in the Program Manager.

2. Double-click the Printers icon as shown in Figure 17-13.

Figure 17-13:
The Printers icon looks like a printer.

```
┌─────────────────────────────────────────────────────────┐
│ ─                    Control Panel                    ▼  │
├─────────────────────────────────────────────────────────┤
│ Settings   Help                                          │
│                                                          │
│   ▥▥       A⅗C      ▱       ⬠       ▦       ⌨          │
│   Color    Fonts    Ports   Mouse   Desktop  Keyboard    │
│                                                          │
│   ▱        ◉        ▦       ▦       ▦       ▦           │
│  Printers  International Date/Time MIDI Mapper 386 Enhanced Drivers │
│                                                          │
│   ✿        ♫☏       ✿                                    │
│ Orchid Setup Sound  Audio Setup                          │
├─────────────────────────────────────────────────────────┤
│ Installs and removes printers, and sets printing options │
└─────────────────────────────────────────────────────────┘
```

3. Double-click the Add button.

This makes the bottom half of the menu appear, as shown in Figure 17-14. Déjà vu! It's the same list of printers you saw when you first installed Windows 3.1.

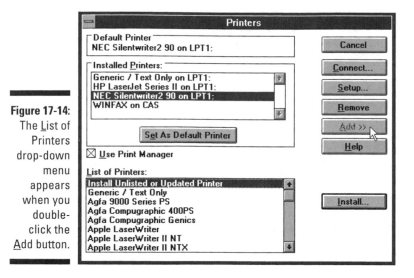

Figure 17-14:
The List of
Printers
drop-down
menu
appears
when you
double-
click the
Add button.

4. Choose your new printer from the list.

Press PgUp or PgDn on your keyboard until you see the name of your new printer. Press Enter or double-click the printer's name. Windows 3.1 then asks you to stick one of its setup disks into a drive. Insert the disk, press Enter, and listen to the grinding noises as Windows 3.1 grabs its appropriate printer driver files. After awhile, the new printer's name appears in the box.

5. Click the Set As Default Printer button and click the Close button.

That's it!

✔ Printer not listed? Then look for the printer it *emulates.* Chapter 9 talks about this emulate stuff.

If you don't want to wade through all those printer names, just press the first letter of your printer: *W* for *WangLDP8,* for example. Windows 3.1 automatically jumps down to the printers starting with the letter W. This slick trick works in just about any list Windows 3.1 tosses at you.

✔ If Windows 3.1 still doesn't recognize your new printer, make sure that you plugged your new printer into the same spot that your old one held on the back of your computer. Then check the old printer's settings, listed under the Connect button. Double-check that your new printer matches the same settings listed there.

✔ After your new printer's working fine, remove your old printer from your Windows 3.1 menus. Follow Steps 1 and 2 from the preceding steps. Then click your old printer's name and click the Remove button. Done!

I Want More Colors and Higher Resolution!

Most video cards can display more than one video *mode*. For example, some let you choose between seeing 16 or 256 colors on the screen. Others let you change *resolutions* and pack more information onto the screen.

Just as some people prefer different brands of toothpaste, some people prefer different video modes. To figure out which mode's right for you, try all the modes your card has to offer and stick with the one you think looks best.

Adjusting colors and resolution in Windows 95

To change video modes in Windows 95, follow these steps:

1. **Right-click anywhere on your screen and choose Properties from the pop-up menu that appears.**

   The Display Properties dialog box appears, as shown in Figure 17-15.

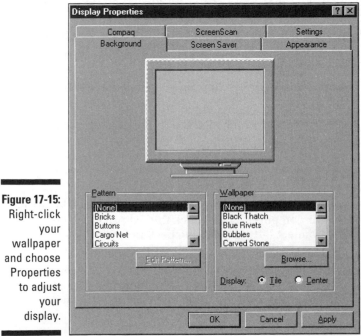

Figure 17-15: Right-click your wallpaper and choose Properties to adjust your display.

2. **Click the Settings tab.**

   The Settings menu lets you change the number of colors the screen can display, as well as its resolution.

3. **To change your amount of colors, click the Color palette drop-down menu.**

4. **To change your video resolution, slide the Desktop area bar from left to right.**

   Sliding to the right gives you more resolution; sliding to the left gives you less. Your video card has to work extra hard when it displays either a lot of colors or a lot of video resolution, so it rarely lets you display both at the same time. In other words, the more colors you choose, the less desktop area Windows 95 allows.

5. **Click the Apply button for a preview of the new look.**

   Like the new amount of colors and resolution? Move ahead to Step 6. Otherwise, head back to Step 3 and fiddle with the controls for awhile.

6. **Click OK.**

   When you're satisfied with your selection, click OK to save your choices. If you changed the amount of colors, Windows 95 probably wants to reboot your computer. (Luckily it gives you the chance to save your work first.)

Adjusting colors and resolution in Windows 3.1

Windows 3.1 users need to follow these steps to adjust their color and screen resolution.

1. **Double-click the Windows Setup icon in the Program Manager's Main window.**

2. **Press and release these three keys in this order: Alt, O, C.**

3. **Click the Display option.**

   Now choose between VGA, SuperVGA, or any other modes your video card can dish out. In fact, if your video card came with a drivers disk, click the Other display (Requires disk from OEM) box.

4. **Follow the directions on the screen, pressing Enter when asked.**

5. **Finally, click the Restart Windows button.**

   Windows reboots and returns in its new video glory!

✔ Sometimes Windows 3.1 *doesn't* return in its new video glory. In fact, it doesn't return at all. If so, tiptoe to the sidebar "I changed video modes, and now Windows 3.1 is broken!" for the cure.

✔ When Windows reappears on the screen after you switch between video modes, part of it sometimes hangs off the edge of your screen. If this happens, feel around the edge of your monitor for its vertical and horizontal control knobs. When you find them, turn them back and forth until you center Windows 3.1 on your screen.

✔ If you switch the video mode from 16 colors to 256 colors, be sure to try the Windows 3.1 wallpaper called 256COLOR.BMP. Almost all Windows programs use only 16 colors, so that wallpaper lets you see why you spent the extra money on your fancy video card.

✔ Switching to higher resolutions and more colors makes Windows look prettier, but don't get carried away. Windows works a lot slower when it has to push all those graphics around.

My Driver's Too Old and Cruddy to Work Right!

After you buy a new piece of hardware — a sound or video card, for example — it's not going to change as it sits inside your computer.

But its *driver* will change. Drivers, like any other piece of software, are subject to perpetual tinkering. As months pass, the manufacturers add bits of code here and there, making drivers faster and less likely to start arguments with other pieces of software.

Some companies release a new driver every two months. When a gadget doesn't work right or conflicts with some other part, your first step should be updating the gadget's driver.

In fact, that's usually the *second* thing you hear if you call the company's tech support line: "Are you using the latest driver?" (The first thing you hear usually is, "All lines are busy right now.")

✔ All versions of Windows work best when you're using the latest driver for all your gadgets.

✔ Your best bet is to call up the gadget's manufacturer. Sometimes the manufacturer will mail you a new driver for free. Other times they will direct you to their Web page or BBS. If you know how to use a modem, you can dial the Internet or BBS and download the latest driver.

I changed video modes, and now Windows 3.1 is broken!

Windows 3.1 is an accommodating program. In fact, it's so accommodating that it cheerfully lets you choose a new video mode your video card can't even display.

Trust me, you know right away if you choose a video mode that's past your computer's limits: When you reboot Windows 3.1, it doesn't reappear. Instead, Windows 3.1 flashes an error message that moves too fast for you to read. Then it leaves you sitting at the DOS prompt. Or the screen may stay blank, looking like a movie that never starts.

To bring Windows 3.1 back to life, use the DOS version of the Windows Setup program. Follow these steps:

1. **Move to your Windows directory.**

   From the DOS prompt, change to your Windows directory. If your Windows directory is on drive C, type these two commands, pressing Enter after each one:

```
C:\> C:

C:\> CD \WINDOWS
```

These commands bring you to drive C and leave you in the Windows directory. If your copy of Windows lives on drive D, however, substitute D: for C: in the first command.

2. **Type** SETUP **and press Enter.**

```
C:\WINDOWS\> SETUP
```

The DOS version of the Windows Setup program appears on the screen.

3. **Change your Windows settings.**

The DOS version of Setup, shown in the accompanying figure, works almost identically to the Windows 3.1 version, described in this chapter . Change the video mode back to VGA or a mode you're *sure* your card and monitor can handle.

```
Windows Setup

    If your computer or network appears on the Hardware Compatibility List
    with an asterisk next to it, press F1 before continuing.

    System Information
        Computer:          MS-DOS System
        Display:           Fahrenheit Enhanced VGA (Small Fonts)
        Mouse:             Microsoft, or IBM PS/2
        Keyboard:          Enhanced 101 or 102 key US and Non US keyboards
        Keyboard Layout:   US
        Language:          English (American)
        Codepage:          English (437)
        Network:           No Network Installed

        Complete Changes: Accept the configuration shown above.

    To change a system setting, press the UP or DOWN ARROW key to
    move the highlight to the setting you want to change. Then press
    ENTER to see alternatives for that item. When you have finished
    changing your settings, select the "Complete Changes" option
    to quit Setup.

 ENTER=Continue  F1=Help  F3=Exit
```

(continued)

(continued)

Feed your computer any disks the Setup program asks for. When the setup is done, the program closes, saving your changes. When Windows 3.1 boots back up, you should be able to see it this time.

The DOS version of Windows 3.1 Setup comes in handy whenever Windows 3.1 refuses to load. Feel free to use it if Windows 3.1 doesn't like your choice of mouse or keyboard, either.

The Windows 3.1 DOS Setup program can get confused if you're not working in the Windows directory when you call it up. If the Setup program starts talking about *installing* Windows — not merely *changing* its settings — press F3 twice to exit. Then make *sure* that you're in the Windows 3.1 directory before trying again.

- ✔ If you subscribe to CompuServe, GEnie, AOL, or other online services, join one of the Windows forums. They usually have the latest drivers within a few days of their release.

- ✔ Know how to get to the Internet? Head for Microsoft's Web Page (http://www.microsoft.com) for a plethora of drivers.

- ✔ Don't like working on computers? Then leave the driver dirty work to somebody else. CyberMedia's Oil Change for Windows 95 searches through your computer for hardware and then checks against its master list to see if every bit of hardware has the latest driver. If anything's lagging, CyberMedia commandeers your modem, dials its database, and updates your computer's drivers.

- ✔ If your new driver doesn't come with an installation program, install it as explained in the "Telling Windows about New Hardware" section. Then click the New button when Windows asks whether you want to use the New driver or the Current driver. (Windows 95 users can also find the answer to driver installation problems in the "Changing drivers in Windows 95" section in this chapter.)

Fine-Tuning Windows 95 System Properties

Unlike its predecessors, Windows 95 comes with a toolbox for tinkerers. When something's going wrong, your first step should be the System Properties dialog box. There, you can find a list of all the hardware that Windows 95 thinks is inside your computer, and whether or not any of the hardware is acting up.

To get to the System Properties dialog box, right-click the My Computer icon and choose Properties from the pop-up menu. From here, you can manipulate Windows 95 in a wide variety of ways.

Changing drivers in Windows 95

Windows 95 works best with updated drivers, that's for sure. Finding the updated driver is the hard part; after you locate the driver, be it on the Internet or directly from a company, Windows 95 makes installing the driver easy.

1. **Right-click the My Computer icon and choose P̲roperties from the pop-up menu.**

2. **Click the Device Manager tab.**

   The dialog box in Figure 17-16 appears, displaying all the goodies connected to your computer.

3. **Double-click the item that needs the new driver.**

   For example, if you've downloaded a new video driver, double-click the Display adapters listing to see your current driver.

4. **Click the current driver and click the P̲roperties button at the bottom of the dialog box.**

   Windows 95 reveals information about the current driver.

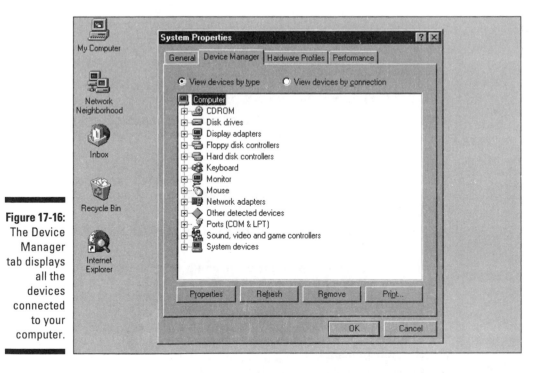

Figure 17-16:
The Device Manager tab displays all the devices connected to your computer.

5. **Click the Driver tab, click the Change Driver button, and click the Have Disk button from the next window.**

6. **Tell Windows 95 where the new driver lurks — on your hard drive or a floppy disk.**

   Windows 95 grabs the driver, puts it in its place, and begins using it. (Chances are you have to reboot the computer first, though.)

While you're on the Device Manager page, click the Print button. Choose the All devices and system summary option and click OK to send a complete technical report of all your computer's internal organs to the printer. That page may be a lifesaver down the road.

Checking the Windows 95 system and performance gauges

Afraid Windows 95 isn't working at its fullest capacity? You can analyze your computer's efforts to see if they're up to snuff using Windows 95's built-in troubleshooting program. Again, it's the System Properties area that comes through.

1. **Right-click the My Computer icon and choose Properties from the pop-up menu, then click the Performance tab.**

   The System Properties dialog box in Figure 17-17 appears, displaying technical information about your computer.

2. **Click the File System button.**

   Leave the Settings area box set to Desktop computer unless you're running Windows 95 on a laptop or network.

3. **If you have a CD-ROM drive, click the CD-ROM tab along the top.**

   Enter your CD-ROM drive's speed into the Optimize access pattern for box; Windows 95 automatically places the correct number in the Supplemental cache size box.

4. **Click OK, then click the Graphics button on the System Properties dialog box.**

   If your computer display has been acting weird, try sliding the Hardware acceleration knob to the left.

5. **Click OK and click OK again.**

   Unless you have very good reason, don't click the Virtual Memory button. It can almost always do a better job of juggling its own memory than any human.

   By tweaking these options after adding new parts to your computer, you can make Windows 95 run smoother and with more gusto.

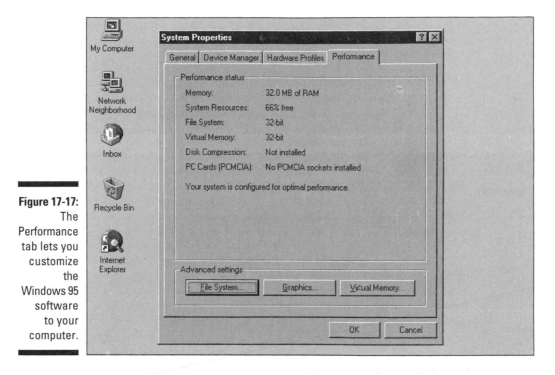

Figure 17-17:
The Performance tab lets you customize the Windows 95 software to your computer.

Finding device conflicts in Windows 95

When two parts aren't getting along in Windows 95, you know about it several ways. First, the computer won't work right. And second — luckily — Windows 95 points out the squabbling devices and help make amends. Again, it's the Device Manager that rules against the unruly.

1. **Right-click the My Computer icon and choose P̲roperties from the pop-up menu.**

2. **Click the Device Manager tab.**

3. **Look for an exclamation point or red X marking a particular part.**

   An exclamation point usually means two parts are squabbling over the same resource — an IRQ, for example, as I explain in Chapter 18.

   A red X as shown in Figure 17-18 means that device is disabled.

   After you find the culprit, click the Start button, choose H̲elp, and click the Contents tab along the window's top. Double-click Troubleshooting to see the list of possible problems, and double-click the area that's giving you trouble.

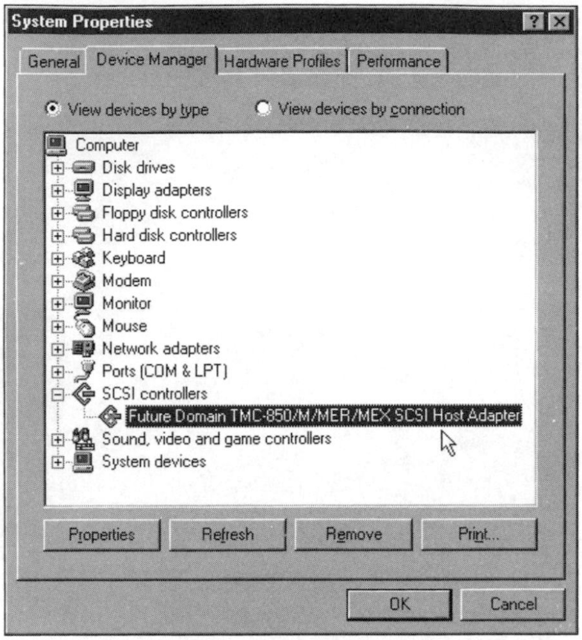

Figure 17-18:
A red X
over a part
means it's
not set up
correctly
and is
disabled.

The Wizard walks you through the steps needed to shake loose the conflicting hardware demons.

If the Help wizard uses unfamiliar language, head for Chapter 18. That chapter tackles things like IRQs, COM ports, and other things that computer gadgets fight over.

Chapter 18
Fiddling with Settings

· ·

In This Chapter

▶ Figuring out COM ports

▶ Resolving irritating IRQ conflicts

▶ Avoiding DMA and address conflicts

▶ Yanking jumpers

▶ Flipping DIP switches

▶ Understanding the CMOS scene

· ·

*T*his is by far the book's scariest chapter. It's full of disturbing, psychoanalytical words like *conflicts* and *interrupts*. If your computer's acting normally, you don't need to bother with this chapter at all.

But if things start to go haywire after you install a new part — or if the part simply refuses to work — you need to muddle through this conflict and interrupt stuff.

See, some new parts will work as is, right out of the box. Your computer embraces them like old friends and invites them to dinner, and nobody spills wine on the tablecloth.

Other new parts, however, can start arguing over territory with the older parts, and the resulting brawl can get ugly fast. The solution? You need to change some of your computer's settings so each part can get its own space.

This chapter tells you how to change the settings on your computer, as well as those on some of your newest gadgets. Tweak a few settings here and there, and nobody gets snubbed, especially you.

My COM Ports Are Arguing!

Chapters 6 and 7 cover all you need to know about plugging a mouse or modem into a serial port. But you probably wound up in this section because of a computerized eccentricity: Computer gadgets don't like to share serial ports.

If a gadget like a modem needs a serial port, it needs its *own* serial port. A mouse or a scanner often want its own serial port, too. If you inadvertently set up two gadgets to use the same port, fisticuffs break out and neither gadget works.

Gadgets that plug into the back of your computer usually don't cause much of a problem. You can plug a mouse into one port, for example, and a modem into the other. As long as your mouse and modem software know which part's plugged into which port, everybody's happy. (Chapter 6 tells how to figure out which one's plugged into which port.)

But things get trickier when you plug cards inside your computer. For example, sometimes you plug an internal modem card inside your computer, but it doesn't work. Not only that, it knocks your once-healthy mouse or scanner out of commission, too.

That usually happens because the modem and mouse or scanner are fighting over the *same* serial port. They've both been told to use the same port, but when they try, they see the other part blocking the way.

The answer is to cajole the internal modem into using a different serial port. You usually do that by a moving a *jumper* or *DIP switch* on the modem's card — a relatively simple, anesthesia-free operation that I describe later in this chapter, in the section entitled "Jumper Bumping and DIP Switch Flipping."

Don't know what COM port to assign to your latest internal gadget? Let Table 18-1 be your guide.

Table 18-1   What COM Port Should I Give My Internal Gadget?

If Your Computer's Like This COM Port	Let Your Internal Gadget Use This
No COM ports at all	COM2
Only COM1 is installed, but something's plugged into it	COM2
Only COM2 is installed, but something's plugged into it	COM1
Both COM1 and COM2 are installed, but something's plugged into COM1	COM4

If Your Computer's Like This COM Port	Let Your Internal Gadget Use This
Both COM1 and COM2 are installed, but something's plugged into COM2	COM3
Both COM1 and COM2 are installed, and something's plugged into both of them	Buy an A/B switch, described in the following section
Golly, I don't know what a COM port looks like or who's using it	Turn to Chapter 3

✔ A serial port and a COM port are the same thing: a "doorway" through which your computer passes information. If two gadgets try to pass information through the same doorway at the same time, everything gets stuck.

✔ Computers can access *four* serial ports, but there's a catch: You can use only *two* of those ports at the same time. You find two serial ports on the back of many computers. The bigger one is usually COM2; the smaller one is usually COM1. (You may want to check out the cool COM port pictures in Chapter 6.)

✔ If you assign one gadget to COM1 and a second to COM2 but they're still fighting, try reversing them. Assign the second gadget to COM1 and the first to COM2.

✔ How do you assign a serial port — a COM port — to a gadget? Usually by checking its manual and moving the right jumpers or DIP switches, as I describe in the section called "Jumper Bumping and DIP Switch Flipping."

After you assign a COM port to your modem, you usually need to tell your modem software what COM port your modem's hogging. Some modem software is getting a little smarter, however; a few programs can find the right port all by themselves. It's about time, too.

✔ You can assign gadgets that plug inside your computer to COM3 and COM4. However, you can't use COM1 and COM3 at the same time, and COM2 and COM4 can't be used at the same time either. Short attention span, those computers.

If you want a gadget to use either COM3 or COM4, you need to use at least DOS version 3.3 or later. Otherwise, your moldy old computer's stuck with two serial ports, COM1 and COM2.

✔ Some older internal modems only like serial ports COM1 and COM2. If COM1 and COM2 are already being used, free up a port with an A/B switch, described in the following tip.

Don't have enough COM ports? Buy an *A/B serial port switch.* It's a little box with a switch on the front. You plug a cable from the box into one of your computer's COM ports. Then you plug two gadgets into the two ports on the box — for example, a serial printer into the box's A port and plug an external modem into the B port. To use the printer, flip the box's switch to A. To use the modem, flip the switch to B. Don't be surprised if you forget to flip the switch back to the printer when you want to print; everybody does.

✔ As you figure out which gadget's using which COM port, fill out Table 18-2. You can save yourself the trouble of figuring everything out again the next time this hassle comes up.

Table 18-2	Who's Using My COM Ports?
The Port	*The Owner (Mouse, Modem, Scanner, or Other Gadget)*
COM1	
COM2	
COM3	
COM4	

How to Resolve Irritating IRQ Conflicts

Like squabbling siblings, computer gadgets often argue over *interrupt* rights.

Computers, like harried parents, concentrate on one thing at a time. When a parent's cooking dinner and a kid wants some attention, the kid pulls on the parent's pant leg. Computer gadgets work the same way. Computers have pant legs known as *interrupts.*

An interrupt, often dubbed an *IRQ,* is sort of a virtual pant leg that gadgets can tug on to get your computer's attention. When you move your mouse, for example, it tugs on one of your computer's pant legs — an interrupt — and tells the computer that it moved. The computer takes note and updates the mouse arrow's position on-screen.

Just as a pair of pants has only two legs, a computer has a limited number of interrupts. And if two gadgets — a sound card and a scanner, for example — try to use the same interrupt, the harried computer doesn't know which one to listen to. So it usually ignores both of them and keeps on cooking dinner.

The solution is to assign a different interrupt — a different IRQ — to each gadget. Sounds simple enough, eh? But here's the problem: When you try to assign an interrupt to a new part, you find that gadgets such as disk drives and keyboards have already grabbed most of the available interrupts for themselves, as you can see in the horribly technical Table 18-3.

Table 18-3		Interrupts and Who Usually Gets Them
Interrupt	*Owner*	*Comments*
IRQ 0	Timer	Your computer already grabbed this one.
IRQ 1	Keyboard	Your computer already grabbed this one. (Your keyboard interrupts your computer each time you press a key.)
IRQ 2	Some video cards on AT and faster computers	This one's usually up for grabs if you have an *XT* computer, not an AT, 386, or faster computer.
IRQ 3	COM 2, COM 4	These two serial ports share this interrupt. (That's why you can't use both of these COM ports at the same time.)
IRQ 4	COM 1, COM 3	These two serial ports share this interrupt. (That's why you can't use both of these COM ports at the same time, either.)
IRQ 5	Second printer port	Try this one on AT, 386, and faster computers.
IRQ6	Floppy Disk Controller	Your computer's already grabbed this one.
IRQ 7	First printer port	Try this one.
IRQ 8	Your computer's clock	Your computer's already grabbed this one.
IRQ 9	Network stuff	This one *may* be free, if you don't work in a connected cluster of other computers.
IRQ 10	Nothing	This may be free, but gadgets rarely let you choose it.
IRQ 11	Nothing	This may be free, but gadgets rarely let you choose it.
IRQ 12	Nothing	This may be free, but gadgets rarely let you choose it.
IRQ 13	Coprocessor	Your computer's already grabbed this one.
IRQ 14	Hard drive	Your computer's already grabbed this one.
IRQ 15	Nothing	This may be free, but gadgets rarely let you choose it.

✔ For such a laborious subject, interrupts have amazingly simple names. They're merely numbers, like 3 or 12.

✔ When a gadget wants an interrupt on an AT, 386, or faster computer, try assigning it to IRQ 5 or IRQ 7. If you're installing a gadget on a tired, old PC or XT model, try IRQ 2 or IRQ 7.

✔ How do you assign an interrupt to a computer part? For the most part, by moving a jumper or by flipping a DIP switch (a hobby I describe later in this chapter, in its own section). Other gadgets let you choose interrupts from their installation software.

✔ If you inadvertently choose an interrupt that another part's already holding onto, nothing explodes. Your new gadget just doesn't work. Keep trying different interrupts until one finally works. It's like driving around in front of the grocery store until you find a place to park. The parking process can be bothersome, but it's quickly forgotten after you're inside looking at the fresh strawberries.

✔ If you don't feel like using trial and error to find an unused interrupt, write down which interrupts your computer's gadgets are using. When a new IRQ-hungry part comes along, you'll know which interrupts are unavailable. Table 18-4 provides a handy spot to write down your IRQ assignments. Put the name of the part (such as *sound card* or *internal fax/modem*) in the first column and write down which IRQ the part snapped up in the second column.

Table 18-4	My Computer Parts Use These IRQs
This Gadget	*Currently Uses This IRQ*
My internal modem	
My scanner	
My sound card	
My video capture card	

If you don't want to use the chart, at least write down the IRQ on the front of the gadget's manual. Chances are, you need to dish out that information to any software that wants to play with the gadget.

Address and DMA Stuff

Some gadgets get greedy. They not only ask for things like an IRQ, described in the preceding section, but also for more arcane bits of weirdness such as an *address* or *DMA*.

Your computer assigns an address to some of its parts so it can find them later. Not all gadgets want or need their own addresses. But some newly installed gadgets ask for their own addresses and expect you to act as a knowledgeable real estate agent.

Because your computer usually has plenty of addresses to spare, most gadgets simply choose an address at random, hoping nobody else is using it. But if some other gadget's already living at the address, the two parts start bickering and neither one works.

The same thing happens when a newly installed gadget grabs a DMA channel that another gadget already snagged. The new gadget simply won't work.

DMA stands for *Direct Memory Address* channel. But who cares?

A DMA channel lets a part squirt information directly into your computer's memory. That's why havoc breaks out if two parts try to squirt in the same place.

The solution is to change your new gadget's address or DMA. You usually need to fiddle with jumpers or DIP switches on a card in order to do this. But sometimes you can change the DMA and address through the gadget's installation software — you don't even need to pop off your computer's case.

Which address or DMA should you choose? Unfortunately, your best bet is the trial-and-error approach. Just keep trying different addresses or DMAs; it shouldn't take long to stumble upon a home that nobody's claimed.

You can't damage anything by inadvertently choosing the wrong address or DMA. Your gadget just won't work until you choose an address or DMA that's vacant.

After you choose a DMA or address, write it down on the front of the gadget's manual. You'll probably need to give that information to any software that wants to play with the gadget.

I/O addresses for *memory* and I/O addresses for *hardware* are different. Software (spreadsheet programs, word processors, and so on) looks for addresses in memory; hardware (sound cards, scanners, and the like) looks for hardware addresses. The two kinds of addresses — memory and hardware — are on completely different streets.

Jumper Bumping and DIP Switch Flipping

Most people talk to their computer by typing on the keyboard. But sometimes you need to probe *deeper* into your computer's psyche. To talk to your computer on a "low grunt" level, you need to move around its little *jumpers* and *DIP switches*. By wiggling these little doodads around, you can tell your computer parts to behave in different ways.

You can easily change a gadget's jumpers or switches. All you need is the gadget's manual and a magnifying glass. These little switches are *tiny*.

Moving jumpers around

A *jumper* is a little box that slides on or off little pins. By moving the little box around to different sets of pins, you instruct the computer part to act in different ways.

The part's manual tells you what pins to fiddle with. The pins themselves have little labels next to them, giving you a fighting chance at finding the right ones.

For example, see the little numbers and letters next to the little pins in Figure 18-1? The jumper box is set across the two pins marked *J1.* That means the jumper is set for J1.

If the manual says to *set jumper J2,* slide the little box up and off the J1 pins and slide it down onto the pins marked *J2.* The pins then look like the ones shown in Figure 18-2.

Quick and easy. In fact, the concept was *too* easy for computer designers, so they complicated matters. Some jumpers don't use *pairs* of pins; instead, they use a single row of pins in a straight line, as shown in Figure 18-3.

In Figure 18-3, the jumper is set between pins 1 and 2. If the manual says to move the jumper to pins 2 and 3, slide the jumper up and off. Then slide it back down over pins 2 and 3, as shown in Figure 18-4.

By moving the little box from pin to pin, you can make the gadget use different settings. It's sort of a gearshift knob for computer circuitry.

- ✔ The hard part of moving jumpers is grabbing that tiny box thing so you can slide it on or off. A pair of tweezers or needle-nose pliers can help.

- ✔ Dropped the little box inside your computer? The last section of Chapter 2 offers tips on fishing out dropped articles.

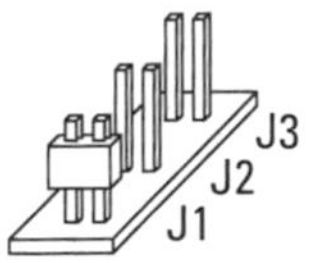

Figure 18-1:
This jumper is set for J1.

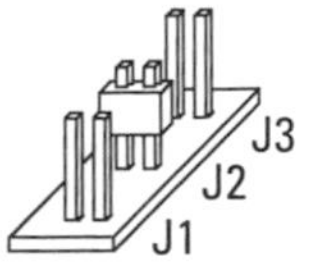

Figure 18-2:
This jumper is set for J2.

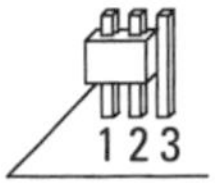

Figure 18-3:
This jumper is set between pins 1 and 2.

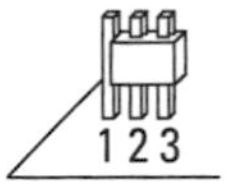

Figure 18-4:
This jumper is set between pins 2 and 3.

 If the manual says to remove a jumper, *don't* remove it! If you slide the little box off the pins, it can camouflage itself amid the paper clips in your desk drawer, and you may never find it again. Instead, leave the little box thing hanging on *one* prong, as shown in Figure 18-5. The computer will think you removed the jumper. But because the jumper's still attached to a pin, it's handy if you ever need to slide it back on.

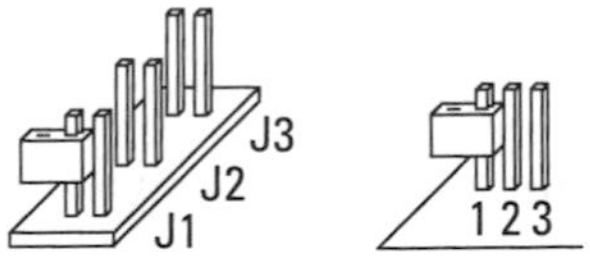

Figure 18-5:
If you're told to remove a jumper, just leave it dangling off one pin. That way it won't get lost and will be handy if you ever need it again.

✔ When the little box is over a pair of pins, that jumper circuit is considered *closed*. If the box is removed, that jumper is called *open*.

✔ Sometimes a jumper's little box comes with wires attached. For example, the wires leading from your computer's reset button probably push onto pins sticking up from your motherboard, as illustrated in Figure 18-6. You can pull that little wire thing on or off, just like any other jumper. The wires stay connected to the little box; the little box just slides on and off.

Figure 18-6:
Little wires
connect to
this jumper.

REMEMBER

Don't know which wire should connect to which pin? Look for little numbers printed near the base of the pins. The red wire always connects to pin #1.

✔ If you don't have a manual, how do you know which jumpers relate to which setting? You don't. You have three options: Call the gadget's manufacturer and ask for a new manual, see if the store has a manual lying around, or keep moving the jumpers around until you stumble across the combination that works.

Flipping a DIP switch

The first personal computer didn't have a keyboard. Its owners bossed it around by flipping dozens of tiny switches across the front of the computer's case. Sure, balancing their checkbooks took a *long* time, but hey, they were pioneers.

Today's computer owners still have to flip little switches, but not nearly as often. And thank goodness! The few remaining switches have shrunk to microscopic level. In fact, they're too small to flip with your finger. You need a little paper clip or ballpoint pen to switch them back and forth.

These little switches are called *DIP switches.* Figure 18-7 shows a few different switch varieties.

See the little numbers next to each switch? And see how one side of the switch says *On*? When you push or flip a switch toward the On side, you turn on that numbered switch.

In Figure 18-7, both DIP switches show switch numbers 4 and 6 turned on. All other switches are turned off.

Figure 18-7:
The DIP
switch on
the left has
sliding
controls;
the one on
the right
has rocker
switches.

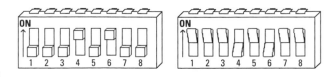

Figure 18-7:
The DIP
switch on
the left has
sliding
controls;
the one on
the right
has rocker
switches.

✔ DIP switches and jumpers are pretty much on their way out. Some of the latest cards and motherboards let you control all the settings using software. The process is just as aggravating, but at least you don't need a magnifying glass.

Before flipping any DIP switches, draw a little picture of the way they're currently set. If something dreadful happens, you can flip them back to the way they were.

✔ The left-most DIP switch pictured in Figure 18-7 has *sliding* controls. You slide the little box toward *On* to turn on that numbered switch. Slide it away from *On* to turn it off.

✔ The DIP switch on the right in Figure 18-7 has *rocker* controls. You press the switch toward *On* to turn on that numbered switch. Press the switch *away* from *On* to turn it off.

Feel free to flip a DIP switch with the tip of a ballpoint pen, but don't use a pencil. The tip of a pencil can break off and jam the switch, leading to much embarrassment.

✔ You need to flip DIP switches on almost *all* XT motherboards when you add memory.

✔ Although some 386 and 486 motherboards make you push around DIP switches, the switches show up mostly on cards. (Chapter 15 has all the card-playing instructions.)

✔ Some manufacturers felt that labeled switches were too easy for consumers to figure out. So they left out the words *On* and *Off* and put a little arrow on one edge of the switch. Just remember that the arrow points in the *On* direction.

✔ To further confuse things, some manufacturers use the word *Open* instead of *Off* and *Closed* instead of *On*.

✔ Some really offbeat manufacturers label their DIP switches with a *1* for *On* and *0* for *Off*.

Nobody needs to know that the "DIP" in "DIP switch" stands for *Dual In-line Package*.

Sailing the CMOS Sea

A *CMOS* — found in AT, 386, and faster computers — is like the sticker in the window of a new car. It lists the machine's most important accessories.

Instead of listing accessories like air-conditioning and driver's side air bag, however, the CMOS (pronounced *see-moss*) keeps track of more computer-nerdish details: the size of your disk drives, the size of your hard drive, how much memory you could afford to buy, and other geekoid facts.

Old PC and XT computers don't have a CMOS. Instead, they keep track of what's inside themselves by looking at the way the DIP switches and jumpers are set on the motherboard. (DIP switches and jumpers got their due in the preceding section.)

A CMOS provides a much more convenient system. You can update it by typing stuff in from the keyboard. That's a lot faster than trying to figure out what DIP switches to flip after you install some extra memory.

- ✔ Your computer's CMOS remembers all this stuff even when the computer's turned off or unplugged. A little battery inside your computer keeps the information backed up on a tiny chip.

- ✔ If that little battery ever dies, however, the information in your CMOS disappears, giving your computer a bad case of amnesia. When you turn the computer on, it won't remember the time, or the date, or the fact that it has a hard drive. (You can find out how to replace a dead battery in Chapter 10.)

- ✔ You need to update your CMOS when you change your computer's battery, type of disk drives (floppy or hard), memory, motherboard, video card, math coprocessor, or a plethora of other parts. The next section provides more specific details.

- ✔ If you have an AT (286) computer, you probably need a CMOS disk or Setup disk to change your CMOS. The disk should have been packaged with your computer. Most IBM PS/2s come with a Setup disk as well.

Keep track of what's in your CMOS in case the battery ever dies. Table 18-5 provides a handy spot. Dunno what words like *LZ* and *RAM* mean? Those nerdy details are covered in the sidebar entitled "Cylinders, heads, and other hard drive hazards."

Table 18-5	My CMOS Says This Stuff
This	***Is Set Up Like This***
Drive A	(circle one)
	Uses 1.44MB and 3¹/₂-inch disks (most common)
	Uses 1.2MB and 5¹/₄-inch disks
	Uses 720K and 3¹/₂-inch disks
	Uses 360K and 5¹/₄-inch disks
Drive B	(circle one line)
	Uses 1.44MB and 3¹/₂-inch disks (most common)
	Uses 1.2MB and 5¹/₄-inch disks
	Uses 720K and 3¹/₂-inch disks
	Uses 360K and 5¹/₄-inch disks
Drive C	Type ____
	Cylinders ____ Heads ____ W-Pcomp ____ LZone ____
	Sec ___ Capacity ___
Drive D	Type ____
	Cylinders ____ Heads ____ W-Pcomp ____ LZone ____
	Sec ___ Capacity ___
Amount of RAM	Base memory _____
	Extended memory _____
Notes	

How Do I Change My CMOS?

Of course, it would be too simple if you could use the same method to update the CMOS in all computers. So here's a rundown of the most common ways to update your computer's master inventory list.

Old PC or XT: These oldsters don't have a CMOS. You have to pull off the case and move jumpers or DIP switches, as per the manual's instructions. Your computer looks at those jumpers and switches to figure out what's packed inside it.

AT/286: These computers usually come with a Setup program. This program calls the CMOS information to the screen, where you can update it.

386/486/586/Pentium: These computers keep their CMOS information locked up inside a chip on your motherboard. You don't have to pry out the chip to change your CMOS, though. In fact, you don't have to pop the computer's cover, either.

Instead, you need to figure out what *secret access code* your CMOS uses. Different brands of computers use different codes, but the following paragraphs provide some of the more common ones. Give 'em all a shot before rooting through the file cabinet for your motherboard's manual. (The code is usually listed in the manual under *BIOS.*)

When you reboot your computer, look for words like these:

```
Press <DEL> If you want to run SETUP or DIAGS
```

If you see that message, press Delete quickly, before the message disappears. If you press Delete before the message clears, you're in: Your computer brings its master list of parts and settings to the screen. This list may look something like the CMOS shown in Figure 18-8.

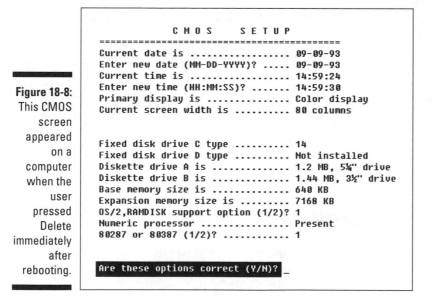

Figure 18-8: This CMOS screen appeared on a computer when the user pressed Delete immediately after rebooting.

```
             C M O S     S E T U P
=============================================
Current date is .................. 09-09-93
Enter new date (MM-DD-YYYY)? ..... 09-09-93
Current time is .................. 14:59:24
Enter new time (HH:MM:SS)? ....... 14:59:30
Primary display is ............... Color display
Current screen width is .......... 80 columns


Fixed disk drive C type .......... 14
Fixed disk drive D type .......... Not installed
Diskette drive A is .............. 1.2 MB, 5¼" drive
Diskette drive B is .............. 1.44 MB, 3½" drive
Base memory size is .............. 640 KB
Expansion memory size is ......... 7168 KB
OS/2,RAMDISK support option (1/2)? 1
Numeric processor ................ Present
80287 or 80387 (1/2)? ............ 1

Are these options correct (Y/N)? _
```

Other computers take different approaches. On my Dell 450DE, I press Ctrl, Alt, and Enter simultaneously at the C:\> prompt. The screen clears, and the CMOS appears, as shown in Figure 18-9.

On my wife's 486 clone, I press Ctrl, Alt, and Esc simultaneously to access the CMOS screen. On my IBM ThinkPad 755CE laptop, I hold down F1 while turning on the computer.

```
                        Dell Computer Corporation
   Screen 1 of 2                System 450DE Setup

   Time:  15:12:25   Date: Sun  Jun  6, 1993   This category sets the time in
                                               24-hour format (hours:minutes:
      Diskette Drive A:   3.5 inch, 1.44 MB    seconds) for the built-in system
      Diskette Drive B:   5.25 inch, 1.2 MB    clock.

   Hard Drives   Type  Cyls  Hds  Pre  L2  Sec   To change the value in a field,
      Drive 0:    46    683   16   -1  683  38    enter digits or use the left- or
      Drive 1:    39    919   16   -1  919  17    right-arrow key to decrease or
                                                  increase the value.
         Base Memory:         640 KB
         Board Memory:        640 KB           Changes take effect immediately.
         Fast Video BIOS:     On
         Extended Memory:     11264 KB
         CPU Cache:           On

         CPU Speed:           50 MHz
         Num Lock:            On                     System BIOS: A09
         Speaker Volume:      High                    Video BIOS: Disabled
                                             Math Coprocessor: Internal
                                                 Total Memory: 12288 KB

   TAB,SHIFT-TAB change fields|←,→ change values|Alt-P page|Esc exit|Alt-B reboot
```

Figure 18-9:
This CMOS screen appears on my Dell 450DE when I press Ctrl+Alt+Enter at the C:\> prompt.

If none of these tricks works for you, it's time to grab the manual for your computer or its motherboard.

Got the CMOS up on the screen? The following list covers things you need to change:

Battery: When you change your computer's battery, your CMOS turns off like a flashlight. It won't remember anything when you turn it on, so you have to reenter all the information. Hopefully you entered the most important stuff in Table 18-5 before the battery died.

Time/Date: Because your CMOS has a constant battery backup, it's a convenient place to keep track of the current time and date. You can change the time and date here. Or you can change the time and date simply by typing **TIME** or **DATE** at any C:\> prompt.

Floppy drives: The CMOS usually lets you choose between four different types of floppy drives, all listed in Table 18-5. If you swap the cables between your drive A and drive B, be sure to swap the drive's settings in your CMOS, too. You can't choose the higher-density disk drives in some of those old XTs, though. You may have to upgrade your computer's BIOS (Chapter 10) or get a new *controller card* (Chapter 12).

Hard drives: If you're lucky, you can find a Type number for your hard drive somewhere in your hard drive's manual. Put that number — which is usually between 1 and 47 — into the hard drive's Type area within your CMOS.

Cylinders, heads, and other hard drive hazards

If you can't find a Type number listed either in the hard drive's manual or your CMOS, you have to dig through the manual for numbers assigned to these words: Number of cylinders (Cyls), Number of heads (Hds), Write Pre Compensation (W-PComp), Landing Zone (LZone), Sectors (Sec), and Capacity (Size).

Then you have to enter those numbers in the user-defined area of the CMOS hard drive chart. You can usually get there by entering Type number 47 or 48 and filling in the blanks.

Can't find these numbers? Check with the store where you bought the drive or call the drive's technical support line or Web site. You also can try calling a local BBS via your modem and asking if somebody has the same kind of disk drive. You'll be able to track the numbers down eventually.

Can't find a Type number? Well, if you're using an IDE drive, try choosing the Type number of any drive that comes closest to, but not over, the capacity of your hard drive.

Not using an IDE drive? Then you're stuck with the agonizing technical details in the sidebar, "Cylinders, heads, and other hard drive hazards."

Memory: Your CMOS needs to know when you pop in some more memory chips, but the job's pretty easy.

Your computer automatically counts all the available memory whenever you turn it on or reset it. If your computer's quick little tally doesn't match the tally currently stored in your CMOS, your computer gets cautious: It sends out an error message and says to update your CMOS through the setup.

You merely have to call up your CMOS setup and confirm that, yes, the computer _did_ count up the memory total correctly — the numbers didn't match because you added some more memory! Sometimes, the CMOS already reflects the computer's new count; you just have to save the new total and exit the CMOS screen.

Some older motherboards make you flip a DIP switch to show how much memory you added. If you don't flip the switch, these motherboards won't be able to find the memory. (They won't even bother looking for it, either.) Check your motherboard's manual to figure out which DIP switches to flip. You'll probably still have to update the CMOS setting for those lazy little beggars.

The CMOS of a 286, 386, or faster computer usually calls your first 640K of memory _base_ memory; it calls the rest _extended_ or _expansion_ memory.

Motherboard: When you buy a new motherboard, you deal with a different CMOS, too. Before removing the old motherboard, call up its CMOS settings and write them down. Then enter the same settings into the new motherboard's CMOS.

Some of the latest motherboards have several pages of advanced settings that are far too authoritarian for this easygoing book. However, make sure that you turn on any memory caches. Your computer will run much faster. If you're searching for speed, try turning on some of the *ROM shadows;* if you run into trouble, change the setting back. It's important to make your changes *one at a time* so you can identify the culprit if your computer freaks out after a change. Just turn that ROM shadow back off, and all will be well.

Math coprocessor: Some computers automatically recognize a newly installed math coprocessor. Others can't figure it out for themselves. Some can't even tell if you installed a 287 or a 387 coprocessor. Fill out the appropriate line in the CMOS, and the computer should recognize your new chip. If it doesn't, you may need to flip some switches or move some jumpers on your motherboard. That means it's time to dig out the manual.

Display: Sometimes, you have to update the CMOS when you install a new video card. Usually, you only have to choose between *monochrome* or *color.* Some picky systems make you choose between *CGA* or *EGA/VGA.* And some picky motherboards make you flip one of their switches or move a jumper.

After you change a CMOS setting, look for a menu item that *saves* your changes. If you don't specifically tell the CMOS to save your changes, all your work will be for naught.

> ✔ Most computers don't let you access your CMOS while you're working in Windows. You usually need to be at the C:\> prompt before any of those weird access-code key combinations take effect. (Try using your System disk, which I describe in Chapter 2, to get to the C:\> prompt.)

> ✔ After you update your CMOS and tell it to change the information, your computer either resets itself or tells you to punch the reset button. When the computer comes back to life, it should recognize your new part.

Part V
The Part of Tens

The 5th Wave   By Rich Tennant

"HOLD ON, THAT'S NOT A PROGRAM ERROR, IT'S JUST A BOOGER ON THE SCREEN."

In this part . . .

Those of you with sharp eyes will realize something scandalous right away: Some of the lists in this section don't contain ten items. Actually, very few of them do. Most have a wee bit more information or a wee bit less.

But by the time most people get to this part of the book, they're tired of counting numbers anyway. In fact, these lists *aren't* numbered. They're just a bunch of facts tossed into the basket.

So when you read these lists, remember that it's quality, not quantity, that matters. Besides, would you want to read a fake tip about 8255 PPI (U20) just because one of the lists needed a tenth tip?

Chapter 19
Ten Cheap Fixes to Try First

● ●

In This Chapter

▶ Making sure that the computer's plugged in

▶ Turning the computer on and off again

▶ Removing disks before booting up your computer

▶ Checking for overheating

▶ Booting from a system disk

▶ Reseating cards, chips, and connectors

▶ Cleaning card connectors with a pencil eraser

▶ Installing a new power supply

▶ Running CHKDSK

● ●

*B*efore spending any money at the shop, try these cheap fixes on your computer. You might get lucky. If you're not lucky, give yourself a good stretch and flip back to Chapter 4 for some more system-sleuthing tips.

Plug It In

Sure, it sounds silly. But industry experts get paid big bucks to say it's the leading cause of "electrical component malfunction." Check your PC's power cord in *two* places: It not only can creep out of the wall outlet but also out of the back of your computer.

Sometimes a yawning leg stretch can inadvertently loosen the cord from the wall. Rearranging a computer on the desk almost always loosens cables that aren't screwed tightly into the back of the computer.

And, uh, the machine's turned on, isn't it? (That's the leading cause of printer malfunction, by the way.)

Turn the Computer Off, Wait 30 Seconds, and Turn It Back On

Sometimes the computer just gets confused for no apparent reason. If your computer drifts off into oblivion, with no return in sight, try tapping the spacebar a few times. Try pressing Esc.

Still no return? Then it's time to get ugly. The next few steps may cause you to lose any work that hasn't been saved to either your hard disk or a floppy disk. Sorry!

✔ Try rebooting the computer: Press the Ctrl, Alt, and Delete keys simultaneously. Sometimes that's enough to wake up Windows 95, whereupon it offers you a chance to snuff out the troublemaking program.

✔ If the computer's still acting like an ice cube, head for the next level of attention grabbing: Press the reset button.

✔ If the computer's *still* counting marbles on some virtual playground, turn it off. Then wait 30 seconds. (That 30-second part is important.) Finally, turn the computer back on and see if it returns in a better mood.

You'd be surprised how much good a little 30-second vacation can accomplish.

Remove Your WordPerfect Floppy and Then Turn On Your Computer

Ever turn on the computer only to be greeted by a message like this?

```
Non-System disk or disk error
Replace and press any key when ready
```

Chances are, you got that message because a floppy disk is sitting in drive A, where it's confusing the computer's start-up process.

Remove the floppy and, as the saying goes, "press any key when ready." A tap of the spacebar does the trick. Your computer returns to life.

Check for Overheating

Nobody likes to work when it's too hot, and your computer's no exception. Your computer normally works naked, but after a few months it wears a thick coat of dust.

Your first step is to look at the fan's round grill on the back of the computer. See all the dust flecks clinging to the grill, swapping barbecue stories? Wipe them off with a rag, being careful to keep the worst grunge from falling inside.

Don't just *blow* on them, either. The microscopic flecks of spittle in your breath can cause problems with the computer's moisture-sensitive internal components.

 Don't tape cards or "cheat sheets" across the front of your PC's case. That can block your PC's air vents, which are often disguised as avant-garde ridges across the front of the case. When air can't circulate inside your PC, your computer heats up in a hurry.

Don't keep your computer pushed up directly against the wall. It needs some breathing room so its fan can blow out all the hot air from inside the case.

Boot from a System Floppy Disk

If a program says it needs more memory to run, try booting it from a system disk. That makes your computer bypass its AUTOEXEC.BAT and CONFIG.SYS files and run as cleanly as possible.

System disks, described in Chapter 2, contain nothing but the bare-bones basics required to make your computer run. Sometimes they're all a program needs.

After making your system disk as described in Chapter 2, put it in drive A and reboot your computer. Then try running your recalcitrant program. When you're done running the program, remove any disk from drive A and reboot your computer to bring things back to normal.

Reseat Cards, Chips, and Connectors

When your computer's been running for a while, it heats up and expands. When you turn your computer off, it cools off and contracts. This constant expanding and contracting can play subtle tricks on your computer's internal components. Specifically, it can make those internal parts slide out of their little compartments.

If your computer acts up, turn it off, remove the case, and give all the cards a little extra push into their slots. Give the chips a little extra push into their sockets as well. That can cure memory errors. While you're in there, make sure that all those internal cables are plugged snugly into their connectors.

Sometimes taking this step clears up some intermittent problems, especially the ones that appear after the computer's been turned on for a while.

Clean Card Connectors with a Pencil Eraser

Is your computer still acting up, even after you pushed the cards a little more deeply into their sockets? Then try this:

1. **Turn off your PC, unplug it, and remove its cover.**

   If you've never gone spelunking inside your computer before, check the Cheat Sheet at the front of this book. It offers complete cover-removal tips.

2. **Unscrew one of the cards and remove any cables from it.**

   You can find complete instructions in Chapter 15. Basically, you need to remove that little screw along the top that holds the card in place. Then unscrew or pull out any cables connected to the card.

3. **Pull the card from its slot and clean the card's contacts**.

   Pull the card straight up out of its slot, being careful not to damage any of the electronic gizmos hanging on to it. Handling the card by its edges, using clean hands, is best.

   Now, see the little copper-colored connectors on the card "tab" that plugs into the slot? Take a pencil eraser and carefully rub it against the tab until the copper-colored connectors look shiny.

   Be careful not to bend the card while cleaning the contacts; doing so can damage the card.

4. **Replace the card and cables. Then repeat the process with the next card.**

   By removing any corrosion from the cards, you let your computer talk to them more efficiently.

Be sure to screw the cards back in. That single screw provides an electrical connection between the card and the computer.

Install a New Power Supply

When older computers simply refuse to turn on and do anything fun, it's probably because the power supply died.

Power supplies have become increasingly reliable over the past few years. Still, be sure to replace the power supply, which costs less than $100, before replacing the entire motherboard, which always costs *more* than $100.

Chapter 14 provides complete power-supply replacement instructions.

Run the Weird-Sounding CHKDSK and Defragmentation Programs

Here's a quick fix that's free! If your computer's sending weird error messages or you're running out of hard disk space, give this trick a try. It doesn't hurt anything, and it can often help.

Don't run CHKDSK while you're currently running an older version of Windows, like Windows 3.1. Instead, exit Windows by closing down the Program Manager. Then it's safe to run CHKDSK by doing this:

Type the following command at the C:\> prompt:

```
C:\> CHKDSK /F
```

That is, type **CHKDSK**, a space, a forward slash, and **F**, and then press Enter. Your computer responds with some computer jargon. But if the program asks you whether you want to Convert lost chains to files (Y/N)?, press Y.

Your computer then gathers any file scraps and stores them in files with names like FILE000.CHK, FILE001.CHK, FILE002.CHK — you get the picture. Feel free to delete those files. They don't contain anything worthwhile, as you'll soon discover if you try to open them with your word processor.

If your computer doesn't ask you for permission to convert lost chains to files, CHKDSK won't fix anything for you — it didn't find anything wrong.

Still, feel free to run CHKDSK every couple of weeks, especially if your computer was turned off while a program was still running.

If you're running Windows 95, head for the end of Chapter 17 for tips on the new Windows 95 version of CHKDSK and its friendly gang of disk-nursing programs.

Chapter 20

The Ten Hardest Upgrades

*E*verybody wants to save money by avoiding the computer repair shop. But how can you tell which fix-it jobs you can do on your dining room table and which ones require experienced technicians who work in sterile rooms, drinking out of Batman coffee cups while holding expensive probe-things with curly wires?

Turn to this chapter when trying to decide whether *you* should hold the screwdriver or pass the job on to somebody else.

Upgrading The Really Ancient PCs

Unfortunately, the computers most in need of upgrading are the hardest machines to upgrade. These oldsters set the stage for everything to come.

But just as the Wright brothers would have trouble finding parts for their old Kitty Hawk cruiser, you'll have increasing trouble finding parts for your old IBM PC, XT, or PCjr. These computers don't accept most of the latest cards. They're too old to run most of the latest software, too. You can forget about Windows and OS/2.

Sure, you can scrap together a few parts here and there from garage sales and mail-order outfits. After all, the Wright brothers built their airplane from scratch in their bike shop. But if you decide to keep your oldster going, you're probably tossing your money down a hole. Consider saving your money and buying a new computer, rather than keeping the old one running.

So what do you do with your old computer when you get the new one? Hang on to it. It's destined to be a collectible.

- A German calculator from the 1820s fetched $11.8 million at Christie's in London, a record auction price for a scientific instrument. How many calculators have you thrown away in the past ten years? (Including the free ones that come with magazine subscriptions?)

- The Altair, the first personal computer, is now selling for thousands of dollars as a collector's item.

- Your old computer may have to be passed down for several generations before it can be cashed in as a collectible. And your great-grandchildren will always remember you as a technoweenie. But at least they'll be able to live comfortably.

Installing Scary Internal Modems

Ask any grizzled, backroom repair shop technician about the computer upgrade that causes the most problems. The words *internal modems* will be mumbled with the fullest force.

Modems toss out obstacle after obstacle. You need to plug them into the right place on your computer and make sure that the modem's software is working. Then you need to make sure that the software's working on the other side — on the computer you're trying to call. And all the while, the phone line itself can toss in some glitches.

With an internal modem, the problems loom larger. Is the modem card pushed far enough into its slot? Is it assigned the right COM port, one that no other parts have already staked out? Many internal modems don't even label their telephone jacks, so you can't tell whether or not you plugged the phone cord into the right jack.

Yes, internal modems cause the most headaches of any upgrade by far. (However, you can cut through most of the fat by checking out Chapter 15 and then flipping to Chapter 18 if the thing doesn't work.)

Replacing the Motherboard

Conceptually, replacing a motherboard isn't too difficult. You merely un-screw one part and screw a new part in its place. The problem comes with all the stuff that's *attached* to the motherboard.

Replacing the motherboard is like replacing the shelves in a bedroom closet. The project sounds simple at first: Just pull out the long board that's sagging over all the shirts and bolt some newer, fancier shelves in its place. Unfortunately, you have to remove *everything* from the closet — all those shirts, hangers, and boxes of old checkbooks must come down from the top shelf. Then after the new shelves are up, all that stuff has to go back on. And if you upgraded the shelves, everything's going to be put back in a different location.

When you replace your computer's motherboard, you can simply screw it in by using the same screws that held down the old motherboard. But all the little wires will plug onto slightly different connectors. You'll have to move little DIP switches and jumpers around, too. And where does the speaker wire connect? The reset button wire?

Then you have to put all the cards back in their slots, with all the right cables plugged into the back of them. Finally, you have to fill out a new CMOS — your computer's master inventory list. Chances are, it'll be filled with new, upgraded words like `Fast Gate A20 Option`.

No, replacing the motherboard is not for the squeamish. Unless you have a lot of patience, leave it for the folks at the shop. Besides, you can't even add a new motherboard to most XTs; the latest motherboards won't fit inside.

Adding a Second Hard Drive to an Ancient, Early Model Hard Drive

Hard drives have made some great advances in the past few years. Unfortunately, they've also left their predecessors in the dust. Most new hard drives don't get along with the older-style hard drives. To install one of the newer IDE hard drives, you probably have to yank out your old drive. The two kinds of drives just don't like to work together.

If you're using a hard drive that's more than five years old, be sure to read Chapter 13 before heading to the store and picking out a new hard drive.

Adding a second IDE drive to your first IDE drive can sometimes be a problem, too. In fact, your best bet is to buy your second IDE drive from the same manufacturer as the first. That usually guarantees that the two drives will be happy roommates.

When buying a second hard drive, make sure that the salesperson lets you bring it back for a refund if it doesn't get along with your first hard drive.

Adding Memory to an Old Motherboard

Sometimes a stroke of good fortune greets you when you lift off your computer's case and peer at its motherboard: You find some empty sockets that are ready to accept new memory chips. Other times, you're in for a disappointment — your memory sockets are already stuffed full of chips.

However, you can still add more memory to your computer; that's not the disappointing part. The disappointing part is that you have to remove some of the old chips and replace them with memory chips that have a higher capacity. For example, you have to yank out a few of your eight rows of 4MB memory chips — those 8 rows of 4MB chips can't create more than 32MB of memory — and replace a few of the chips with 8MB or 16MB chips in order to upgrade your computer's memory.

Sure, this upgrades your computer, and Windows runs much faster. But you're stuck with a handful of extra memory chips and no place to put them. If you're lucky, your local chip merchant will let you trade in your older chips, giving you a discount on the new ones. Otherwise, you'll do what everybody else does: Stick them in a Ziploc baggie and keep 'em in a drawer.

Another alternative is to buy a memory card to add more memory to your computer. The card will work more slowly, however, and probably cost just as much as adding memory chips. If you have a tired old XT, however, it's pretty much your only alternative. Those old XTs don't have room for any more memory chips on the motherboard.

Connecting Computers to a Network

This brutal upgrade has caused much grief and consternation over the years, especially for all those workers who have been left helpless simultaneously when their computer system crashed.

Installing a network is not a job for the novice, which is why I decided not to cover it in this book. Basically, installing a network involves placing cards in each computer and then linking them in peculiar ways with cables. After the hardware's in place, software constantly runs in the background so the computers can talk to each other.

To get a hint at whether or not you'd want to tackle the task, drop by the bookstore and get ahold of my book *More Windows 95 For Dummies* (IDG Books Worldwide, Inc.). After reading a few sections, you should get a feel for the level of computer oomph required.

Chapter 21

The Ten Easiest Things to Upgrade

Some of the most effective automobile upgrades are the easiest. You can simply hang some dice from the rearview mirror, for example. It looks cool, it's cheap, and you don't have to read any complicated manual to figure out which direction the dice should hang.

A few computer upgrades are almost as easy. They're collected and listed here for your upgrading pleasure.

Adding a Keyboard

By far, the easiest computer part to upgrade or replace is the keyboard. Just turn off your computer, pull the keyboard's plug out of your computer, and take your old, coffee-soaked keyboard to the computer store. Buy another one, plug it back into your computer, turn the computer on, and keep typing, being careful to keep the coffee cup a little farther away this time.

You do need to make sure that the little plugs on the end of the cables match and that the number of keys matches. If your old keyboard had 101 keys, the new one should have 101 keys as well. The salesperson can tell at a glance what type of replacement you need, so don't bother counting the keys.

If your computer is particularly old, the salesperson also can sell you a small converter that lets your new keyboard plug into the old computer's hole.

Unlike other upgrades, adding a keyboard doesn't involve fiddling with any software, tools, or files. Just plug and play. Yay! Oh, and see Chapter 5 for some more keyboard information — you may be able to fix the keyboard instead of replacing it.

Adding a Mouse

Adding a mouse can get a little tricky, but usually it's a pretty easy upgrade.

Chances are, you have a mouse port on the back of your computer. (Look in Chapter 3 for a picture of a mouse port; you're probably using the PS/2-style.) If nothing's plugged into the port, just plug in your new mouse and run the little creature's installation program. You don't have to take off your computer's case and run the risk of letting the snakes out. Quick and easy.

To replace a mouse, turn off your computer. Then unplug the dead one, take it to the store, and buy another just like it. Plug it into the same spot, and you're through. The complete steps — as well as a lot more mice trivia — are dissected in Chapter 6.

Adding Cards

Cards often get a bum rap. Adding cards sounds scary because you have to take off your computer's case. Then you have to decipher the inside-the-case vocabulary, which includes words like *slots, 8-bit,* and *16-bit.*

But for the most part, installing a card is pretty simple. Physically, it's kind of like pushing a credit card into an ATM machine. That, and tightening a single screw, is the whole procedure.

Most cards are designed to work with a wide variety of computers. So unless your computer's set up a little differently than most, the card probably will work right off the bat. If it doesn't, head for Chapter 18 for information to help you figure out what the card's manual means when it says to *set DIP switches 2, 4, and 5 to On,* and *set jumpers J2 and J4.*

It's a *lot* easier than it sounds. Promise.

Replacing a Monitor

Adding a new monitor is another easy upgrade, as long as you understand one key point: Monitors work in pairs with *video cards*. Video cards are the things that live inside your computer and give the monitor a place to plug into.

Your video card is responsible for creating an image and spitting it out. Your monitor merely grabs that image and puts it on the screen for you to show your friends. If you're looking to upgrade your monitor, you'll probably want to upgrade your video card as well. Otherwise, your new monitor probably will display the same image that your old monitor displayed.

✔ Even if you buy a huge monitor to go with your VGA video card, for example, you won't see any more information on your new screen. Your word processor will still fill the entire screen, and your windows will still overlap, just as they did on your other monitor.

✔ The solution? Buy your video card at the same time you buy your monitor. Then you can be sure that your monitor can display the highest quality image that the card can spit out.

✔ You probably have to buy a new card with that new monitor anyway because some of the newer monitors won't even plug into older video cards.

✔ You can find more of this video card/monitor stuff in Chapters 8 and 15.

Installing a Floppy Drive

Floppy drives are a snap to install — *unless* you're trying to install a newer, high-capacity floppy drive into an old IBM PC or XT. Those old guys just can't stand the pressure, and you have to add a whole bunch of reinforcement parts before they can handle it.

In other computers, new floppy drives simply slide on in. In fact, one of the most popular upgrades these days is installing those new *combo drives*. (You can see a picture of a combo drive in Chapter 3.) These drives squeeze a large, $5^1/_4$-inch floppy drive and a $3^1/_2$-inch floppy drive into a single floppy drive.

By combining the two floppy drives into one little unit, you free up enough room to stick in a new hard drive, a tape backup unit, a compact disc player, or a pencil holder. And best of all, the double-decker drives are easy to install. Details abound in Chapter 12.

Adding a Power Supply

Power supplies come in zillions of sizes, but even so, adding a power supply is an easy upgrade. How come? Because you install all power supplies in pretty much the same way.

Just unscrew the old one, making sure to save the screws. Then disconnect all the power supply's wires (write down where the different wires connect before you remove them).

Next, drag the old power supply into the store and get another one that's the exact same size. Screw the new power supply in and reconnect the wires. You're done! (You can find *complete* instructions in Chapter 14.)

While you're shopping, consider buying a power supply with a higher wattage, as I discuss in Chapter 14.

Don't ever try to repair or take apart power supplies. They soak up electricity like a sponge and can give you a serious zap if you poke around inside them.

Chapter 22

Ten Ways to Make Your PC Run Better

. . . .

In This Chapter

▶ Buying utility programs

▶ Keeping track of your computer's CMOS information

▶ Adding more memory

▶ Buying a graphics accelerator card

▶ Not smoking around your PC

▶ Keeping the Turbo switch on

▶ Avoiding the cheapest parts

▶ Avoiding turning your PC on and off quickly

▶ Keeping your old parts

▶ Tuning Windows 95 to your computer parts

. . . .

*I*f you're in an office somewhere and some tired-looking person is responsible for looking after your computer, don't bother browsing through this chapter. That person is paid to keep your PC running smoothly and probably already knows the tricks in this chapter.

But if *you're* the one who has to handle the screwdriver, this chapter's designed to keep it locked up in the toolbox for as long as possible. It shows you some simple ways to keep your computer healthy and happy.

Buy Some Utility Programs

The words *utility program* reek with a nerdish aroma. Utility programs aren't designed to let people do fun things; they're designed to let the *computer* do maintenance work. What a bore!

That's why the nerds snap them up. Norton Utilities, for example, comes with an advanced hard disk defragmentation program that organizes your hard drive more logically so the computer doesn't have to work as hard to grab stuff off the drive. (Windows 95 comes with a smaller, freebie version, which I describe in Chapter 13.) Because the computer isn't working as hard, it's less likely to break down.

Many utilities also contain diagnostic programs to help you figure out why your computer suddenly goes on strike. Still others can examine the way your computer's memory was set up and offer suggestions to make it run faster or smoother.

 Ever wish that something could poke around inside your computer, figure out what software and drivers were out of date, and swap all the ailing ones with their updated replacements? CyberMedia's *Oil Change* does just that (contact them at 310-581-4700 or www.cybermedia.com). After identifying the software and hardware drivers on your PC, Oil Change checks to see if it knows of any available updates and newer drivers. If any match, Oil Change downloads them from the Internet and installs them onto your PC.

Write Down Your CMOS Information

I describe this tip in Chapter 18, but it's important enough to emphasize here. Your computer's CMOS works like its secretary. The CMOS keeps track of all the parts currently installed inside your computer. Should something happen to your CMOS information, your computer will be as lost as a blue-suited executive whose secretary leaves for three weeks.

Call up your computer's CMOS and copy it into the chart in Chapter 18 while the information's safe. If something dreadful happens, you'll be glad you did.

Buy More RAM

The advertising on the Windows 95 box says that Windows 95 needs 4MB of RAM. But if you listen to the Windows 95 box, you'll also be listening to your hard drives whir and grind. With only 4MB of RAM, Windows constantly shuffles information back and forth from your hard drive.

If you're using Windows, upgrade to at least 8MB of RAM; better still, upgrade to 16MB or 32MB if you work with large programs. Windows runs faster and smoother after you upgrade. You can also run more programs at the same time, all the while shifting information between them. And isn't that the whole point of Windows?

Buy a Graphics Accelerator Card

Another quick way to add some spunk to Windows is to buy a graphics *accelerator card.* These small, quick video cards shoulder the burden of updating the screen when you move little windows around on the screen.

That doesn't sound like much to get excited about. But when you see the difference it makes on your screen, you'll be surprised at all the extra zip you get from an accelerator card.

Don't Smoke Around Your PC

You can tell a lot about a PC's owner by looking inside its case. Computer repair folks can quickly tell when someone's been smoking around a PC.

The PC's fan constantly sucks air into the case and blows it out the back to keep the machine cool. If the air's filled with smoke, the PC's internal organs soon are covered with smoke, too.

So smoke outdoors. Ride a horse like the Marlboro man or toss a hat in the air like the Virginia Slims woman. If you can't smoke outdoors, clean the inside of your PC's case regularly. Remove the case and use a can of compressed air to blow away all the gunk, as described in Chapter 2.

Keep the Turbo Switch On

This one's simple, yet it makes a big difference. Many older PCs have a *turbo switch* along the front of the case. Look for the little turbo light along the front of the case. When the turbo light's on, the turbo mode is on, too; your computer's already running as fast as its legs will carry it. But if the light's off, flip the turbo switch to make the computer run a little faster.

(Believe it or not, engineers added the switch years ago so they could slow down their computers to play video games.)

Avoid Really Cheap Parts

When buying computer parts, you inevitably come across three brands of parts that look the same and claim to do the same thing. One will be priced sky-high, another will cost less than dry cat food, and the other will be priced somewhere in the middle.

Don't buy the *cheapest* parts. They're made with the cheapest ingredients tossed together in the cheapest way. They may save you money in the short run, but they cost you in the long run.

For example, the cheapest floppy disks can coat your floppy drives with gunk after a few years of use. The cheapest hard drives don't last as long as the slightly more expensive ones. And the cheapest cables (usually found on the cheapest mice) fall apart more quickly than others costing just a few dollars more.

In addition, some of the cheapest parts aren't as compatible with your other computer parts as the more expensive brands. Finally, if something goes wrong with a cheap part, you usually find that its manufacturer has either gone out of business or doesn't have a technical support staff who listens to you.

Don't Flip the Computer On and Off a Lot

Computers tend to go bad when stressed. Because computers don't worry about credit card interest rates, car stereo thieves, or public restrooms, their most stressful experience comes when they're first powered up and a jolt of electricity flashes through them.

To ease the strain, don't turn a computer on and off repeatedly like you did to make "living room lightning" as a kid. After you turn your computer off, wait 30 seconds before turning it back on again.

Computers also get stressed when the temperature changes. They heat up when they're running, and they cool down when they're turned off. This makes them expand and contract, no matter how slightly. The expansion and contraction can lead to subtle cracks in the motherboard as well as to "chip creep" — parts slowly lifting themselves from their sockets.

If you live in an area where the temperature varies widely, keep your computer turned on all the time. That keeps it running at a constant temperature.

Hang On to Your Old Parts for Emergencies

When you upgrade to a newer or fancier computer part, keep your old one in a closet somewhere. Then you'll have something to help test your computer when things go wrong.

For example, I put a new motherboard in my wife's computer, but it wouldn't boot up. Each time I rebooted, the screen came up blank. So I pulled out the video card and stuck in an older video card from yesteryear. The computer worked!

Of course, I then spent two hours trying dozens of other tricks before stumbling onto the fact that her new motherboard simply didn't get along with the newer video card. But because I still had my three-year-old video card in the closet, I could fix her computer myself; I didn't need to take it into the shop.

- ✔ Duplicate parts always come in handy when you're trying to figure out what's wrong with a computer. By swapping different parts one by one, you can eventually isolate the part that's stirring up trouble.

- ✔ Store your old cards in a Ziploc bag; if they're too big, store them in Saran Wrap or its generic equivalent. Storing cards in this way helps prevent any damage from static electricity.

- ✔ Got an old monitor in the closet? You may be able to plug it into a laptop to provide a better screen when you're working at your desk.

Fine-Tune Windows 95

If you want to get under the hood, Windows 95 comes with a panel of switches that fine-tune its performance. To get your hands dirty, check out Chapter 17.

Chapter 23

Ten Baffling Things Your Computer May Say When You Turn It On

In This Chapter

▶ Bunches of confusing little messages

▶ that pop up on your screen

▶ when you first turn on your computer,

▶ as well as tips

▶ on what you're supposed to do to fix them.

*W*hen you first turn on your computer and it wakes up, it scurries around looking at all its parts. If your computer finds something wrong, it tells you. Unfortunately, it doesn't tell you in English. Instead, your computer sends you some complicated observation about its internal mechanics and then stops working.

This chapter offers some translations for some of the most foreign-looking boot-up messages you may see frozen on your screen.

When My Computer Boots Up, It Spits Out Weird Words

We're talking gut-level error messages here; the kind your computer spits out as a welcome when you first turn it on. (I decipher the other error messages — the ones that turn up after the computer's been turned on for a while — in Chapter 25.)

The error messages I describe in this section are stored in your computer's *BIOS,* the base-level chip that serves as your PC's nervous system. (Check out Chapter 10 for more BIOS basics.)

Different brands of BIOS chips spit out subtly different error messages. However, Table 23-1 shows some of the key words and phrases all BIOS chips use when they find something wrong with your PC.

Table 23-1	Common Boot-Up Messages and How to Get Rid of Them
These Key Words	*Usually Mean This*
64K	Some of your memory has probably gone bad. Your best bet is to pull all of your memory chips (Chapter 11) and have a professional test them.
Bad DMA	Your motherboard may need replacing. Turn to Chapter 10.
Bad or missing command interpreter	Your computer's looking for a file called COMMAND.COM, which is supposed to be in its root directory. Copy that file back to your root directory from your System disk, described in Chapter 2.
CMOS, Configuration	When your computer mentions CMOS, you need to change some of its settings. Head to Chapter 18 to read about CMOS settings.
Drive Failure	Head for Chapter 13 and make sure that your hard drive's cables are plugged in snugly. Is the drive getting power from the power supply? Also check out Chapter 18 to make sure that the drive is listed correctly in your computer's CMOS.
Memory and Failure	When combined in the same message, these two words usually mean something's wrong with one or more of your memory chips. Your best bet is to have your memory chips professionally tested (Chapter 11). You may need to replace the motherboard (Chapter 10).
Non-system disk or disk error	Take out the disk that's in drive A and press the spacebar for a quick fix. If your computer sends this message about your hard drive, you need to copy COMMAND.COM over to the hard drive from your System disk, described in Chapter 2.
Parity	Your memory's acting up. Head for Chapter 11 and try pushing the chips more firmly into their sockets.

These Key Words	Usually Mean This
Partition table	Your hard drive's acting up. Your best bet is to buy a hard drive installation utility, described in Chapters 13 and 18, and let the utility try to fix the problem.
Sector not found or Unrecoverable error	This means a disk is starting to go bad. Programs such as Norton Utilities or PC Tools can help recover any information before it's too far gone to retrieve.
Timer	Problems with timers usually mean that your computer's motherboard is defective.

What Do Those Little Numbers Mean?

Some of the genuine IBM computers and a few older clones just flash some code numbers on the screen when they're having problems getting on their feet. They don't bother listing any more helpful details about what's bothering them and what they'd like you to do about it. Table 23-2 explains what some of those cryptic numbers mean and also tells you which chapters offer more information about fixing the problem.

One note about the table: See how the codes have the letter *X* in them, as in *1XX?* The X stands for *any* number. The code 1XX can mean any three-digit number starting with the number 1, such as 122, 189, or something similar.

Table 23-2	Numeric Codes and What They Mean	
This Code	*Usually Means This Is Acting Up*	*Comments*
02X	Power supply	You may need to replace your power supply, described in Chapter 14.
1XX	Motherboard	These numbers often translate to expensive problems. Look up any of your computer's other symptoms in Chapters 24 and 25; Chapter 4 may help as well.
2XX	Memory	Try pushing your memory chips more firmly into their sockets (Chapter 11). If that doesn't work, you probably need to ask a professional to test your memory chips.

(continued)

Table 23-2 *(continued)*

This Code	Usually Means This Is Acting Up	Comments
3XX	Keyboard	Is a book lying across the keyboard, pressing some of the keys as your computer boots up? Another possible solution is to turn off your computer, unplug the keyboard, shake out any dust, and try rebooting the computer. See Chapter 5.
4XX	Monochrome video or adapter	Only XTs complain about this one. Your monochrome video card is acting up. See Chapters 8 and 15.
5XX	Color video or adapter	Only XTs complain about this problem. Your CGA video card is acting up. See Chapters 8 and 15.
6XX	Floppy drive or adapter	Could there be a bad floppy disk in the drive? Is your CMOS set up for the right type of disk? Better start with Chapters 12 and 18.
7XX	Math coprocessor	Is your math coprocessor seated firmly in its socket? Does your computer's CMOS know that the chip's there? Chapters 10 and 18 should help you fix this one.
9XX	Printer port	Your I/O card may be at fault. See Chapters 3 and 15.
10XX	Second printer port	Your I/O card may be at fault. See Chapters 3 and 15.
11XX	Serial port	Your I/O card may be at fault. See Chapters 3 and 15.
12XX	Second serial port	Your I/O card may be at fault. See Chapters 3 and 15.
13XX	Game card	Your I/O card may be at fault. See Chapters 3 and 15.
17XX	Hard drive or controller	Better give Chapter 13 the once-over: Make sure that your hard drive's cables are securely fastened and that its jumpers are set correctly (Chapter 18). Also make sure that the controller card is set firmly in its slot (Chapters 15 and 19).

Chapter 24

Ten Common Warning Beeps and What They Mean

....

In This Chapter
▶ Lists of little beeps
▶ that fill the air
▶ when you first turn on your computer
▶ and what, for goodness sake,
▶ you're supposed to do about them.

....

*A*nybody who's watched television in the last decade has seen computers that can talk to their owners. Your little desktop computer can talk, too. But instead of using the more common vowels and consonants, your computer does the best it can: It strings together some beeps.

By carefully counting all the beeps, you can figure out what your computer's trying to say. Although your computer is no opera singer, it can give you a clue as to what's wrong even if you can't see any error messages on your monitor.

What's This BIOS Beep Business?

Sometimes your computer freaks out while it's booting up or being turned on. But if it finds something wrong before it gets around to testing the video card, it can't flash an error message on the screen. So the computer beeps to say what's wrong.

Unfortunately, no clearly defined "beep standard" exists. All PC manufacturers know their computers should beep when something's wrong, but because there aren't any hard-and-fast rules to follow, they all assign different "beep codes" to different problems.

The secret beep codes are stored in your computer's BIOS chip (which I describe in Chapter 10). By figuring out what BIOS your computer uses, you can tell which beep codes your computer uses.

Watch the screen carefully when your computer first boots up or is turned on. Look for some words about BIOS copyright — that legalese stuff you usually ignore.

Do you see a company name? It's probably AMI — short for American Megatrends — or else it's Phoenix. These two companies are the biggest BIOS makers. Don't be confused by the *video card* BIOS copyright stuff that may pop up on the first line; you're looking for the computer's *real* BIOS information. Can't figure out what BIOS you're using? Chapter 10 has more tips.

When your computer makes some beeps and then stops working, count the number of beeps you hear. Feel free to turn the computer off, wait 30 seconds, and turn it back on again. When you're sure that you counted the right number of beeps, look in the table in this chapter that corresponds to your brand of BIOS. The table translates different beep codes for you.

- ✔ If your computer's down to the beep stage and you've tried all the "cheap fixes" I list in Chapter 19, something's usually seriously wrong.

- ✔ Many of the errors mean that a chip is bad on your computer's motherboard. Unfortunately, it's usually easier to replace the entire motherboard than to isolate the problem chip, remove it, and solder another one in its place.

- ✔ Still, if you have computer hacker friends, see if you can cajole them into giving you a hand. If you explain the specific problem — a bad timer chip, for example — they may know whether it's something they can fix or whether the whole motherboard's a goner.

AMI BIOS Beeps

Normally, computers using the AMI BIOS don't bother with beeps. When they can't muster the energy to boot up, they flash an error message on the screen. To figure out what the computer's trying to tell you, look up the message in Chapter 23.

But if something's wrong with the video card or the computer's so confused it can't even put any words on the screen, it falls back on the ol' beep trick. Table 24-1 explains what your AMI BIOS beeps are trying desperately to tell you.

Don't take these beep codes as the absolute truth. They provide a clue as to why your computer's acting up, but they don't always finger the exact culprit.

Table 24-1	AMI BIOS Beeps and What They Mean
Number of Beeps	*What It Means*
No beep	You're *supposed* to hear one beep. If you don't hear anything, your computer's suffering from a bad power supply, a bad motherboard, or a speaker that doesn't work.
1 beep	Normally, computers issue one self-assured beep when everything's working fine. But when nothing appears on the screen, you'd better check your monitor (Chapter 8) and your video card (Chapter 15). If those two parts appear to work well, the single beep can mean that your motherboard's struggling with some bad chips. This is a job for the people in the white lab coats. You probably can't fix it yourself.
2 beeps	Your computer's complaining about its memory. Make sure that the chips are seated firmly in their sockets (Chapter 11). If that doesn't fix the problem, you probably need to pull out the chips and have them tested at the chip store. If the chips are good, you may need a new motherboard. Again, this problem may be beyond your help.
3 beeps	Same as the 2 beeps message.
4 beeps	Almost always the same as the 2 beeps message.
5 beeps	Your motherboard's acting up. Try reseating all the chips, especially your CPU (Chapter 10). If that doesn't work, you may have to spring for a new motherboard.
6 beeps	The chip on your motherboard that controls your keyboard is acting up. Try reseating it (if you can find it) or try a different keyboard. You may want to take this one to the shop.
7 beeps	Your motherboard's acting up. Try reseating all the chips, especially your CPU (Chapter 10). If that doesn't work, you better spring for a new motherboard.
8 beeps	Your video card may be incorrectly installed. Better hit Chapter 15; you may need to replace your old video card.

(continued)

Table 24-1 *(continued)*

Number of Beeps	What It Means
9 beeps	Your BIOS (Chapter 10) is acting up; you probably have to replace it.
10 beeps	Your motherboard (Chapter 10) is acting up; if this problem persists, you have to replace the motherboard.
11 beeps	Your motherboard's cache memory has problems. You'd best take this one to the shop.

Genuine IBM BIOS Beeps

If you have a "True Blue" IBM computer, the kind that says *IBM* on its case, Table 24-2 lists some of the beep codes you may hear.

Don't take these beep codes as the absolute truth. They provide a clue as to why your computer's acting up, but they don't always finger the right culprit.

Table 24-2	Beep Codes for *Real* IBM Computers
These Beeps	Mean This
No beep	You're supposed to hear one beep. If you don't, your computer either has a bad power supply, a bad motherboard, or a speaker that's broken or not connected.
Constant beep	Your power supply (Chapter 14) isn't working right.
Short, repetitive beeps	Your power supply (Chapter 14) isn't working right.
One long beep, one short beep	Your motherboard (Chapter 10) isn't working right.
One long beep, two short beeps	Your video card (Chapters 8 and 15) or its cables are messing up.
One long beep, three short beeps	Your EGA card (Chapters 8 and 15) or its cables are messing up.

Phoenix BIOS Beeps

If you see the word *Phoenix* on the screen when you reboot or turn on your computer, your system uses the Phoenix BIOS.

So? Well, Phoenix honed the beep code concept to a fine art. Listen to the beeps carefully: The computer gives you *three* sets of beeps, with a pause between each set.

For example, if you hear BEEP BEEP, a pause, BEEP BEEP BEEP, another pause, and BEEP BEEP BEEP BEEP, that translates to two beeps, three beeps, and four beeps. That all boils down to this code: 2 – 3 – 4. You need to look up 2 – 3 – 4 in Table 24-3 to find out what your Phoenix BIOS is complaining about this time.

Don't take these beep codes as the absolute truth. They provide a clue as to why your computer's acting up, but they don't always finger the right culprit.

Table 24-3	Phoenix Beep Codes
These Beeps	*Usually Mean This*
1 – 1 – 3	Your computer can't read its CMOS (Chapter 18), so your motherboard's complaining (Chapter 10).
1 – 1 – 4	Your BIOS probably needs replacing (Chapter 10).
1 – 2 – 1	A timer chip on your motherboard is acting up; you probably have to replace the motherboard (Chapter 10).
1 – 2 – 2	The motherboard is bad (Chapter 10).
1 – 2 – 3	You have a bad motherboard (Chapter 10) or memory (Chapter 11).
1 – 3 – 1	The motherboard (Chapter 10) or memory (Chapter 11) is bad.
1 – 3 – 3	The motherboard (Chapter 10) or memory (Chapter 11) is bad.
1 – 3 – 4	You probably have a bad motherboard (Chapter 10).
1 – 4 – 1	You probably have a bad motherboard (Chapter 10).
1 – 4 – 2	Some of the memory is bad (Chapter 11).
2 – ? –?	Any beep series starting with two beeps means some of your memory is bad (Chapter 11). Better get the chips tested professionally.
3 – 1 – 1	One of the chips on your motherboard is acting up; you probably have to replace the whole thing.

(continued)

Table 24-3 *(continued)*

These Beeps	Usually Mean This
3 – 1 – 2	One of the chips on your motherboard is acting up; you probably have to replace the whole thing.
3 – 1 – 3	One of the chips on your motherboard is acting up; you probably have to replace the whole thing.
3 – 1 – 4	One of the chips on your motherboard is acting up; you probably have to replace the whole thing.
3 – 2 – 4	Your keyboard (or the chip on the motherboard that controls it) is acting up. Visit Chapter 5.
3 – 3 – 4	Your computer can't find its video card. Is there one in there? (See Chapter 15.)
3 – 4 – 1	Your video card is acting up (Chapter 15).
3 – 4 – 2	Your video card is acting up (Chapter 15).
3 – 4 – 3	Your video card is acting up (Chapter 15).
4 – 2 – 1	Your motherboard has a bad chip; you probably have to replace the whole thing (Chapter 10).
4 – 2 – 2	First, check your keyboard (Chapter 5) for problems; if that doesn't fix the problem, your motherboard's probably bad.
4 – 2 – 3	Just as with the beeps above, first check your keyboard (Chapter 5) for problems; if that doesn't fix the problem, your motherboard's probably bad.
4 – 2 – 4	One of your cards (Chapter 15) is confusing your computer. Try pulling your cards out one by one to isolate the culprit.
4 – 3 – 1	Your motherboard has probably gone bad.
4 – 3 – 2	Again, your motherboard has probably gone bad.
4 – 3 – 3	One of the timer chips died. You probably have to replace the motherboard.
4 – 3 – 4	Try calling up your CMOS (Chapter 18) and checking the date and time. If that doesn't fix the problem, try changing your computer's battery (Chapter 10). Still acting up? Try a new power supply before breaking down and buying a new motherboard.
4 – 4 – 1	Your serial port's acting up; try reseating (or replacing) your I/O card (Chapter 15).
4 – 4 – 2	Your parallel port's acting up; try reseating (or replacing) your I/O card (Chapter 15).
4 – 4 – 3	Your math coprocessor's acting up. Run the program that came with it to see if it's *really* fried or just pretending.

Chapter 25

Ten Common Error Messages (And How to Avoid Them)

Computers come with great gobs of error messages. You find the ten most popular — actually, the most *un*popular — error messages in this chapter. You also find some tips on how to shut 'em up.

Insert disk with COMMAND.COM in drive A Press any key to continue

If you haven't moved up to Windows 95, this message usually means that your computer can't find its life-giving pieces of DOS. Stick a System disk in drive A and press Enter. Or, if your computer usually boots off your hard drive, remove any errant floppy disks that may be sitting in drive A and press Enter. (Dunno how to make a System disk? Troop back to Chapter 2.)

Invalid media or Track 0 unusable Format terminated

When your computer hides its most important files on a System disk, it sticks them in some front-row seats called *Track 0*. If those seats are damaged — they're full of gum or something even worse — the computer can't stick its important stuff on them.

That's what happens when this message appears. Throw the disk away and try another. If you get this message when you're trying to format your hard drive, you're in *deep* trouble. Head for Chapters 12 and 13 for some possible fixes.

Sector not found

DOS is having trouble finding information on a disk. Try running CHKDSK, which I describe in Chapter 19. If you haven't backed up your disk — whether it's a hard disk or a floppy — do it as quickly as possible. Your hard drive (Chapter 13) may be on its last legs or in need of reformatting.

Access denied

You're probably trying to write (or delete) something on a write-protected floppy disk. If you're *sure* that you want to change the disk, disable its write-protection. If you're working with a 3½-inch disk, slide the little tab away from the hole in the disk's top corner. (On a 5¼-inch floppy, remove the little piece of tape from the edge of the disk.)

You may also receive this message if you try to delete a protected file on the hard disk. Or perhaps you're trying to read or write to a file that is used or manipulated by another program in Windows.

Divide Overflow

This one leaves you no choice but to reboot the computer. Your computer's fine, but the software did something that has confused everybody since their first math course: It tried to divide by zero.

Try reinstalling the software onto your hard disk from the original disks. If that doesn't work, try cajoling the folks on the software's tech support line to send you a new, working copy of the program. Also, make sure that you have the most current drivers, as discussed in Chapter 18.

Drive not ready Abort, Retry, Ignore, Fail?

The computer's probably startled because it tried to find a file on a drive but couldn't even find a floppy or compact disc in the drive. If you *did* put a disk or a CD in there, is the drive's latch closed? Is the disk or CD right-side up? Make sure that the disk or CD is in the correct drive and press R for Retry. (You may have to give the drive a few seconds to recognize the disk, especially with CDs.)

A:\ is not accessible. The device is not ready.

Windows 95 usually shoots this one out when you shut down your computer while displaying the contents of a floppy drive. Then if you remove the floppy disk and restart Windows, it tries to reread the information from the disk in order to display it on the screen again. When the disk's not there, Windows 95 complains.

The moral? Don't leave the contents of a floppy disk on your monitor when you shut down your computer.

Track 0 Bad — Disk Unusable

If you're using an older computer, then you're probably trying to format one of those high-density, 1.2MB floppies in a 360K floppy drive. It just can't be done.

If you're *not* using an old, 360K drive, the floppy disk itself is probably bad.

Finally, if this message refers to your hard drive, it's particularly bad news. Head to Chapter 19 for a possible cheap fix, and then see Chapter 13 for some more detailed tips.

Insufficient disk space

When you see this message, your disk — hard drive or floppy disk — doesn't have enough room on it to store the incoming files. You have to delete some files from it to make room. Of course, you could just put in a clean floppy disk or buy another hard disk, as I describe in Chapter 13.

Insufficient memory

Your computer doesn't have enough memory to run this particular program. Or perhaps the memory you do have isn't set up right.

If you're using DOS or trying to run a DOS game, put your System disk (described in Chapter 2) in drive A and reboot your computer. When your computer reboots from the boot disk, it'll come up "clean" of anything that's sucking memory from the available pool. Don't try to run Windows after this trick, though.

If your Windows programs complain of "Insufficient memory," you have two options: First, try shutting down all your extraneous programs so all your memory is available for your current program. Second, buy more memory and install it, as I describe in Chapter 11.

Bad command or filename

You probably typed something at the C:\> prompt, and your computer couldn't figure out what you were trying to do. You may have spelled something wrong or typed in the name of a program your computer couldn't find.

If you see these words when your computer's first booting up, one of the lines in your AUTOEXEC.BAT file is confusing your computer. (That weird-sounding file's described in Chapter 16.)

Bad or missing filename

If you see this message when you boot up your computer, it probably means that the computer couldn't find a driver listed in your CONFIG.SYS file. Look at Chapter 16 and then check your CONFIG.SYS file to see what's amiss. Otherwise, your computer's telling you it couldn't find a file. Check out the information on *paths* in Chapter 16.

General failure

When DOS has trouble trying to read information from a hard drive or floppy disk, it offers a specific error message. But when it's *really* confused, it slings out this one. Check to make sure that your hard drive is configured correctly (Chapters 13 and 18). On a floppy drive, check to make sure that your disk's formatted properly, that it's inserted right-side up, and, if you're using a low-density drive, that the floppy isn't a high-density disk.

Incorrect DOS version

This message usually pops up when the commands and programs in the computer's DOS directory come from a version of DOS that's different from the version that boots up from its hard drive.

Suppose that your old computer's hard drive is formatted to boot up and start running under DOS 3.3. Then you take a friend's backup disk of DOS 6 and copy all those DOS 6 commands to your DOS directory.

The computer still thinks that it's running in DOS 3.3. When you type one of the DOS 6 commands, the computer gets confused: The two versions of DOS don't match each other. The solution? Don't mix versions of DOS. Buy the latest version of DOS and always run the installation program that comes with it.

Internal stack failure, system halted

Reboot your computer. You may need to use a System disk, described in Chapter 2, before the computer will stop flinging out this message and come back to life.

Next, add the following line to your hard disk's CONFIG.SYS file, a process described in Chapter 16:

```
STACKS 9,256
```

When you reboot your computer, it should be back to normal. If not, try changing the 9 in the STACKS line to 12. Still getting the message? Then increase the number to 15. Don't change the 256 number, though. That won't help.

A new MS-DOS resident program named 'Black Widow Tea' may decrease your system performance. Would you like to see more information about this problem?

Windows 95 users should click Yes. The Performance tab in Windows' System Properties area jumps up and usually identifies the program that's out of line. Also, it often has instructions on how to kick the program and its evil drivers off your computer's hard drive.

What's the point of the warning? Although Windows 95 sounds as calm as a doctor in a waiting room, it's really trying to identify viruses sneaking into your computer by describing themselves as a hardware's sidekick device driver.

Parity Error

Any message containing the unpleasant words Parity Error can pop up on just about any computer at any time. Windows 95 frames the words in a pleasant blue background; its grandfather, DOS, just slaps the words onto the screen. Either way, the solution's the same: Restart your computer.

Parity errors usually mean your memory's acting up, meaning you should head for Chapter 11.

My computer puts that C:> thing onto the screen, not Windows 95!

When Windows 95 refuses to come out on stage, it has usually broken a leg — and not in a good way. If you recently installed some software, the incoming software may have damaged some Windows files. Or, if you just tried to install Windows 95, the installation process may not have worked all the way.

To fix everything, run Windows 95 Setup program again. This time, choose the Verify option to make Windows 95 check all files and replace any that are missing or damaged.

Index

(continued)

IDG BOOKS WORLDWIDE BOOK REGISTRATION

Register This Book and Win!

We want to hear from you!

Visit **http://my2cents.dummies.com** to register this book and tell us how you liked it!

- Get entered in our monthly prize giveaway.

- Give us feedback about this book — tell us what you like best, what you like least, or maybe what you'd like to ask the author and us to change!

- Let us know any other *...For Dummies* topics that interest you.

Your feedback helps us determine what books to publish, tells us what coverage to add as we revise our books, and lets us know whether we're meeting your needs as a *...For Dummies* reader. You're our most valuable resource, and what you have to say is important to us!

Not on the Web yet? It's easy to get started with *Dummies 101®: The Internet For Windows® 95* or *The Internet For Dummies®,* 4th Edition, at local retailers everywhere.

Or let us know what you think by sending us a letter at the following address:

...For Dummies Book Registration
Dummies Press
7260 Shadeland Station, Suite 100
Indianapolis, IN 46256
Fax 317-596-5498

BUSINESS AND **GENERAL REFERENCE BOOK SERIES FROM IDG**

COMPUTER BOOK SERIES FROM IDG